the Bourbon Cookbook

the Bourbon Cookbook

by Tom Hoge

Stackpole Books

THE BOURBON COOKBOOK

Copyright © 1975 by Tom Hoge

Published by STACKPOLE BOOKS
Cameron and Kelker Streets
Harrisburg, Pa. 17105

All rights reserved, including the right to reproduce this book or portions thereof in any form or by any means, electronic or mechanical, including photocopying, recording, or by any information storage and retrieval system, without permission in writing from the publisher. All inquiries should be addressed to Stackpole Books, Cameron and Kelker Streets, Harrisburg, Pennsylvania 17105.

Printed in the U.S.A.

Library of Congress Cataloging in Publication Data

Hoge, Tom.
    The bourbon cookbook.

    Includes index.
    1. Cookery (Bourbon)   I. Title.
TX726.H65   641.6'2   74-26731
ISBN 0-8117-0417-3

CONTENTS

Foreword   9

What Is Bourbon?   11
    Congress defines the genuine article.

Bourbon: The Whiskey for Suppin'   13
    Creative cooks everywhere are discovering the amazing versatility of bourbon as a cooking ingredient in everything from tangy dips and hearty soups to savory pot roasts and epicurean desserts.

Appetizers   17
    The haunting, nutty flavor of bourbon imparts distinction to the most prosaic ingredients: the plebeian hot dog becomes an aristocrat when cut in chunks and simmered in a piquant bourbon sauce, cheese spreads and sour cream dips take on a new pungency when laced with bourbon, and humble chicken livers are transformed into elegant pâtés when blended with America's authentic native spirit.

Contents

Soups   32
> Seafood bisques and chowders and bean, onion, cheese, and pepperpot soups really perk up with a dash of bourbon.

Salads   40
> Old favorites—chicken, avocado, and lettuce salads—will never seem the same again, once you've tried making them with bourbon.

Omelettes and Soufflés   42
> Here is an intriguing array of egg dishes featuring flaming omelettes and dessert-type soufflés.

Fondues   48
> Melted cheese, bourbon, and crusty bread combine their goodness to provide many tasty morsels.

Seafood   51
> Bourbon does wonders for these easy-to-fix top-of-the-stove and oven-baked dishes featuring prawns, shrimp, lobster tails, clams, crabmeat, and flounder.

Fowl   64
> Whether it's used in sauces, marinades, basting juices, or stuffings, bourbon adds its unique excitement to these recipes for chicken, capon, Cornish hens, goose, duck, and turkey.

Beef   87
> From flaming sirloin steaks and filet mignon to robust roasts and stews, bourbon bestows an aura of luxury upon even the most princely of meats.

Lamb   108
> These recipes for marinated and broiled, roast, and skewered lamb—many with the exotic touch of the Middle East—will add the spice of adventure to your daily bill-of-fare.

Pork and Ham   116
> Sweet 'n' spicy sauces and glazes get star billing in recipes for saucy spareribs and pork chops and glazed pork loin roast, ham steak, and canned ham; savory meat tarts and pies are also featured.

Veal   125
> Whether it is used to flame or simmer the meat, bourbon glamorizes veal cutlets and scallopini.

Contents

Mixed Meats   128

    Five versions of the famed Kentucky burgoo, in which varied combinations of beef, pork, veal, lamb, and chicken are simmered with bourbon, and a pork, veal, and beef stuffing for sourdough French bread prove that bourbon can work its wonders for several meats at once.

Game   134

    If you don't believe bourbon and game were made for each other, just try this distinctive American liquor in a marinade for venison steaks or quail stuffing; for flaming quail, partridge casserole, and wild ducks; for simmering squirrel, and to make a cream sauce for pheasant.

Vegetables   140

    Bourbon and oven-baked beans go together like love and marriage, but this fabulous liquor works its sorcery equally well on baked onions, broccoli, sweet potatoes, and squash and creamed carrots and mushrooms.

Marinades and Sauces   151

    As the key ingredient in marinades and barbecue and basting sauces for main dish meats and fish, bourbon excels, as it does in dessert sauces for cakes, puddings, ice cream, and fruit.

Fruit Desserts   165

    For a real taste thrill, try peaches, bananas, cherries, and baked apples flamed with bourbon; or use bourbon to steep watermelon, stew figs, poach apricots, preserve peaches, or make hot fruit compote.

Mousses   174

    The outstanding flavor of bourbon—when combined with chocolate instant pudding, cocoa, coffee and vanilla ice cream, macaroons, candied fruit, oil of peppermint, canned figs, chopped nuts, and cooked pumpkin—produces unforgettable frozen desserts.

Pies   181

    The flavor of chocolate, the perfect complement to bourbon, is featured in the crusts as well as the fillings of many of these pies, while eggnog, nuts, coffee, mincemeat, pumpkin, and sweet potatoes contribute to the mouth-watering goodness of many others.

Puddings   197

    Whip-and-chill, custard, steamed, and oven-baked puddings are something special when made with bourbon, fruits and nuts, carrots, yams, and sweet potatoes.

Contents

Jellies and Jam   210

Bourbon not only makes old favorites—cherry and apple jellies, peach butter, grapefruit-orange marmalade—truly memorable, but is also the key ingredient in confections, like jellied old-fashioneds, that are in a class by themselves.

Candy   215

With bourbon, it's a snap to make the fanciest candies from the simplest ingredients; for instance, you can use vanilla wafer crumbs, corn syrup, and bourbon as a base to make a wide assortment of candy drops with the addition of easily available flavorings no farther away than your cupboard or neighborhood supermarket.

Cake   221

When it comes to cakes, bourbon is a jack-of-all-trades, making the frostings and sauces as well as the cakes themselves—and what cakes! festive cakes for holidays—Thanksgiving, Christmas, New Year's, Saint Patrick's Day, Flag Day, and the Fourth of July; fruit and nut cakes galore, and delicious miniatures—petits fours, raisin-and-nut bars, date-nut squares, and many others.

Cookies   248

These cookies come in many styles—plain, glazed, decorated with confetti sugar, double-decked with luscious buttery filling—and in many shapes—round and puffed, round and flat, oblong, tricorn—but they all are enhanced with the hearty, provocative flavor of bourbon.

Breads   262

When you serve bread, biscuits, muffins, rolls, french toast, and pancakes made with bourbon, your guests will keep coming back for extra helpings.

Bourbon: The Whiskey for Sippin'   269

Nothing concerning bourbon seems to be beyond dispute; and arguments about its geographical origin, the identity of its inventor, the proper methods of processing, the merits of sour mash bourbon versus others, how to judge the quality of a bourbon, and the authentic formula for a mint julep have been as lively as the drink itself.

Drinks   276

It's easy to be your own bartender with these simple but elegant recipes for mint julep, eggnog, milk punch, hot mulled cider, and other favorites made with bourbon.

Index   283

Foreword

There is a decided trend toward gourmet cookery among food-minded people today. All of us who like to cook and enjoy good eating are constantly in search of ways to add touches which make recipes special. Within recent years, a wider use of "spirits" in American cookery has been evident, and bourbon has proved a favorite.

It is fun experimenting with new ideas, and when experiments concern food, sampling the results can be a delightful experience. Bourbon is a fine flavor mate with meats, poultry, seafood, fruits, and vegetables. The mellowness of bourbon enhances a dish with gourmet taste and a note of glamour. Flaming bourbon specialties have an allure all their own; both 86-proof and 100-proof bourbon are recommended for this purpose.

I recommend this collection of tested recipes with the hope that you and your friends will find pleasure in preparing and savoring them. And may the discovery of bourbon in food inspire you to make this distinctively American product a staple in your kitchen as well as at your bar.

W. J. Marshall
Vice Admiral, U.S.N. (Ret.)
President, The Bourbon Institute (1958-1974)

What Is Bourbon?

Bourbon is a truly American liquor, born and bred in this land and made mainly from native corn. As Scotch is to Scotland and Irish whiskey is to Ireland, bourbon is to America—our authentic, native spirit. It is the only liquor ever to be honored by the United States Congress. On May 4, 1964, the two houses acknowledged bourbon in a joint resolution, declaring it to be a "distinctive product of the United States."

By this act, Congress decreed that true bourbon must be distilled to no more than 160 proof from a fermented mash of not less than 51 percent corn grain. It must then be reduced to 125 proof or less and finally aged to a minimum of two years in previously unused charred barrels made from staves of white oak.

No material whatever may be added to bourbon, except distilled water to adjust the proof. Bourbon is not bourbon unless the label says so.

All of which inspired former New York Mayor Lindsay to go

before the House of Representatives as a congressman in 1964 and recite the following doggerel:

> The nectar of Scotch
> is very urban
>
> But is there a man
> with soul so dead
> who never to himself
> has said:
>
> "This is my own, my
> native Bourbon."

Bourbon
The Whiskey for Suppin'

Not long ago, Julia Childs led off her TV cooking show with a tip on how to brighten up a spaghetti dinner. Then she flamed some apples with bourbon. This bears repeating for one reason. Ten years ago no one would have thought of using bourbon for flaming anything. Such fireworks fell within the realm of brandy—except in the Southland where bourbon was born.

Using bourbon as a flambé, or as a condiment for that matter, is virtually an untried art that has a vast potential, considering the depth and fullness of this native American liquor. But as far back as my childhood, in the days following World War I, there were hints of things to come down South, where the folks had a more profound knowledge of bourbon than those Yankees.

My first contact with bourbon was at the age of ten while spending the Christmas holidays at the home of my grandparents in Staunton, Virginia. About a week before the Big Day, a package arrived from a great-uncle who lived in Louisville, Kentucky. It contained a damp, dark fruit cake redolent of spices. Nestled against the cake was a squat flask of bourbon and attached to it it a note exhorting my grandmother to douse the cake with the whiskey each day to keep it "good and moist" for the Yuletide. I have tasted a lot of fruit cakes since then, including some from that same convivial uncle. But none have seemed as pungent and rich as that first one which my grandmother doled out cautiously to us kids.

Another early memory of the South was of rich plum puddings with a crown of blue flames atop. Britain, where this noble dessert is said to have originated, and the rest of the world, might use brandy to flame plum pudding, but the homes I visited in both Kentucky and Virginia used bourbon. At the end of a typical Christmas dinner, the guests would pull back their chairs and wait expectantly while the host pulled a bottle from the sideboard. Pouring a couple of ounces into a big silver ladle, he would light it, then spoon the dancing flames over the fragrant pudding.

The haunting, nutty flavor of bourbon has been known to connoisseurs of fine whiskey for nearly two centuries, but its value as a culinary aid from soup to dessert is still a mystery to many amateur cooks. Even the names of established bourbon recipes baffle them. Bourbon on a Cloud is not an advanced stage of inebriation as some think, but a delicate dessert. And Beef Bourbonnaise is not a misspelling of the French classic Boeuf à la Bourgignonne.

How many know that bourbon has a special affinity for chocolate that can turn a simple pudding into a Lucullan delight? And it was not until food and liquor writer Emanuel Greenberg and his wife, Madeline, brought out their book on cooking with various types of booze that I realized that bourbon and peaches in most any form have a celestial quality. Every day, housewives and some husbands are making new discoveries about bourbon as a condiment.

Several months ago my friend Al Durante, an amateur chef and veteran bourbon sipper, stumbled onto one. It seems that Al's wife had asked her church choir group home for Sunday brunch without realizing that the family cupboard was virtually bare.

A crisis was in the making but Al, a good man in a tight situation, spotted two big cans of baked beans in the nearly empty larder. Nearby was a box of raisins and in the ice box some oranges and a lemon. With an ingenuity that would have roused the envy of Escoffier, Al went to work. Combining the beans, some molasses, and ginger with the raisins and sliced fruit, he tossed in a few ounces of bourbon, offered up a silent prayer, and let the mixture simmer in the oven for an hour while he and his guests knocked back a few bourbon sours.

Bourbon: The Whiskey for Suppin'

How did they like the lunch?

"They went crazy over it," said Al with simple eloquence.

Did you ever notice how an onion dip or a fragrant slice of Bermuda aboard a cracker is improved when washed down with a highball? Carry that a step further and try onion soup laced with bourbon and simmered about thirty minutes. Then you'll realize how well the spirit and the bulb blend.

Bourbon can brighten up many soups. Try it with a can of tomato and throw in a spoon or so of heavy cream to give richness. Italian minestrone takes on an added dimension with bourbon added. So does navy bean. Just be sure, unless the recipe reads otherwise, that the mixture is simmered long enough for the bourbon to blend in and lose its identity.

Beef and bourbon make a natural union, and a couple of slugs of the whiskey can turn a pot roast into an epicurean dream. It also works with the cheaper forms of beef. Recently I had some leftover hamburger and hashed it up with chopped onions, celery, and a little beef broth. As an afterthought, I tossed in a couple of drams of bourbon and let it simmer about half an hour. My wife and three daughters devoured it. Then, out of curiosity, I made the same dish a week later, adding some cognac instead of bourbon. My culinary effort bombed.

I've discovered that pepper steak improves greatly with a little bourbon thrown in. But again, don't forget to let it simmer a while. And never get carried away and drown the food in whiskey. Too much can ruin any dish. As the late Lyndon Johnson once said; "If you take a glass at a time, it's fine. But if you drink a whole bottle you have troubles."

Most or all of the alcohol dissipates when you simmer bourbon in a dish, but too much is still too much.

Seeking some expert opinion on the growing popularity of bourbon as a condiment, I talked to three chefs at one major hotel and two well-known restaurants in New York City, where I live.

Edmond Kaspar, executive chef of the big, bustling Americana Hotel, was emphatic in his preference for bourbon over other liquors as an aid to cookery. He features several bourbon dishes, including a unique salad.

"Bourbon gives food a really different flavor. It gives a depth and richness," said Kaspar, as we sat in his glass-walled office from which he can survey his domain and watch a small army of assistant chefs prepare meals for the endless procession of guests.

"Brandy is what most cooks have been using in the past," said Kaspar, "but I have found that brandy evaporates much faster and loses its flavor more quickly than bourbon. Besides, bourbon has a stronger bouquet than brandy."

These views were generally shared by Joseph Montalbano, director of the attractive Ground Floor Restaurant, a popular tourist spot in Manhattan.

Montalbano, who offers a unique cheese soup laced with both bourbon and dry red wine, referred proudly to this distinctive marriage.

"The combination of red wine and bourbon is unusual," said he. "The bourbon definitely adds interest and the recipe is frequently requested by Ground Floor patrons."

Horst Semper, who is boss of the kitchens at Ma Bell's Restaurant, another favorite of tourists and New Yorkers as well, weighed in with a simple but delicious cheese spread composed solely of a tangy cheddar, hot cayenne pepper, and bourbon.

"Bourbon is the secret ingredient of this delicious and very simple recipe," said Semper. "It's subtle, with just enough tang to make diners ask what's in it. All in all, a perfect accompaniment for cocktails."

Dishes from the three above places and several other noted hotels and restaurants are included in the recipes in this book.

As mentioned earlier, beef and bourbon form a natural union. Which explains why so many restaurants dedicated to fostering this delightful match are popping up. To cite a few: Chicago has a "Bourbon and Beef" restaurant, and in New York it's the "Beef and Bourbon." New Orleans, home of Bourbon Street, and a stronghold of the whiskey, has a "Beef and Bourbon" restaurant in the heart of the French Quarter. And half a world away in Sydney, Australia, there is a "Bourbon and Beefsteak Bar" in Kings Cross, the hub of the city's restaurant and night club area.

Appetizers

Bourbon Pâté No. 1

   1½ *lb. liverwurst*
    1 *cup butter*
   ¼ *cup bourbon*
   ½ *teaspoon pepper*
   ½ *cup chopped black olives*

    Let liverwurst and butter stand at room temperature until soft enough to mash.
    Mash liverwurst with a fork until free of lumps. Add butter and mix well. Add bourbon, pepper, and black olives and mix thoroughly. Pack into a crock or lightly oiled 1-quart mold. Chill.
    Serve directly from crock, or unmold onto serving plate. Serve with crackers, melba toast rounds, or quartered, lightly buttered slices of hot toast. Serves 6.

Bourbon Pâté No. 2

½ lb. butter
1 small onion, chopped
1 lb. chicken livers
1½ cups chicken broth
2 teaspoons sweet sherry
½ teaspoon paprika
⅛ teaspoon allspice
½ teaspoon salt
⅛ teaspoon white pepper
1 clove garlic, minced
½ cup bourbon
1 envelope plain gelatine
1 cup chopped walnuts

Melt butter; add onion and chicken livers. Cook 10 minutes, stirring occasionally. Add ¾ cup broth, sherry, paprika, allspice, salt, pepper, and garlic. Cook 5 minutes. Remove from heat; add bourbon. Soften gelatine in remaining ¾ cup broth; cook over boiling water until dissolved. Place chicken liver mixture in blender; blend until smooth. Stir gelatine and walnuts into chicken liver mixture. Turn into 5- or 6-cup mold. Chill until firm.

Bourbon Pâté No. 3

1 small onion
1 lb. butter
1 lb. fresh chicken livers
1½ cups clear chicken broth
2 tablespoons dry white wine
½ teaspoon paprika
⅛ teaspoon allspice
½ teaspoon salt
⅛ teaspoon white pepper or Tabasco
1 clove garlic, minced
⅓ cup straight bourbon
1 cup pecans, chopped
1 envelope unflavored gelatine

Appetizers 19

Sauté onion in ½ pound butter until tender. Add chicken livers cut in small pieces. Cook for 10 minutes, stirring occasionally. Add half of the broth, together with the wine, paprika, allspice, salt, pepper, and garlic. Cook for 5 minutes more.

Place mixture in electric blender. Gradually add remaining butter (melted) and bourbon. Blend until smooth. Stir in pecans.

In saucepan, sprinkle gelatine over remaining broth. Heat and stir until gelatine is dissolved. Pour part of the gelatine-broth into a 1½-quart mold and arrange any garnishes desired. Chill mold for 10 minutes. Fill mold with chicken liver mixture and top with remaining broth. Keep in refrigerator for at least 8 hours before unmolding and serving. Serves 8-10.

Bourbon Mist Pâté

4 *oz. pork liver pâté*
1 *teaspoon bourbon*
1 *tablespoon chopped almonds*

To liver pâté, add bourbon and chopped almonds. Mix well and allow to stand, uncovered, at room temperature at least 25 minutes "to allow the flavors to marry." Serves 2-4.

Chicken-Cream Pâté

4 *lb. chicken livers*
1 *medium onion, finely minced*
2 *tablespoons salt*
1 *cup sweet butter*
2 *cups (1 lb.) cream cheese*
⅓ *cup bourbon*
1 *tablespoon dry mustard*
1 *teaspoon nutmeg*
   freshly ground pepper to taste
   watercress, cherry tomatoes, and radish roses for garnish

Put livers in saucepan with onion and salt, add ¼ inch water, cover pan, and simmer until livers are cooked through. Drain and mash livers and onion, removing the stringy membranes, and put through sieve or puree in electric blender.

Cream butter and cheese together; blend with livers. Add bourbon and seasonings to taste. Spoon evenly into 2 aspic-lined 6-cup ring molds, cover with aspic, and chill thoroughly until set.

Unmold on serving plate; garnish with watercress, cherry tomatoes, and radish roses. Serve with thin-sliced toast. Serves 25.

Quick Bourbon-Chicken Liver Spread

½ *lb. fresh chicken livers, cut into quarters*
1 *medium onion, chopped*
½ *teaspoon salt*
½ *teaspoon sugar*
¼ *teaspoon pepper*
1 *oz. bourbon*
   pinch of thyme
2 *tablespoons butter*
1 *3-oz. package cream cheese, cut into small cubes*

Sauté onion in butter for 3 minutes; then add chicken livers and sauté about 5 minutes more, or until onions are brown and livers are cooked through but not well done. Put livers and onion into an electric blender together with other ingredients and blend at top speed 15-20 seconds or until completely smooth. Spoon mixture into covered dish or crock and store in refrigerator. Serves 4-6.

Bourbon Pâté Balls

½ *lb. chicken livers*
½ *onion, minced*
1 *tablespoon bacon fat or butter*
2 *hard-cooked eggs, yolks and whites separated*
1 *tablespoon bourbon*
   salt, pepper

Sauté liver and onion in fat until meat is just cooked through. Chop this mixture finely, or puree in blender, with egg yolks. Add bourbon to make firm paste; add salt and pepper to taste.

Chill mixture; shape into small balls. Grate or chop hard-cooked egg whites finely; roll balls in this to coat. Serves 4-6.

Bourbon Aspic No. 1

  6 *oz. bourbon*
  2 *cans beef bouillon*
     salt and pepper
     garlic salt
  1 *oz. butter*
  8 *oz. liverwurst*
  2 *oz. chopped celery*
     monosodium glutamate

Pour 4 ounces of bourbon into 2 cans of bouillon. Salt and pepper to taste. Add garlic salt. Make sure mold is buttered for easy removal from dish.

Prepare liver pâté by adding liverwurst to chopped celery, 1 to 2 ounces of bourbon (depending on consistency), salt, pepper, garlic salt, and monosodium glutamate.

After beef bouillon is jelled, remove the middle portion of pan and stuff with the pâté. The portion that is removed is reheated and poured over entire dish. Refreeze, remove from mold, and serve. Serves 6.

Bourbon Aspic No. 2

  1 *10½-oz. can condensed consommé*
  2 *envelopes unflavored gelatine*
  ½ *cup bourbon*
  1 *can chicken liver pâté*
  ½ *cup sliced black olives*
  ½ *cup blanched almond halves*

Sprinkle gelatine on ½ can consommé to soften. Stir over low heat until gelatine dissolves, about 3 minutes. Add remaining consommé and bourbon. Chill until mixture is syrupy.

Chill two 6-cup ring molds. Pour ½ cup aspic in each mold and tip to coat evenly. Chill until set.

Arrange almond halves and black olives on aspic, cover with another thin layer of aspic, and chill until set. Spoon pâté over set aspic and cover with remaining aspic. Chill well before unmolding. Serves 20-30.

Ham-Bourbon Balls

6 *hard-boiled eggs, chopped*
1 *tablespoon minced onion*
1 *cup ground ham, cooked*
pepper
3 *tablespoons bourbon*
½ *cup pecans, ground*

Mix eggs, minced onion, ham, pepper, and bourbon together into a smooth consistency. Roll into balls the size of a nickel, and roll balls, a few at a time, in ½ cup ground pecans.

Refrigerate; serve with festive toothpick in each. Makes 36 balls.

Bourbon Beef Balls No. 1

1 *lb. chuck, ground*
1 *tablespoon oil*
1 *8-oz. can tomato sauce*
½ *teaspoon crumbled bay leaves*
salt and pepper to taste
¼ *cup bourbon*

Shape beef into 1-inch balls. Heat oil; add beef balls and cook over low heat until browned on all sides. Drain off drippings. Pour tomato sauce over meat balls. Stir in bay leaves, salt and pepper. Cover and cook over low heat 20 minutes. Remove from heat. Add bourbon and stir lightly. Serve with cocktail picks.

The meat balls may be frozen after they are cooked. To serve, reheat in a skillet or chafing dish with sauce. Serves 12.

Bourbon Beef Balls No. 2

Meat Balls
1½ lbs. *chopped chuck*
1 *egg, well-beaten*
1 *teaspoon salt*
1 *tablespoon tomato catsup*
¼ *cup water*
1 *slice of white bread, crumbled*

Sauce
2 *tablespoons Spanish olive oil*
1 *small onion, minced*
1 *garlic clove, crushed*
¼ *teaspoon salt*
¼ *teaspoon oregano*
1 *teaspoon flour*
1 *beef bouillon cube*
1 *cup water*
1 *teaspoon dry mustard*
  dash of bitters
¼ *cup bourbon*
2 *tablespoons sweet vermouth*

Combine meat, egg, salt, catsup, ¼ cup water, and bread crumbs; form into smooth, bite-size balls.

Sauté meat balls in olive oil until brown on all sides; remove. Sauté onion and garlic in same pan until soft. Add salt and oregano; then stir in flour.

Add remaining sauce ingredients and bring to a boil; cook hard until reduced and slightly thickened, stirring to dissolve bouillon cube.

Replace meat balls in sauce; simmer 5 minutes.

Refrigerate 24 hours before serving; reheat when needed. Keep hot on serving. As appetizer serves 20.

Holiday Meat Balls Flambé

 2 *lb. chuck*
 ¾ *lb. smoked ham*
 3 *slices bread*
 2 *cups water*
 1 *tablespoon oil*
 1 *medium onion, minced*
 2 *eggs beaten lightly*
 2 *teaspoons salt and freshly ground black pepper*
 ¼ *cup bourbon*
 2 *medium potatoes, boiled and mashed*
 6 *tablespoons butter*

Have meats ground together twice. Soak bread in water. Heat oil in small skillet and cook onion until translucent. In deep bowl, beat eggs with salt, pepper and ¼ cup of bourbon. Add meat, bread soaked in water, and sautéed onion. Mix with large fork and stir in mashed potatoes. Work gently to make a light, spongy mixture. Form into walnut-size balls.

Heat butter in chafing dish or in large skillet, and brown meat balls all around, turning carefully and shaking to keep round shape. Lift out and keep warm until sauce is ready. Serves 10-12.

Bourbon Sauce for Meat Balls

 4 *tablespoons butter*
 3 *tablespoons flour*
 ½ *cup bourbon*
 3 *cups beef bouillon*

Heat butter in saucepan, stir in flour to make a paste, and cook slowly for 5-6 minutes. Add 3 cups stock, stirring rapidly until smooth and slightly thickened. Stir in ¼ cup bourbon and cook a few minutes.

Add meat balls to sauce and cook over low heat approximately 35-45 minutes. Ten minutes before serving, flame ¼ cup bourbon and pour over all.

Bourbon Cheese Spread

    8 *oz. cheddar cheese*
    1 *oz. bourbon*
    tip of a teaspoon cayenne

Whip the cheddar cheese and bourbon together to a fluff. Add cayenne. Chill and serve in a pottery crock. Serves 6-8.

(Ma Bell's Restaurant, New York City)

Cheddar and Bourbon Mix

    12 *oz. soft cheddar cheese*
    2 *oz. bourbon*
    2 *oz. minced onion*
    ¼ *teaspoon Tabasco*
    ½ *teaspoon worcestershire sauce*

Mix above ingredients. Chill in glass or crockery jar and chill at least 24 hours in refrigerator. Serves 16-20.

Cheese Coquettes

    1 *lb. imported Swiss cheese, grated*
    ¼ *cup bourbon*
    1 *egg, beaten*
    salt
    pepper
    paprika
    4 *slices toast*

Mix cheese, bourbon, egg, salt and pepper. Spread mixture over toast; dust with paprika. Place under broiler until cheese is slightly melted and the top is a delicate brown. Serve hot. With toast cut into quarters, serves 16.

Cheddar-Cream Spread

 2 *cups grated or shredded cheddar cheese*
 2 *tablespoons olive oil*
 2 *tablespoons bourbon*
2-4 *tablespoons cream cheese or butter*

Combine ingredients and beat until smooth. Age at least two days before serving. Makes 2 cups cheese spread. Remove from refrigerator at least 1 hour before serving.

Roquefort Spread

4 *oz. roquefort cheese*
8 *oz. cream cheese, soft*
3 *tablespoons bourbon*

While the roquefort is still cold and firm, turn it into a fine mesh strainer, set over a mixing bowl. With a spoon press the cheese through the strainer. Add the soft cream cheese and thoroughly stir together until combined. Add the bourbon. Pack into a wide-mouth glass jar that will hold 1½-2 cups. Be sure the jar has a screw-type cover. Cover tightly and refrigerate for at least 1 week to allow flavors to blend and develop. Makes about 1½ cups.

Spiked Cheese Pastries

2 *cups unsifted flour*
½ *teaspoon salt*
1 *cup butter*
½ *lb. grated cheddar cheese*
3 *tablespoons bourbon*
1 *egg, beaten with 1 tablespoon water*
 sesame seeds, caraway seeds, coarse salt

Measure flour and salt into a bowl. Cut in butter and blend in cheese, as for piecrust. Stir in bourbon. Gather dough into a ball, wrap in plastic wrap, and chill for at least ½ hour. Roll out about ¼ inch thick on well-floured board. Cut as desired. Brush with beaten egg and sprinkle with seeds and coarse salt.

Bake on ungreased cooky sheets in preheated 375-degree oven for 8-10 minutes, until lightly browned. Makes about 4 dozen.

Teriyaki Appetizers

1 *lb. beef round in 1-inch cubes*

Sauce
½ *cup soy sauce*
2 *tablespoons sugar*
1 *teaspoon grated fresh ginger*
1 *clove grated garlic*
1 *tablespoon bourbon*
  dash of monosodium glutamate

Soak beef 90 minutes in sauce. Drain and broil.

Sausage and Bacon Tidbits

1 *lb. vienna sausages*
½ *lb. bacon (each strip cut in half)*
2 *oz. bourbon*

Wrap sausages in bacon, heat in moderate oven, blaze in 2 ounces bourbon, and serve.

Drunken Hot Dogs

2 *lb. hot dogs*
½ *cup brown sugar*
½ *cup bourbon*
1½ *cups tomato catsup*
½ *cup water*
2 *tablespoons minced onion*

Cut hot dogs into bite-size pieces. Combine all. Simmer for one hour. Serve with toothpicks in fondue pot.

Bourbon Hot Dogs

    1 lb. hot dogs
    ¾ cup bourbon
    1 teaspoon worcestershire sauce
    ⅛ teaspoon Tabasco
    1½ cups tomato catsup
    ½ cup brown sugar
    1 tablespoon grated onion

Cut hot dogs into half-inch slices. Simmer with remaining ingredients for one hour in frying pan. If liquid dries out too much, add a little bourbon. Serve hot from chafing dish.

Bourbon Wieners

    1 lb. vienna sausages
    1 cup bourbon
    1 cup tomato catsup
    ½ cup brown sugar
    1 teaspoon sweet sherry
    ¼ teaspoon nutmeg (or to taste)

Cut vienna cocktail wieners into ½-inch sections. Into a mixing dish pour bourbon, catsup, and brown sugar. Add sherry and nutmeg. Stir and pour into saucepan. Add wiener sections and simmer, without boiling, over very low fire for about 1 hour. Serve in chafing dish with toothpicks. Serves 8.

Cocktail Sandwich Filling

    1¾ cups butter, softened
    ½ cup bourbon
    salt

Blend well and spread on bread. Cover with thinly sliced salmon or ham. Cut into small squares.

Bourbon-Banana-Bacon Tidbits

3 *medium-sized bananas*
¼ *teaspoon curry powder*
2 *tablespoons lemon juice*
2 *tablespoons lime juice*
¼ *cup bourbon*
12 *slices bacon, cut in half*
1 *teaspoon cornstarch*

Cut bananas into ¾-inch slices. Combine curry powder, lemon juice, lime juice, and bourbon; add bananas. Let stand 1 hour, stirring frequently. Drain bananas; reserve bourbon mixture.

Wrap each banana slice in half-slice of bacon. Secure with toothpick. Broil bacon-wrapped banana slices 3-4 inches from source of heat 3 minutes.

Meanwhile, gradually add bourbon mixture to cornstarch to blend. Cook over low heat, stirring constantly, until thickened and clear. Turn banana slices; broil 2 minutes. Brush with bourbon mixture and broil 1 minute, or until bacon is desired degree of doneness. Makes about 2 dozen.

Bourbon-Walnut Mushrooms

30 *medium-sized mushrooms*
2 *tablespoons chopped onion*
1 *tablespoon melted butter*
½ *lb. ground beef*
   salt and pepper to taste
2 *tablespoons chopped parsley*
¼ *cup coarsely chopped walnuts*
¼ *cup bourbon*
2 *eggs, well beaten*
⅓ *cup fine dry bread crumbs*

Remove stems from mushrooms. Sauté onion in butter until lightly browned; add beef and brown well. Season mixture with salt and pepper; stir in parsley. Remove from heat.

Mix walnuts and bourbon into meat mixture; stir in eggs and bread crumbs. Pile meat mixture into mushrooms. Dust top lightly with bread crumbs and dot with butter, as desired.

Arrange mushrooms in greased shallow baking pan. Bake in moderate oven (375 degrees) about 20 minutes. Makes 2½ dozen.

Bourbon-Black Bean Dip

1 *can condensed black bean soup*
1 *cup tomato sauce*
1 *cup grated cheddar cheese*
¼ *cup bourbon*

Simmer bean soup, tomato sauce, and grated cheese. Stir in bourbon. Serve warm with potato chips.

Sour Cream Dip

1 *tablespoon bourbon*
1 *cup sour cream*
1 *teaspoon finely chopped dill*
pinch garlic salt
½ *teaspoon lemon juice*

To sour cream add bourbon, chopped dill, garlic salt, and lemon juice. Mix well and let stand a few hours. Serve with raw vegetables cut in bite-size pieces. Makes about 1 cup.

Bourbon Clam Dip

1 *7½-oz. can minced clams*
1 *1¼-oz. envelope dehydrated tomato soup mix*
2 *cups sour cream*
½ *cup bourbon*

Combine undrained clams and remaining ingredients; mix well. Chill at least 1 hour. Serve as a dip with potato chips or crackers. Makes about 3 cups dip.

Kentucky Corn Dip

      6 *strips bacon*
      1 *cup mayonnaise*
      1 *cup dairy sour cream*
      1 *clove garlic, finely chopped*
        chopped parsley
      1 *12-oz. can Mexicorn corn with sweet peppers, drained*
    ¼ *cup bourbon*
    ¼ *teaspoon Tabasco*

Fry bacon until crisp; crumble. Combine with remaining ingredients; chill thoroughly.

Serve with cherry tomatoes, cucumber strips, scallions and radishes. Yield: 3 cups dip.

Bourbon Hors d'Oeuvres

      1 *lb. ground chuck*
      1 *tablespoon salad oil*
      1 *8-oz. can tomato sauce*
    ½ *teaspoon crumbled bay leaves*
        salt and pepper to taste
    ¼ *cup bourbon*

Shape beef into 1-inch balls. Heat oil; add beef balls and cook over low heat until browned on all sides. Drain off drippings. Pour tomato sauce over meat balls. Stir in bay leaves and salt and pepper. Cover and cook over low heat 20 minutes. Remove from heat. Add bourbon and stir lightly. Serve with cocktail picks. Serves 8.

Soups

Corn-Oyster Chowder

  1 *7-oz. package frozen oysters, thawed*
  2 *tablespoons butter*
  ⅛ *tablespoon salt*
  ⅛ *teaspoon onion powder*
  ¼ *teaspoon paprika*
  ⅛ *teaspoon garlic powder*
  1 *jar strained corn (baby food)*
  1 *cup light cream*
  1 *tablespoon bourbon*

Put thawed oysters with their liquid, salt, onion powder, paprika, garlic powder, corn, cream, and 1 tablespoon butter in saucepan. Heat quickly. As edges of oysters start to curl, add bourbon. Stir several times and remove from heat. Top with remaining tablespoon butter. Serves 2.

Shrimp Bisque

    1 *can condensed tomato soup*
    1 *can condensed pea soup*
    2 *cups milk*
      dash cayenne
      dash worcestershire sauce
    1 *lb. shrimp, cooked, shelled, and deveined*
  1½ *oz. bourbon*

Blend tomato and pea soups, spices and milk. Heat slowly to boiling point, stirring occasionally. Add shrimp and bourbon. Continue cooking till shrimp are heated through. Serves 6.

Black Bean Soup

    1 *can black bean soup*
    1 *tablespoon lemon juice*
    1 *hard-boiled egg, sliced*
      dash Tabasco
    1 *oz. bourbon*
      salt and pepper to taste

Heat soup with salt and pepper, lemon juice, and Tabasco. When heated, add bourbon. Stir and let simmer 3 minutes longer. Garnish each portion with slice of egg sprinkled with paprika.

Crabmeat Kentucky Chowder

   ¼ *cup butter*
   4 *large mushrooms, sliced thin*
   2 *tablespoons grated onion*
   2 *fresh tomatoes, peeled and cut into eighths*
  ¾ *lb. fresh crabmeat, or two packages frozen crabmeat, thawed*
  ½ *teaspoon salt*
    pinch cayenne
    dash worcestershire sauce

dash Tabasco
1 cup heavy cream
2 teaspoons minced parsley
1 teaspoon minced chives
¼ cup bourbon

Melt butter in large skillet. Add mushrooms and cook, stirring gently till browned; about 5 minutes. Add onion and tomatoes. Cook and stir 5 minutes more. Add crabmeat, salt, cayenne, worcestershire, and Tabasco, stirring gently to keep meat in big pieces. After one minute stir in cream. When it bubbles, add parsley, chives, and bourbon. Serve at once over hot, cooked rice.

Clam Corn Soup

1 no. 1 can whole kernel corn
1 7-oz. can minced clams
2 cups heavy cream
2 tablespoons butter
3 oz. bourbon
½ teaspoon salt
¼ teaspoon paprika
dash Tabasco
½ teaspoon fine ground pepper
croutons

Blend corn and clams, including liquid from cans, in blender till smooth. Pour mixture into top part of double boiler. Add cream, salt, paprika, Tabasco, pepper, and butter and heat. When soup is at boiling point add bourbon. Serve with croutons.

Bean Soup Flambé

2 10½-oz. cans black bean soup
1 10½-oz. can condensed beef bouillon
2 soup cans water
dash paprika
dash Tabasco

    salt and pepper to taste
2 oz. bourbon
    lemon slices

Blend soups, adding water and seasonings. Heat, stirring often. Pour into heat-proof chafing dish. Heat bourbon in a ladle, ignite with match, and lower flaming ladle into soup. Stir slowly and serve, garnishing each dish with a lemon slice. Serves 6.

Pepperpot Soup

1 lb. honeycombed tripe, cut into 1-inch cubes
2 veal knuckles (about 1 lb. each)
2 quarts water
2 bay leaves, crumbled
½ teaspoon marjoram
¼ teaspoon thyme
1 teaspoon basil
2 teaspoons salt
¼ teaspoon cayenne
2 teaspoons crushed peppercorns
4 chicken bouillon cubes
1 cup chopped parsley
1 medium-sized green pepper
2 medium-sized onions, sliced
½ cup chopped celery
3 cups cubed potatoes
1½ cups milk
8 oz. bourbon

Place tripe and veal in soup kettle or large saucepan, add water, seasonings, and bouillon cubes. Heat to boiling point over medium heat. Cook, covered, 10 minutes. Skim, if necessary. Cover and cook over low heat 3 hours. Remove bones. Prepare vegetables and add to stock. Cover and simmer 40 minutes. Add milk and peppercorns, crushed if desired. Simmer few minutes longer and serve. Put two tablespoons bourbon into each serving. Serves 8.

Tomato-Pea Soup

    1 11¼-oz. can condensed green pea soup
    1 10¾-oz. can condensed tomato soup
    2 soup cans water
    2 beef bouillon cubes
       dash Tabasco
    1 oz. bourbon

Stir soups till smooth. Gradually blend in water, adding bouillon cubes and Tabasco. Add bourbon and heat, stirring occasionally; bring to boiling point. Serves 6.

Bourbon Cheese Soup No. 1

    1 cup water
    1 11-oz. can condensed cheddar cheese soup
    ½ teaspoon worcestershire sauce
    ¼ teaspoon Tabasco
    2 oz. bourbon
    4 slices bacon, cooked, drained, and crumbled

Slowly stir water into soup and add spices. Heat slowly to boiling point. Add bourbon and heat to serving temperature, stirring constantly. Pour into serving cups. Garnish with bacon. Serves 4.

Bourbon Cheese Soup No. 2

    1 cup flour
    5 cups beef bouillon
    1 cup red wine, dry
    3 cups cold water
    ½ onion, chopped fine
    1 bay leaf
    2 oz. bourbon
       salt and pepper to taste
    2 slices white bread
    4 tablespoons grated Swiss cheese

Put flour in skillet and stir steadily over low heat till golden brown. In a pot, combine onion and wine and reduce over heat to half volume. Mix cold water with browned flour till smooth. Add to beef bouillon, together with wine, onion, bay leaf, and bourbon, and simmer 45 minutes. Cut white bread into small cubes and sauté golden brown. Strain soup into soup bowls. Sprinkle each bowl with 1 tablespoon Swiss cheese and one-fourth of the croutons. Serves 4.

(Ground Floor Café, New York City)

Cream of Shrimp Soup

    1 *can cream of shrimp soup (frozen)*
    1 *soup can of milk*
  ⅛ *teaspoon Tabasco*
  ⅛ *teaspoon paprika*
      salt and pepper to taste
    3 *oz. frozen shelled and deveined shrimp*
    3 *tablespoons bourbon*

Heat shrimp soup and milk slowly. Add thawed shrimp to milk, soup, and spices. Heat thoroughly but do not boil. Add bourbon and serve. Serves 3.

Onion Soup, Kentucky Style

    1 *10½-oz. can condensed onion soup*
    1 *soup can water*
  ½ *teaspoon worcestershire sauce*
    2 *oz. bourbon*
      salt and pepper
  ¼ *teaspoon garlic powder*
    1 *cup croutons*
    1 *tablespoon grated parmesan cheese*

Prepare soup as label directs. Heat to boiling point. Add bourbon, worcestershire, garlic powder, salt and pepper, and stir well. Cook over low heat five minutes, stirring from time to time. Mix croutons and cheese together lightly. Pour soup into serving bowls. Top each serving with croutons. Serves 4.

French Onion Soup Flambé

    1 *quart thinly sliced onions*
    4 *tablespoons butter*
    2 *cloves garlic, minced*
    1 *quart plus 1 pint beef bouillon*
    1 *teaspoon worcestershire sauce*
      dash Tabasco
      dash paprika
      salt and pepper to taste
  12 *thin slices narrow French bread, toasted*
    4 *slices processed Swiss cheese*
      grated parmesan cheese
      paprika
      salad oil
    4 *oz. bourbon*

    Melt butter in soup pot. Add onions and garlic. Sauté slowly, stirring frequently till onions are yellow. Add broth and spices. Simmer 20 minutes.
    Pour soup into 4 bowls. Preheat oven to 425 degrees. Float 3 thin slices of bread on top of each portion. Place a third of a slice of Swiss cheese on each bread slice. Sprinkle with parmesan. Sprinkle lightly with paprika and oil. Place bowls in baking pan with about half an inch of water. Bake about 20 minutes, till tops are well browned. At table, spoon about 1 ounce bourbon atop each portion and ignite. Serves 4.

Onion Soup, Italian Style

    5 *cups thinly sliced yellow onions*
    3 *tablespoons olive oil*
    3 *tablespoons flour*
    1 *cup bourbon*
    2 *quarts chicken broth*

½ teaspoon basil
dash oregano
dash garlic powder
6 slices Italian bread, toasted
½ cup grated Swiss cheese

In a 3-quart, flameproof casserole, sauté onions in vegetable oil till soft. Stir in flour to form a paste. Add bourbon, stirring slowly. Stir in broth and season with spices and garlic powder. Simmer about 40 minutes. Top soup with toasted slices of Italian bread. Sprinkle with cheese and place under broiler till cheese is golden and bubbly. Serves 6.

Crab Bisque

2 7½-oz. cans crabmeat
1 can condensed tomato soup
1 can condensed pea soup
1 beef bouillon cube
dash cayenne
dash worcestershire sauce
1½ cups milk
4 oz. bourbon

Heat two cans of soup in saucepan, adding milk, bouillon cube, cayenne, and worcestershire. Heat well but do not boil. Add crab, stirring to avoid its sticking to pan. Do not boil. Just before serving stir in the whiskey. Serves 4.

Salads

Chicken Salad with Bourbon

    2 *cups chicken, cooked and cubed*
    ¼ *cup chopped celery*
    ¼ *cup green pepper, diced*
    2 *tablespoons onion, minced*
    ⅓ *cup sour cream*
    1 *tablespoon bourbon*
    ¼ *teaspoon salt*
    ¼ *teaspoon dry mustard*
    ½ *bunch watercress, trimmed and washed*
    1 *lemon, quartered*

In bowl, combine chicken, celery, green pepper, and onion. Place in refrigerator to chill. Prepare dressing of sour cream, bourbon, salt, and dry mustard. Fold dressing into chicken mixture and serve on bed of watercress with lemon wedges as garnish. Serves 4.

Avocado Salad

    2 *medium avocados*
   ½ *medium Bermuda onion, sliced thin*
    2 *oz. raisins*
    4 *oz. salad oil*
    3 *tablespoons lemon juice*
   ½ *teaspoon sugar*
    3 *tablespoons bourbon*
       salt and pepper
       dash Tabasco
       dash horseradish
    1 *orange*
       shredded lettuce

Peel avocados and cut into cubes. Combine in bowl with sliced onion and raisins. Mix with salad oil, lemon juice, sugar, bourbon, salt, pepper, Tabasco, and horseradish. Before serving add the orange, peeled and cut in sections. Serve salad on the shredded lettuce.

Limestone Lettuce Flambé

    5 *heads Kentucky limestone lettuce*
       juice 1 lemon
       salt and pepper to taste
    2 *slices fresh bacon*
    1 *teaspoon olive oil*
    1 *teaspoon grenadine*
    1 *oz. bourbon*
    2 *tablespoons wine vinegar*
       dash Angostura bitters
       dash worcestershire sauce

Sauté bacon till crisp. Add oil, then grenadine. Set aflame with bourbon and add vinegar, worcestershire, and bitters. Pour over lettuce to which lemon juice, salt and pepper have already been added. Serves 4.

(Hotel Americana, New York City)

Omelettes and Soufflés

Strawberry Omelette Flambé

    2 *eggs, separated*
  ¼ *teaspoon salt*
    1 *teaspoon lemon juice*
      dash vanilla
    2 *tablespoons sugar*
    1 *tablespoon clarified butter*
    2 *tablespoons bourbon*
    1 *cup strawberry preserve*

    Beat egg whites with salt till foamy. Gradually add 1 tablespoon sugar, beating till stiff. Beat egg yolks with lemon juice and vanilla till thick and lemon-colored. Fold yolks into whites. Heat clarified butter till bubbly, but not brown in an 8-inch omelette pan or skillet that has a cover. Pour in omelette mixture, smooth top

Omelettes and Soufflés 43

lightly, cover, and cook over very low heat 7 minutes or till top is dry and a knife inserted comes out clean. Make indentation in center of omelette, cutting through almost to bottom. Spoon strawberry preserve onto half of the omelette, fold other half of omelette over, and slide onto plate. Sprinkle top with remaining tablespoon sugar. Warm bourbon in a ladle, ignite, and pour flaming over omelette. Serve when flames go out. Serves 2-3.

To clarify butter: heat one stick of butter in small pan till just melted. Skim off foam and spoon off golden butter, leaving white sediment. Refrigerate clarified butter till needed.

Bourbon Omelette Ala Moana

    8 *eggs*
      salt
    2 *tablespoons brown sugar*
    2 *tablespoons bourbon*
      powdered sugar
    1 *oz. butter*

Beat eggs in bowl and add pinch salt, sugar, and 1 tablespoon bourbon. Warm butter in a pan and pour in beaten egg mix, thickening till it starts to firm by stirring with a large fork. Fold omelette as soon as it detaches from pan, and invert it with one stroke on a platter. Cover omelette with powdered sugar and glaze with an omelette heating iron, decorating top in any desired fashion. Serve omelette after pouring another tablespoon bourbon into bottom of the dish and setting afire. Serves 4.

(Ala Moana Hotel, Honolulu)

Bourbon Soufflé

    3 *tablespoons butter*
    3 *tablespoons flour*
    ¾ *cup milk*
    ½ *cup sugar*
    4 *eggs, separated*

pinch salt
  dash mace
2 oz. bourbon
¼ teaspoon almond extract

Melt butter in saucepan. Blend in flour and stir in milk. Cook till thickened, stirring till smooth. Add sugar. Stir till dissolved. Beat in lightly beaten egg yolks. Cool. Add salt and mace to egg whites. Beat till stiff. Fold into pudding mixture with bourbon and almond extract. Turn into a 1½-quart buttered soufflé dish. Bake in preheated oven at 375 degrees for 45 minutes. Serve at once with Bourbon Chocolate Sauce. Serves 6.

Bourbon Chocolate Sauce
1 cup semisweet chocolate pieces
½ cup dairy sour cream
¼ cup bourbon

Melt chocolate over hot water. Add sour cream and stir smooth. Pour bourbon into hot sauce, ignite, and pour over soufflé.

Raisin Bourbon Soufflé

⅓ cup butter
⅔ cup flour
2 tablespoons honey
4 oz. bourbon
  dash vanilla
½ cup raisins, blended to a puree
5 egg yolks
6 egg whites
¼ cup raisins

Make roux of butter and flour by melting butter, gradually adding flour till smooth. Slowly stir in honey, bourbon, and vanilla. Cook till mixture is thickened. Add blended raisins and egg yolks and cook 1 minute longer. Cool slightly. Beat egg whites till stiff but not dry and fold into mixture. Fold in raisins. Pour into buttered and sugared 1½-quart soufflé dish and bake in 375-degree oven for about 35 minutes. Serve with whipped cream. Serves 4-6.

Mocha Soufflé with Bourbon Sauce

    1 *cup milk*
    2 *squares (2 oz.) unsweetened chocolate*
    1 *tablespoon instant coffee powder*
    ⅓ *cup all-purpose flour*
    ¼ *teaspoon salt*
    4 *eggs, separated*
    1 *teaspoon almond extract*
    ¼ *teaspoon mace*
    ⅓ *cup sugar*

Combine ½ cup milk, chocolate, and coffee powder over boiling water and cook, stirring constantly till coffee is melted. Gradually stir remaining ½ cup milk into flour and salt to blend. Stir flour mixture into chocolate mixture and cook over boiling water, stirring constantly till very thick. Remove from heat; beat till smooth. Add yolks, one at a time, beating till smooth. Add almond extract and mace and mix well. Beat egg whites till soft peaks form. Gradually add sugar, beating constantly till smooth, stiff, and glossy. Fold chocolate mixture into egg whites. Turn into greased 1½-quart casserole. Bake in hot oven, about 425 degrees, for 35 minutes or till soufflé is done. Serves 6.

Bourbon Sauce

    ½ *cup sugar*
    2 *tablespoons cornstarch*
    ⅛ *teaspoon salt*
    1½ *cups water*
    ¼ *cup butter*
    ½ *cup bourbon*

Combine sugar, cornstarch, and salt; gradually add water and cook over low heat, stirring constantly, till thick and clear.

Remove from heat; add butter and bourbon. Stir till butter melts. Pour over soufflé.

Ham Soufflé

    8 oz. *sliced cooked ham*
  ⅓ *cup butter*
  ⅓ *cup flour*
1½ *cups milk*
    9 *eggs, whites and yolks separated*
    2 *tablespoons finely chopped fresh chives*
  ¼ *teaspoon caraway seed, ground*
1½ *oz. bourbon*
     dash cayenne
     dash Tabasco
     salt, pepper to taste

Preheat oven at 350 degrees. Put ham through grinder, using fine blade. Put butter, flour, and milk in saucepan. Bring to boil, stirring constantly. Remove from flame. Beat egg yolks well and add to sauce. Heat over low flame 1 minute, stirring constantly. Remove from flame. Add ham, chives, caraway seed, bourbon, Tabasco, cayenne, and salt and pepper to taste. Beat egg whites till stiff and glossy. Add one-quarter of beaten egg whites to ham mixture. Stir well. Slowly add ham mixture to balance of egg whites, folding in very carefully and lightly. Turn into 2-quart soufflé dish greased on bottom only. Fit dish with aluminum collar extending 2 inches above rim. Place dish in shallow pan with 1 inch boiling water. Bake 60-70 minutes or till well browned.

Mushroom Omelette

2 *eggs*
1 *tablespoon bourbon*
  dash Tabasco
  dash chervil
  salt and pepper
2 *tablespoons butter*
  cup of sliced fresh mushrooms

Beat eggs with bourbon till light, adding Tabasco, chervil, salt and pepper. Combine with mushrooms sautéed in 1 tablespoon butter. Cook omelette in pan greased with remaining butter till light and fluffy. Serves 1.

Old Bourbon Soufflé

> 8 *lady fingers*
> 2 *oz. bourbon*
> 2 *tablespoons butter*
> 1 *tablespoon flour*
> ½ *cup milk*
> ½ *teaspoon vanilla extract*
> 5 *egg yolks*
> 5 *tablespoons sugar*
> 6 *egg whites*
>   *powdered sugar*

Moisten lady fingers in the bourbon. Melt butter in saucepan; add flour and cook slowly till roux turns golden. Stir in milk and add vanilla. Beat in egg yolks with 4 tablespoons sugar and add to sauce. Beat egg whites well; then add 1 tablespoon sugar and blend into mixture throughly by folding over and over. Pour half mixture into buttered and sugared soufflé mold. Cover with lady fingers and fill dish with rest of soufflé mixture. Smooth the top with spatula. Bake soufflé in a 375-degree oven about 20 minutes, or till well puffed and delicately browned. A couple of minutes before removing soufflé from oven, sprinkle it with a little powdered sugar.

(Hotel Shoreham, Washington, D.C.)

Fondues

Bourbon Cheese Fondue

    16 *oz. Swiss cheese*
    1 *tablespoon flour*
    dash baking soda
    dash mace
    dash Tabasco
    dash powdered garlic
    ½ *teaspoon worcestershire sauce*
    1 *pint white wine*
    1 *cup bourbon*

Mix ingredients together, adding wine and bourbon when ready to cook. Cook over high heat in heavy pan till mixture thickens, stirring occasionally. Test to see if it sticks to bread (preferably one-inch cubes of French bread, with part of crust on each piece). Transfer to chafing dish with warmer beneath. Dunk bread cubes in mixture with long-handled forks. Serves 4.

Bourbon Cheese Fondue

Butterscotch-Bourbon Fondue

  2 6-oz. packages butterscotch flavor morsels
    dash nutmeg
  1 oz. sweet butter
  ¼ cup light cream
  ¼ cup bourbon

 Melt butterscotch morsels with cream and butter in a fondue pot over low heat, stirring occasionally until smooth. Stir in nutmeg and bourbon. Keep warm. Makes about 1½ cups.

Bourbon Swiss Fondue

    1 lb. Swiss cheese, shredded
    1 tablespoon flour
1½ cups dry white wine
1½ oz. bourbon
   ½ teaspoon worcestershire sauce
   ¼ teaspoon Tabasco
     apples and pears, cored and cut in chunks

Toss shredded cheese with flour. Pour wine into fondue pot or saucepan and bring just to simmer over low heat. Add cheese, a handful at a time, stirring constantly, and allowing it to melt before adding more. When cheese has melted and mixture is smooth, slowly stir in bourbon and seasonings. Serve with fruit pieces. Serves 4.

Golden Cheese Fondue

    1 lb. cheddar cheese, shredded
    1 tablespoon flour
1½ oz. bourbon
    7 oz. club soda
    1 teaspoon worcestershire sauce
     dash Tabasco
   ¼ teaspoon dry mustard
    1 tablespoon butter
    1 egg, lightly beaten
     French or Italian bread, cut in chunks, each with crust

Toss shredded cheese with flour. Combine bourbon, club soda, seasonings, and butter in a fondue pot or saucepan and bring to a simmer. Add cheese a handful at a time, stirring constantly, and allowing it to melt before adding more. Cook, stirring, until cheese has melted and mixture thickened. Add a little of the hot cheese mixture to the beaten egg and then stir back into pan. Stir smooth. Serve with crusty chunks of bread for dipping. Serves 4.

Seafood

Seafood Special

    1 *envelope unflavored gelatine*
  ¼ *cup hot water*
    1 *lb. prawns, unshelled*
    1 *15-oz. can crushed pineapple*
    4 *oz. cream cheese*
    2 *oz. bourbon*
        juice of 1 lemon
        dash mace
    1 *teaspoon grated orange rind*

Peel prawns and place in a bowl. Pour bourbon over the prawns and set aside. Dissolve gelatine in hot water. Beat cream cheese with lemon juice till smooth. Add crushed pineapple, mace, orange rind, and dissolved gelatine. Allow mixture to thicken slightly and fold in prawns and bourbon. Spoon into a mold and refrigerate till set.

Shrimp in Bourbon

    2 lbs. raw shrimp, peeled and deveined
    4 oz. bourbon
       bay leaf
    1 teaspoon salt
    ¼ teaspoon pepper
    ½ teaspoon horseradish
       dash worcestershire sauce
    2 tablespoons butter
    2 tablespoons flour

Put shrimp in saucepan; add bourbon, bay leaf, salt, pepper, horseradish, worcestershire, and enough water to just cover. Bring liquid to boil. Simmer shrimp 5-8 minutes, till pink. With perforated spoon, remove shrimp to serving dish. Reduce liquid, over high heat, to about 1½ cups and strain. Melt butter, stir in flour, and cook about 90 seconds. Stir in strained stock; cook till smooth and thickened. Add shrimp and reheat. Add salt and pepper to taste. Serve with rice. Serves 6.

Shrimp Flambé

    ½ cup butter
    6 tablespoons vegetable oil
    2 garlic cloves, minced
    2 small onions, grated
    1 cup finely chopped green pepper
   24 oz. raw shrimp, shelled and deveined
       cayenne and black pepper, salt
       dash Tabasco
    6 tablespoons finely minced parsley
       juice of 1 lemon
    3 tablespoons bourbon

Melt butter and oil in deep frying pan. Add garlic, onions, and green pepper. Cook 2 minutes, or till soft but not brown. Add shrimp, salt, cayenne and black pepper, and Tabasco. Cover and simmer 4 minutes, turning shrimp at least once. Add parsley and lemon juice and let simmer a couple of minutes. Turn off heat and add bourbon. Flame and send to table with rice or potato croquettes. Serves 4.

Shrimp and Mushrooms with Whiskey

1 lb. *unpeeled, raw shrimp*
½ cup *butter*
½ lb. *mushrooms*
2 tablespoons *lime juice*
1 tablespoon *minced parsley*
1 *clove garlic, pressed*
½ teaspoon *salt*
  dash black pepper
⅛ teaspoon *cayenne*
  dash worcestershire sauce
2 oz. *bourbon*

Place shrimp in 1 quart boiling water. When water comes to second boil after adding shrimp, cover and lower heat. Simmer about 5 minutes till shrimp turn pink. Peel and devein shrimp.

Heat butter till it bubbles. Add mushrooms and sauté gently. Add shrimp and heat through. Add lime juice, parsley, garlic, salt, black pepper, cayenne, worcestershire, and bourbon. Serve over hot rice.

Broiled Shrimp

1½ lb. *large raw shrimp with shells*
1¼ cups *bourbon*
⅛ teaspoon *worcestershire sauce*
1 tablespoon *salad oil*
1 *clove minced garlic*
2 tablespoons *chopped parsley*
1 teaspoon *lemon juice*
½ teaspoon *salt*
⅛ teaspoon *pepper*

Split unpeeled shrimp lengthwise to tail, leaving shells on. Rinse and remove vein in back and pat dry. (If you prefer, you can shell the shrimp, leaving whole.) Combine remaining ingredients with the bourbon. Dip each shrimp into bourbon mixture and arrange on broiling pan. Pour remaining mixture over the shrimp. Broil shrimp 6 inches below heated broiler 7 to 10 minutes, depending on size. Serves 4.

Wild Oriental Shrimp

 2 *oz. bourbon*
 2 *tablespoons soy sauce*
 1 *clove crushed garlic*
 4 *tablespoons vegetable oil*
  dash mace
  dash Tabasco
 1 *tablespoon candied ginger, minced*
 1 *lb. raw shrimp, deveined and shelled*

Combine 1 tablespoon bourbon, soy sauce, 2 tablespoons oil, garlic, mace, Tabasco, and ginger. Pour mixture over shrimp. Heat remaining oil in skillet and add shrimp. Cook about five minutes, stirring occasionally, till shrimp turns pink. Warm rest of bourbon, ignite, and pour over shrimp in pan; stir slowly till flames die. Serve with rice. Serves 2.

Shrimp Orleans

 ½ *lb. butter*
 2 *teaspoons parsley flakes*
  dash worcestershire sauce
 ¼ *teaspoon onion salt*
 ¼ *teaspoon garlic salt*
 6 *5-oz. cans deveined shrimp*
 4 *4-oz. cans sliced mushrooms*
 3 *oz. bourbon*

Put butter, parsley flakes, worcestershire, onion salt, and garlic salt in 12-inch skillet. Drain shrimp and mushrooms and add to skillet along with the bourbon. Let simmer about 10 minutes till butter is melted, ingredients are hot, and bourbon is assimilated. Serve over hot rice. Serves 8.

Deviled Lobster Tails

    2   *9-oz. packages frozen rock lobster tails*
  ¼   *cup butter*
  ¼   *cup all-purpose flour*
    1   *cup milk*
    1   *teaspoon prepared horseradish*
  ¼   *teaspoon cayenne*
       dash worcestershire sauce
    1   *tablespoon chopped parsley*
    1   *teaspoon salt*
  ⅛   *teaspoon pepper*
    2   *teaspoons lemon juice*
    2   *tablespoons fine dry bread crumbs*
    4   *oz. bourbon*

Boil lobster according to package directions. Drain. Cut away undershell, using scissors, and discard. Remove meat and dice, reserving shells. Melt butter, add flour, and blend. Gradually add milk, horseradish, cayenne, worcestershire, parsley, salt and pepper, and cook over low heat, stirring steadily, till thickened. Add lemon juice and lobster, mix well. Fill lobster shells with creamed mixture. Sprinkle with crumbs and arrange in shallow baking dish. Bake in 400-degree oven 10 minutes. Remove mixture from oven, spoon bourbon over lobster, and serve garnished with lemon wedges and parsley, if desired. Serves 4-6.

Shrimp Calypso

  24   *peeled, deveined raw jumbo shrimp or prawns*
    2   *chopped shallots*

3 red green peppers, cut julienne
 ½ teaspoon minced fresh garlic
 2 tomatoes, diced
 turmeric, oregano, white pepper, and salt to taste
 4 oz. melted butter
 2 oz. bourbon

Sauté shrimp in butter over light heat. Add garlic, shallots, and a dash of turmeric and oregano. Flame with bourbon; then add peppers and tomatoes and season with salt and pepper. Cover and let simmer several minutes. Serve with steamed rice. Serves 4.

(Hotel Americana, New York City)

Rock Lobster Tails Inferno

 4 frozen rock lobster tails (2 10-oz. packages)
 2 oz. butter, melted
 dash Tabasco
 dash A-1 sauce
 2 tablespoons lemon juice
 2 oz. bourbon

Prepare lobster tails for broiling according to package directions. Place tails shell side up on rack of broiling pan. Combine butter, lemon juice, Tabasco, and A-1 sauce. Turn lobster tails and brush with lemon-spice butter. Broil 4 minutes or till lobster flakes easily with fork. Serve in shell with remaining sauce. Upon serving, sprinkle hot lobster with the bourbon and ignite. Serves 4.

Lobster Grand Marnier

 2 tablespoons butter
 1 lb. cooked lobster meat
 1 oz. Grand Marnier
 1 oz. bourbon
 1 can lobster bisque
 ¼ teaspoon paprika

Rock Lobster Tails Inferno

>   dash Tabasco
> 3 tablespoons sour cream
> 1 tablespoon cornstarch
>   juice of half a lemon
>   salt and pepper to taste

Melt butter in skillet. Toss lobster meat in it till hot. Pour Grand Marnier and bourbon over lobster and ignite. When flame dies add bisque, paprika, salt and pepper, Tabasco, sour cream mixed with cornstarch, and lemon juice. Cook till hot, thick, and bubbly. Serve on steamed rice. Serves 4.

Lobster au Whiskey

> 1¾ lb. lobster meat, cut in chunks
> 8   tablespoons butter
> 3   cups heavy cream (scalded)
> 6   oz. bourbon
> 2   tablespoons flour
>   salt, black pepper, and cayenne to taste

Heat two tablespoons butter in heavy, shallow pan. Sauté lobster meat lightly. Add cream and let simmer about 5 minutes. Knead 3 tablespoons of butter with the flour. Add this to lobster, stirring steadily with wooden spoon till it thickens. Season with salt, black pepper, and cayenne. Let simmer another five minutes. Remove from fire; pour in bourbon and the remaining butter. Mix well and serve with timbales of rice and artichoke bottoms stuffed with puree of peas around. Serves 6.

Lobster Queen Anne

> 2 lbs. fresh lobster meat, boiled
> 2 oz. butter
> 1 oz. cognac
> 3 oz. bourbon
> 1 quart heavy cream
> 1 cup chopped shallots

1 tablespoon chopped tarragon
1 tablespoon chopped parsley
1 cup dry white wine

Cut lobster into medium-sized chunks; place in heavy casserole with butter and warm. When hot, flame it with the cognac and 2 oz. of bourbon. Add the shallots and cook 6 minutes. Remove lobster from casserole and set aside. Stir a cup of dry white wine into the liquid in the casserole, reduce the fluid, and add the cream. Reduce again, stirring steadily. Soak the lobster in the hot sauce, add salt and pepper to taste, and add the remainder of the bourbon. Add the tarragon and parsley. Serves 6.

(Hotel Shoreham, Washington, D.C.)

Cioppino

2 cloves garlic, minced
2 onions, chopped fine
2 tablespoons vegetable oil
handful of parsley, chopped
1 medium can tomato sauce
dash oregano, sage, rosemary, and cinnamon
½ peel of 1 lemon
dash Tabasco and dash worcestershire sauce
salt and pepper to taste
1 teaspoon horseradish
1 lb. butter clams
2 lb. flounder fillets, cut up in small pieces
1 lb. shrimp, raw, shelled, and deveined
4 oz. dry sherry
4 oz. bourbon

Brown onions in oil; then add garlic, parsley, tomato sauce, oregano, sage, rosemary, cinnamon, lemon peel, salt and pepper, Tabasco, worcestershire, and horseradish. Add clams and flounder pieces and simmer another 15 minutes. Add shrimp, sherry, and bourbon and simmer 5 minutes more. Good with steamed rice or buttered spaghetti.

Bourbon Seafood Shells

2 tablespoons butter
2 tablespoons all-purpose flour
½ teaspoon seasoned salt
¼ teaspoon paprika
¼ teaspoon monosodium glutamate
⅛ teaspoon pepper
  dash worcestershire sauce
⅔ cup milk
⅓ cup bourbon
1 6½-oz. can crabmeat, drained, boned, and flaked
2 hard-boiled eggs, chopped
1 tablespoon chopped parsley
2 tablespoons chopped chives

Melt butter; add flour, seasoned salt, paprika, monosodium glutamate, pepper, and worcestershire, and blend. Gradually add milk and bourbon and cook over low heat, stirring constantly till thickened. Add crabmeat, eggs, parsley, and chives. Spoon into small seafood shells (clam or scallop will do). Bake in 350-degree oven 10 minutes. Serves about 12.

Crabmeat Bourbonnaise

¼ cup butter
2 cups sliced mushrooms
½ cup chopped green pepper
¼ cup chopped pimiento
1 tomato, medium, peeled and sliced
1 tablespoon minced shallots
4 tablespoons flour
2 cups light cream
1 lb. crabmeat
1 tablespoon minced chives
  salt and pepper to taste
2 oz. bourbon

Bourbon Seafood Shells *(bottom dish)* **and Bourbon-Banana-Bacon Tidbits**
(top dish)

Melt butter in large skillet. Add mushrooms and green pepper and cook over moderate heat, stirring for 5 minutes. Add pimiento, tomato, and shallots. Cook 1 minute. Blend in flour. Add cream, stirring rapidly. Add crabmeat, salt and pepper and heat till it bubbles. Add chives and bourbon. Serve with steamed rice or noodles.

Crabmeat au Crème

2 *oz. butter*
2 *cups sliced fresh mushrooms*
4 *tablespoons chopped pimiento*
½ *cup celery, chopped fine*
1 *tomato, peeled and cut in thin wedges*
1 *tablespoon minced onion*
2 *tablespoons flour*
2 *cups light cream*
2 *6-oz. packages frozen crabmeat, thawed, drained, and flaked*
½ *tablespoon salt*
¼ *tablespoon coarsely ground black pepper*
¼ *teaspoon paprika*
3 *teaspoons minced chives*
2 *oz. bourbon*

Melt butter in large skillet. Add pimiento, mushrooms, tomato, celery, and onion. Cook three minutes. Sprinkle with flour. Slowly add cream, stirring constantly. Add crabmeat, salt, pepper and paprika. Heat, stirring gently till it bubbles. Add chives and bourbon and simmer another minute. Serve over steamed rice. Serves 6.

Seafood Louisiana

3 *oz. butter*
¼ *cup onion, chopped*
12 *oz. lobster meat*

4 oz. bourbon
1 cup mushrooms, sliced
1 green pepper, diced
½ cup celery, diced
1 pimiento, diced
6 tomatoes, peeled and chopped
1 cup tomato sauce
pepper to taste
salt to taste
paprika to taste

Melt 2 oz. butter in heavy shallow pan and cook onion till soft. Add seafood and cook 3 minutes, stirring constantly. Add bourbon. In another pan, melt 1 oz. butter and sauté mushrooms, green pepper, celery, pimiento, and tomatoes till tender. Add tomato sauce and bring to a simmer. Add seafood and mix thoroughly. Season to taste. Serve in a rice ring. Decorate with a little parsley and paprika.

Fowl

Breast of Chicken with Bourbon

   4 *half chicken breasts*
¼ *cup flour*
½ *teaspoon paprika*
½ *teaspoon salt*
   2 *tablespoons butter*
   2 *tablespoons salad oil*
   2 *tablespoons minced onion*
   1 *tablespoon minced parsley*
¼ *cup bourbon*
   1 *4-oz. can mushrooms*
   1 *10-oz. can tomatoes*
¼ *teaspoon sugar*
⅛ *teaspoon monosodium glutamate*
     salt, pepper

Breast of Chicken with Bourbon

Place chicken in a paper bag with flour, paprika, and salt. Shake bag well to coat chicken thoroughly, remove from bag, and shake off excess flour.

In a heavy saucepan melt the butter; add salad oil and sauté the chicken until light brown on both sides. Add onion and parsley. After browning, add bourbon and set aflame for about 10 seconds. Add mushrooms—pieces, stems, and juice—to the pan. Chop the tomatoes coarsely and add with juice to the pan. Cover with a tight lid, and continue to simmer 12 to 15 minutes, stirring occasionally. If necessary, remove the lid and continue to cook until the sauce is medium thick. Skim excess fat from sauce. Add sugar, monosodium glutamate, and salt and pepper to taste. Serve with noodles, vermicelli, or rice in a casserole. Serves 4.

Pears 'n' Chicken

8 *canned pear halves*
½ *stick butter, melted*
¼ *cup orange juice*
2 *tablespoons lemon juice*
2 *tablespoons bourbon*
½ *teaspoon salt*
½ *teaspoon pepper*
2 *broiler-fryers*
whole cranberry sauce

Combine butter, orange and lemon juice, bourbon, and salt and pepper. Use this to brush chicken pieces, placed skin side down in broiler pan. Broil 10 inches from heat about 30 minutes. Baste occasionally with butter sauce. Turn chicken and baste; broil about 30 minutes longer. During the last 10 minutes of broiling, add pear halves generously brushed with butter sauce. Warm cranberry sauce a little and use to fill pear halves. Arrange attractively in a plate. Serves 4.

Chicken and Fruit Sauce

1 *broiler-fryer chicken, cut in serving pieces*
2 *tablespoons bourbon*

2 *teaspoons lime juice*
　　1 *cup sifted cornstarch*
　½ *teaspoon allspice*
　　1 *teaspoon ground ginger*
　　6 *tablespoons corn oil*
　　1 *recipe Fruit Sauce (see below)*

Mix liquor, lime juice. Rub mixture into chicken pieces. Cover and let stand 1 hour. Mix cornstarch, allspice, and ginger and put into a paper bag. Place chicken pieces in bag and coat evenly. Heat corn oil in a heavy skillet over medium heat. Fry chicken, turning as needed, to a light golden brown. Place browned chicken in a 13¼ x 9¼ x 2¼ -inch baking pan. Pour Fruit Sauce over chicken. Bake in preheated 300-degree oven 45 minutes or until chicken is tender. Serves 3.

Fruit Sauce

　¼ *cup currant jelly*
　　2 *tablespoons bourbon*
　　1 *teaspoon honey*
　　1 *13¼ -oz. can pineapple chunks, undrained*

Mash jelly with a fork; blend in liquor and honey. Stir in pineapple.

Chicken Cacciatore

　　1 *3-lb. frying chicken*
　½ *cup olive oil*
　　1 *clove garlic*
　　2 *teaspoons salt*
　½ *teaspoon pepper*
　　4 *tablespoons flour*
　　1 *green pepper, sliced*
　　1 *medium onion, sliced*
　　1 *no. 2 can of tomatoes*
　¼ *teaspoon celery seed*

½ teaspoon ginger
2 tablespoons chopped parsley
½ lb. mushrooms, sliced
2 tablespoons butter
¼ cup sauterne
1 tablespoon bourbon

Cut chicken into serving pieces. Heat olive oil in skillet; brown garlic clove and remove from oil. Rub salt, pepper, and flour into chicken pieces. Brown chicken; add green pepper and onion and sauté lightly.

Add tomatoes, celery seed, ginger, and parsley and simmer on low heat for 30 minutes, or until chicken is tender. Melt butter in small skillet and sauté mushrooms. Add mushrooms, sauterne, and bourbon to chicken. Cook on high heat for about 5 minutes. Serves 4-6.

Chicken Sauté Bourbon

2 broiler-fryers (2½-3 lb. each), cut into serving pieces
flour
3 tablespoons butter
1 tablespoon vegetable oil
salt and pepper to taste
1 medium onion, finely chopped
¼ cup bourbon
2 cups chicken broth
2 teaspoons lime juice
3 tablespoons bourbon

Wash chicken and pat dry. Dredge chicken in flour and shake off any excess. In a very large skillet, heat the butter and oil. Sprinkle the chicken with salt and pepper and sauté, a few pieces at a time, on both sides until nicely browned. As each piece of chicken browns, remove it to a platter. When all the chicken has been sautéed, add the chopped onion to the skillet and sauté until wilted. Put the chicken back in the skillet and pour ¼ cup bourbon over it. Ignite the bourbon and when the flames die down, add the chicken broth and lime juice. Cover and simmer the chicken 20 minutes.

At the end of the cooking period, place the chicken in an ovenproof casserole or baking dish. Over high heat, reduce the sauce in the skillet until slightly thickened. Strain the sauce over the chicken. Use the additional 3 tablespoons of bourbon to flame at table. Serves 6.

Chicken in Orange-Lemon Sauce

2 *small whole chicken breasts, split and boned*
salt and black pepper
3 *tablespoons butter*
6 *oz. frozen orange juice concentrate, thawed*
1 *tablespoon fresh lemon juice*
¼ *cup chopped pecans*
2 *tablespoons bourbon*

Season chicken with salt and pepper. Brown in butter on both sides. Add juices, ½ teaspoon salt, and ¼ teaspoon pepper. Cover and simmer 20 minutes, or until tender. Occasionally spoon sauce over chicken.

Remove chicken to serving plates; sprinkle with nuts. Keep warm. Reduce liquid in pan to consistency of heavy cream by cooking over high heat and stirring. Add bourbon, stir to blend, and pour over chicken. Serves 2.

Creole Chicken

1 *3- to 4-lb. broiler-fryer, cut up*
1 *teaspoon salt*
½ *teaspoon pepper*
dash cayenne
¼ *cup (½ stick) corn oil margarine*
1 *lb. fresh mushrooms, thinly sliced*
1 *cup water*

½ cup bourbon
1 beef bouillon cube
2 tablespoons tomato paste
1 tablespoon flour
1 tablespoon margarine
½ cup pimiento strips

Sprinkle chicken with salt, pepper, and cayenne. Heat ¼ cup margarine in large skillet. Add chicken and brown well. Remove from skillet and set aside. Add mushrooms to skillet; cook 3 minutes, stirring frequently. Stir in water, bourbon, bouillon cube, and tomato paste. Add chicken. Cover; bring to boil. Simmer about 40 minutes, or until chicken is done.

Remove chicken to heated serving dish. Blend together flour and 1 tablespoon margarine. Add to liquid in skillet. Cook until thickened and boiling, stirring constantly. Gently stir in pimiento strips; cook 1 minute. Pour over chicken. Serves 4.

Chinese Walnut Chicken

1 cup bamboo shoots
1½ cup diced celery
½ cup chopped green peppers
1 cup sliced onions
1 clove crushed garlic
8 water chestnuts (1 can)
6 tablespoons plus 4 oz. oil
½ lb. walnuts
1 lb. cubed raw chicken
¾ teaspoon salt
2 tablespoons cornstarch
3-4 tablespoons soy sauce
2 tablespoons bourbon
1 teaspoon sugar
½ cup chicken stock

Sauté first 6 ingredients lightly in 3 tablespoons oil. Remove from pan. Brown the nuts in 4 ounces oil, remove, and drain.

Dredge chicken in a mixture of next 5 ingredients. Sauté in 3 tablespoons oil until tender. Add the chicken stock and heat thoroughly. Add vegetables and nuts; heat and serve.

Chicken Ginger

    1 *3-lb. frying chicken, cut up*
    1 *cup bourbon*
    1 *cup soy sauce*
    2 *heaping tablespoons sugar*
    2 *(or more) tablespoons grated fresh ginger*

Marinate chicken 6 hours in above ingredients, mixed. Bake at 325 degrees, uncovered, for about 2 hours, or until done. Use marinade to baste chicken from time to time. Serves 3-4.

Breast of Capon with White Grapes

    4 *breasts of capon*
    1 *bunch white grapes*
    1 *tablespoon butter*
    1 *oz. vegetable oil*
       salt, pepper
  ½ *cup flour*
    1 *cup chopped shallots*
    3 *oz. bourbon*
    6 *oz. white wine*
    1 *pint light cream*
  ¼ *cup chopped parsley*

Season breasts with salt and pepper. Coat with flour and soak in Sauce Anglaise (see below). Cook in casserole with butter and oil. After about 15 minutes, when breasts are lightly browned, remove from casserole, place in serving dish, and keep in warm place. Discard cooking fat from casserole and put in shallots. Cook 6-8 minutes; then add bourbon and wine, stirring constantly. Reduce the fluid and add the cream. Reduce again for a few minutes. Wash grapes, remove seeds, and place in sauce. Pour sauce over breasts and sprinkle with chopped parsley. Serves 4.

Sauce Anglaise
2 *eggs*
6 *oz. light cream*
salt and pepper

Mix eggs with cream and season with salt and pepper.

Hotel Shoreham, Washington, D. C.

Cornish Hens

¾ *cup onion, chopped*
1¾ *cup melted butter*
¼ *teaspoon Tabasco*
4½ *cups cooked brown rice*
⅔ *cup chopped walnuts, sautéed in butter*
salt to taste
chicken livers, cooked and chopped
½ *teaspoon thyme*
8 *cornish hens*
1¼ *teaspoon salt*
¼ *teaspoon pepper*
½ *cup bourbon*
8 *tablespoons red currant jelly, melted*

Sauté onion in 1 tablespoon butter and mix with Tabasco and rice. Add walnuts, salt, thyme, and ½ teaspoon butter. Mix well. Add already cooked and chopped livers. Stuff hens. Place hens in shallow baking dish. Mix 1¼ teaspoon salt and ¼ teaspoon pepper with ½ cup melted butter. Pour over hens. Roast in 425-degree oven for 20 minutes, basting 3 times with bourbon and remaining butter. Reduce heat to 350 degrees; roast 30 minutes, basting every 15 minutes. Turn breast side down and baste and roast 15 minutes. If liquid evaporates, add ½ cup bouillon. Turn hens; pour melted currant jelly over hens for last 30 minutes of baking.

Bourbon Goose

    1 *goose, 10 to 12 lb.*
    2 *teaspoons salt*
    1 *teaspoon pepper*
    2 *teaspoons caraway seeds*
    1 *cup bourbon*
    3 *cups diced apples*
    2 *1-lb. jars cooked prunes, drained and pitted*
    1 *cup raisins*
1½ *cups bread crumbs*
    1 *onion, chopped*
      salt and pepper to taste
      dash Tabasco

Wipe goose inside and out. Rub inside and out with salt, pepper, and caraway seeds, mixed together, and sprinkle with ¼ cup of the bourbon. Cover loosely and store in the refrigerator 8 hours or more to mellow.

To make the stuffing, simmer apples and prune juice in a covered saucepan until the fruit is soft. Add prunes, raisins, bread crumbs, chopped onion, and another ¼ cup bourbon. Blend well and add salt, pepper, and Tabasco to taste. Cool before stuffing goose.

Fill goose lightly with mixture and fasten opening with skewers or sew together. Truss legs and especially wings tightly against the body of the bird. Roast goose on a rack in a shallow pan in a 350-degree oven for about 2½ hours, draining off the fat as it accumulates. Pour the remaining ½ cup bourbon over the bird and roast for about 1 hour longer or until the goose is tender, basting it occasionally with the pan juices. Test the goose for tenderness by pressing the flesh of the leg. The skin should be very crisp and brown.

Remove the goose to a platter, discard the string and skewers, and garnish with apple slices and prunes.

Kentucky Duck

    1 *3-lb. duck*
       salt and pepper
    1 *pt. thickened veal stock*
  12 *oz. cream*
    4 *oz. butter*
    8 *half apricots*
    2 *oz. bourbon*
    4 *oz. orange juice*

Salt and pepper the duck and cook in a hot oven for 1½ hours; when cooked, take the duck out of pan and drain off the fat.

Mix bourbon and orange juice and put into the pan. Add the veal stock and cream, salt and pepper to taste, and let it reduce until it has thickened.

Put half apricots with a bit of sugar on top to brown under the grill.

Cut the duck up in portions, put on a dish with the half apricots on top, and pour the sauce over the duck.

Marinated Duck

   1 *3-lb. duck*
  ½ *cup lime juice*
   1 *teaspoon Tabasco*
  ½ *cup soy sauce*
   1 *small onion, diced*
     salt
   1 *slice bacon*
  ¼ *cup bourbon*

Thoroughly wash the cavity of the duck. Marinate duck in a mixture of lime juice, Tabasco, onion, and soy sauce for several hours. Remove from marinade; lightly salt the cavity. Place, breast side up, in a roasting pan with the bacon strip on top.

Bake uncovered in a preheated oven 30 minutes at 450 degrees. Reduce heat to 250 degrees. Remove the bacon strip; pour marinade and half of the bourbon over the duck. Cover roaster; bake approximately 2 hours. During the last hour of cooking, pour balance of bourbon over the duck.

Kentucky Duckling

Duck
- 1 *duck, 4 to 6 lb.*
- 1 *orange, quartered*
- 1 *clove garlic*
- ½ *cup lime marmalade*
- 1 *teaspoon salt*
- ½ *teaspoon paprika*
- ¼ *cup melted butter*
- ¼ *cup bourbon*

Preheat oven to 425 degrees. Stuff duckling cavity with the orange quarters, garlic, salt, and paprika. Close cavity with small skewers or toothpicks. Lace with twine and truss. Place duckling on a rack in a shallow roasting pan; brush well with melted butter. Pour bourbon over duckling and roast uncovered for 30 minutes. Reduce heat to 375 degrees. Roast duckling 40 minutes, basting twice with pan drippings. Turn over on its breast; roast 20 minutes. Turn on its back again and roast 30 minutes, basting twice. Spread with marmalade and roast 10 minutes longer. Serve with sauce.

Sauce
- 3 *tablespoons butter*
- 1 *duck liver*
- 3 *tablespoons plus ¼ cup bourbon*
- 2 *tablespoons grated orange rind*
- ½ *teaspoon minced garlic*
- 3 *tablespoons flour*
- ⅛ *teaspoon pepper*
- ⅛ *teaspoon ground nutmeg*
- 1 *teaspoon tomato catsup*
- 1 *teaspoon beef extract*
- 1 *cup orange juice*

>   2 oz. lemon juice
>   1 cup chicken broth
>   ¼ cup burgundy
>   ¼ cup orange marmalade
>   1 navel orange, sliced

Heat 2 tablespoons butter in medium skillet; add liver and brown well. Heat 3 tablespoons bourbon slightly. Light and pour over liver. Add remaining butter, orange rind, and minced garlic. Simmer 2 minutes. Remove from heat. Chop liver fine and set aside. Into skillet stir flour, pepper, nutmeg, catsup, and beef extract until smooth. Add orange and lemon juice, chicken broth, burgundy, marmalade, and ¼ cup bourbon. Bring to boiling point. Reduce heat and simmer 10 minutes. Add sliced oranges and chopped liver.

Thanksgiving Turkey and Dressing

>   1 18-lb. turkey
>   4 lb. white bread
> 2½ lb. chopped onions
>   4 cups chopped celery
>   1 cup raisins
>   ½ lb. chopped chicken livers
>   6 eggs
>   3 oz. bourbon
>   pinch each sage and basil
>   ½ teaspoon mace
>   salt and pepper to taste

Soak and squeeze out bread. Sauté chopped onions and add with all other ingredients to bread. Mix well, stuff turkey, and brush with oil. Roast in 350-degree oven in a covered enamel roaster for 3½ hours. Serves 8.

Turkey and Bourbon

>   1 turkey, 10 to 12 lb.
>   1 cup chopped onions

Fowl

   1 *cup chopped celery*
¼ *cup chopped parsley*
½ *cup chopped walnuts*
   5 *cups soft bread crumbs*
½ *teaspoon salt*
⅛ *teaspoon pepper*
½ *teaspoon ginger*
   6 *oz. bourbon*
   1 *egg, beaten*
½ *teaspoon poultry seasoning*
   2 *ounces melted margarine*

Combine onions, celery, parsley, walnuts, bread crumbs, salt, pepper, ginger, bourbon, egg, and poultry seasoning. Fill turkey cavity with dressing and secure openings. Place on rack in a shallow roasting pan. Brush with melted butter. Bake 5 hours in a 325-degree oven or till meat thermometer registers 190 degrees. Brush with margarine frequently while turkey is roasting.

Roast Turkey, Julep Style

1 *10-lb. turkey*
1 *large white onion*
1 *cup chopped celery*
  chopped parsley
2 *sprigs mint, minced*
  salt, pepper to taste
2 *cups diced stale bread*
½ *cup chopped pecans*
1 *cup bourbon*
1 *tablespoon poultry seasoning*
3 *tablespoons butter*
  paprika
  foil

Make dressing by mixing finely chopped onion and all the other ingredients, except last 3, together. Stuff turkey loosely and sew up both cavities with coarse thread.

Spread butter all over top side of turkey. Salt and pepper a bit; sprinkle generously with paprika. Place breast side up in a large roasting pan and cook 30 minutes at a moderately high heat. Lay large piece of foil over the breast of the bird; add ½ cup of water to drippings in bottom of pan and continue to roast another 90 minutes.

Test for doneness as the bird might need another 20-30 minutes. Remove foil to give the last crisping to the skin.

A bit more water may be added to prevent bird sticking to the pan. Serve with its sauce in a bowl apart.

Roast Turkey with Bourbon Stuffing

    1 *10-lb. turkey*
    1 *large white onion*
  ½ *cup chopped pecans*
    2 *cups dry bread stuffing*
      salt and pepper to taste
    1 *pinch sage*
    1 *pinch basil*
    1 *cup bourbon*
      olive oil
      parsley, chopped
      paprika

Mince onion and mix it with chopped pecans, bread stuffing, salt, pepper, seasoning, and bourbon. Stuff turkey lightly with the mixture. Brush olive oil over the skin of the turkey and dust with parsley and paprika. Skewer firmly and let turn in rotisserie for about 15 minutes per pound.

Braised Turkey

    1 *turkey, 8 to 10 lb.*
      salt, pepper, and ground nutmeg
    6 *cloves*
    1 *medium onion, peeled*

Roast Turkey with Bourbon Stuffing *(top)*, **Bourbon Molds** *(center)*, **and Glazed Sweet Potatoes and Pineapples** *(bottom)*

1 rib celery
2 oz. chopped parsley
1 apple, quartered
1 carrot
flour
2 tablespoons each butter and oil
¼ cup bourbon
1 10½-oz. can condensed chicken broth, undiluted
½ cup dry white wine
4 parboiled yams, peeled and cut in large cubes

Season turkey inside and out with salt, pepper, and nutmeg. Insert cloves in onion and place in turkey cavity with celery, parsley, apple, and carrot. Tie wings and legs close to body with string. Pat outside of turkey dry with paper towels; dust lightly with flour. Heat butter and oil in a large, shallow ovenproof pan and brown turkey on all sides. Warm bourbon in a large ladle; ignite and pour over turkey (the flames will shoot up, but only for an instant). Spoon pan juices over the turkey until flames die down. Add chicken broth and wine. Cover pan with heavy aluminum foil, tucking edges tightly around sides.

Bake in preheated 400-degree oven. After 1 hour uncover and add yams. Cover and cook 1 hour longer. Uncover and bake about 25 minutes to brown turkey. For gravy, skim fat off pan juices, taste for seasoning, and thicken slightly with cornstarch if desired.

Turkey Tetrazzini

½ lb. spaghetti
1 tablespoon butter
4 tablespoons butter
⅓ cup flour
2 cups turkey broth or chicken broth
½ teaspoon Tabasco
1 cup light cream
½ teaspoon parsley, chopped
¼ lb. mushrooms

2 *tablespoons bourbon*
2 *cups diced cooked turkey*
½ *cup grated parmesan cheese*

Cook spaghetti according to package directions. Slice mushrooms and cook in one tablespoon butter until soft and lightly browned. Prepare cream sauce: melt the 4 tablespoons butter, add flour, and blend thoroughly. Add cold broth and Tabasco all at once. Stirring occasionally, cook until uniformly thickened. Add cream and parsley. Season to taste. Add bourbon. Divide sauce in half. Add turkey meat to half, and the well-drained cooked mushrooms to other half. Put spaghetti and mushrooms, mixed, in casserole. Make a hole in center of spaghetti, then pour into it the turkey mixture. Top with cheese. Bake in 400-degree oven until bubbly, about 20 minutes. Serves 5.

Turkey Hash St. Germain

4½ *cups diced boiled turkey or 1½ lb. turkey roll, diced*
1 *lb. split green peas*
1 *medium-size onion, minced*
1 *rib celery, minced*
1 *large clove garlic, minced*
1 *teaspoon salt*
salt, white pepper to taste
½ *teaspoon Tabasco*
8 *tablespoons butter*
2 *packets chicken broth*
1 *cup milk*
2 *tablespoons flour*
3 *tablespoons dry vermouth*
2 *tablespoons bourbon*
2½ *cups light cream*
grated parmesan cheese

In soup pot or large saucepan, put peas, onion, garlic, and celery and cover with cold water. Add 1 teaspoon salt and Tabasco. Bring to a boil; skim. Reduce flame and simmer about 1½ hours until peas are very tender. During cooking, add water as needed to keep peas covered until done. Drain peas well; put them into blender, in batches if necessary, and blend until smooth puree is formed.

Melt 3 tablespoons butter; add to puree. Add chicken broth and salt and pepper to taste. Chill in refrigerator until needed.

Put milk and flour into small saucepan; stir well with wire whip until flour is completely dissolved. Add 2 tablespoons butter and heat over moderate flame, stirring constantly, until sauce is thick. Reduce flame and simmer 5 minutes, stirring occasionally. Add salt and pepper to taste. Remove from flame and keep pan covered.

In large saucepan, melt 3 tablespoons butter over low flame. Add turkey, vermouth, and bourbon. When hot, set ablaze. When flames subside, add cream. Simmer very slowly about 10 minutes. Add white sauce and simmer 5 minutes, stirring frequently. Add salt and pepper to taste and a dash of Tabasco. Preheat oven to 375 degrees. In large shallow casserole or 6 individual shirred-egg dishes, form a border of split-pea puree, using a pastry bag and tube. Spoon turkey hash into center and sprinkle with parmesan cheese. Bake 30 minutes or until heated through. Just before serving, place under broiler flame for a few minutes, watching constantly, until cheese is browned.

Southern Fried Chicken

2 *broiler-fryer chickens, cut up*
1 *oz. lime juice*
¼ *cup flour*
1 *teaspoon salt*
1 *pinch sage*
1 *pinch basil*
1 *pinch garlic powder*
1 *pinch white pepper*
1 *pinch paprika*
¼ *cup butter*
½ *cup chopped onion*
½ *cup seedless raisins*
1 *teaspoon brown sugar*
1 *teaspoon grated lemon rind*

2 *fresh tomatoes, peeled and chopped*
1 *cup crushed pineapple, drained*
4 *oz. bourbon*

Brush chicken parts with lime juice. Sprinkle with mixture of flour and seasonings. Lightly brown chicken parts in butter and transfer to baking dish. To the fat remaining in skillet, add chopped onion and sauté lightly. Add raisins, brown sugar, grated lemon rind, tomatoes, pineapple, and bourbon. Mix well and spoon over chicken in baking dish. Cover and bake 90 minutes in 350-degree oven. Serves 6-8.

Whiskey Fried Chicken

2 *broiler-fryer chickens, cut up*
1½ *cups flour*
garlic powder to taste
2½ *teaspoons baking powder*
½ *teaspoon salt*
dash pepper
1 *egg*
1¼ *cups milk*
¼ *cup bourbon*
oil

Wipe and dry chicken. Combine dry ingredients. Beat egg with milk and bourbon; then beat into flour until smooth. Dip chicken in batter; then fry in deep hot fat (380 degrees) until batter is golden brown and chicken cooked through. Serves 6.

Golden Fried Chicken

2 *2-lb. fryers, cut in serving pieces*
1 *tablespoon salt*
2 *teaspoons monosodium glutamate*
1 *teaspoon onion powder*
1 *teaspoon garlic powder*

    2 *teaspoons paprika*
¼ *teaspoon Tabasco*
    1 *tablespoon Angostura bitters*
    1 *tablespoon lemon juice*
    2 *tablespoons bourbon*
¼ *cup water*
    2 *eggs, beaten*
1½ *cup fine bread crumbs*
½ *cup flour*
    1 *cup vegetable oil*

Sprinkle chicken with dry seasonings, coating each piece well. Place chicken in large glass plate. In a saucepan heat the Tabasco, bitters, lemon juice, bourbon, and water. Bring to boil and pour over seasoned chicken. Let marinate for at least 1 hour at room temperature, turning frequently.

At end of marinating time, drain chicken, reserving liquid. Stir marinade into beaten eggs. Place flour and bread crumbs in separate paper bags. Place chicken first in flour, then in egg mixture, then bread crumbs, coating well.

Fry in large pan in hot vegetable oil about 1 inch deep, until a rich golden brown and tender.

Bourbon Chicken

2 *fryers, quartered*
2 *oz. vegetable oil*
1 *clove garlic, crushed*
1 *teaspoon nutmeg*
1 *teaspoon orange rind, grated*
1 *cup soy sauce*
1 *cup bourbon*

In large kettle over medium heat pour in oil ¼ inch deep. Add garlic, nutmeg, orange rind, soy sauce, and bourbon. Add chicken and baste constantly with the mixture for 30 minutes. Turn chicken and baste 20 minutes. Put on lid and cook 10 minutes more. Serves 4.

Whiskey Chicken

    4 *chicken breasts, 6 to 8 oz.*
    5 *tablespoons butter*
    6 *tablespoons bourbon*
  ½ *cup mushrooms, sliced*
      lemon juice
    2 *cups heavy cream*
    1 *teaspoon flour*
    2 *tablespoons white wine*
      salt, pepper, cayenne

Season chicken breasts with salt, pepper, and cayenne. Heat 2 tablespoons butter in skillet. Place chicken breasts skin down in hot butter and cook, covered, over low heat for 8 minutes. Turn and cook for 8 minutes longer. Add 5 tablespoons bourbon and flame (heat high). Add the wine and cook over low heat, slightly covered, for 15 minutes.

Remove chicken and keep warm. Add to skillet 1 tablespoon butter and mushrooms with a few drops of lemon juice; sauté for a few minutes, add the cream, and bring to a rapid boil for 5 minutes. Stir in mixture of 2 tablespoons butter and 1 teaspoon flour and boil for 3 minutes more.

Return breasts to sauce to reheat, but do not boil them any more. Add 1 tablespoon bourbon. Serves 4.

(Ala Moana Hotel, Honolulu)

Bourbon Baked Chicken

    3 *2½-lb. frying chickens*
      butter
      salt
      white pepper

Sauce
  ¼ *lb. small white mushrooms*
      juice 1 fresh lemon
      onion powder to taste
    3 *tablespoons butter*

3 tablespoons flour
2 cups chicken broth
1 tablespoon (or to taste) dijon mustard
½ teaspoon worcestershire sauce
½ cup heavy cream
3 egg yolks
salt
white pepper
4 oz. bourbon

Have the chickens quartered and the backs removed. Brush all over well with melted butter, sprinkle with salt and pepper, and place in a roasting pan in a preheated 500-degree oven for 20 to 25 minutes or until golden and flesh is tender when pierced with a fork. Baste occasionally with more melted butter.

Wipe the mushroom caps with a fresh, damp cloth, break off the stems, and slice the caps very thin. Place in a flat dish and sprinkle with half the lemon juice. Set aside.

Melt butter; stir in the flour and onion powder until smooth. When foaming, add the broth. Whip with a wire whisk, over a moderate heat, until smooth. Cook, whipping constantly, until sauce has a light consistency. Whip in the mustard and worcestershire until well combined. Stir in the cream, taking care not to allow the sauce to boil. Beat the egg yolks lightly. Add a little of the hot sauce; then combine the two, beating constantly. Bring almost to a boil. Add the mushrooms and the remaining lemon juice. Bring almost to a boil again. Take off the heat; add salt and white pepper to taste.

Take the chicken out of the oven, pour half a cup of warmed bourbon over the pieces, and ignite. When flames die out, arrange chicken on a warm serving platter. Stir the pan juices into the sauce, scraping down any particles that cling to the pan. Pour the sauce over the chicken; garnish with a bouquet of parsley. Serves 6.

Beef

Sirloin Steak Flambé No. 1
(For Backyard Barbecue)

>   1 *sirloin steak, 1-1½ inches thick*
>   1 *cup bourbon*
>   ¼ *cup lime juice*
>   2 *tablespoons brown sugar*
>   3 *tablespoons melted butter*
>   *salt and pepper to taste*
>   ¼ *cup cognac*
>   *quilted broiling foil*

Place steak in shallow pan or dish. Combine bourbon, lime juice, and brown sugar. Pour over steak, cover, and marinate for 1 hour. Line firebox with broiling foil and prepare fire.

When coals are covered with gray ashes, place steak on greased rack. Add melted butter to remaining marinade; baste steak generously and continue to baste frequently during the grilling.

When steak is well browned on the underside, turn and season with salt and papper. At the desired degree of doneness, place steak on heated platter; pour cognac and ignite for serving. Serves 4.

Sirloin Steak Flambé No. 2

    1 *sirloin steak, 1¼ inches thick*
    1 *cup bourbon*
  ¼ *cup lime juice*
    2 *tablespoons brown sugar*
  ½ *stick melted butter*
  ¼ *cup bourbon*
     salt and pepper to taste

Cut the fat cover of the steak at intervals all around. Place it in a shallow baking dish.

Mix together the bourbon, lime juice, and brown sugar. Blend well. Pour the mixture over the steak. Set aside at room temperature and marinate for 3 or 4 hours. Then remove the steak from the marinade and drain well.

Pour the marinade into a small saucepan. Set it over low heat and add the butter. When the butter has melted, blend well.

Place the steak over hot coals on the grill, or under the broiler of the kitchen range. Brush with the marinade.

Broil on both sides as usual. Brush steak frequently with the marinade. When done to the desired degree, remove the steak to a hot platter. Dust with salt and pepper to taste. Dot with butter.

Warm the bourbon. When the steak is served, ignite the liquor and pour it over the steak, flaming. Serves 4.

Sirloin Steak Flambé No. 3

    1 *sirloin steak, about 3 lb.*
    2 *tablespoons prepared mustard plus 1 tablespoon dry mustard*
  ½ *cup light brown sugar*
  ¼ *cup bourbon*

Wipe steak with a damp paper towel. Blend prepared and dry mustards and brown sugar. Spread half of mixture on one side of steak. Place on grill, spread side down. Brush remaining mixture over top. When steak is well browned on bottom, turn and complete grilling until desired degree of doneness is reached. Meanwhile, heat bourbon in a small pan. When steak is done, ignite the bourbon and pour over the steak ablaze or transfer to a warm platter and flame. Serves 6-8.

Sirloin Steak Flambé No. 4
(For Backyard Barbecue)

- 2 lb. prime sirloin, cut thick
- ½ teaspoon salt
- ½ teaspoon hickory-smoked salt
- black pepper
- 3 tablespoons butter
- 1 tablespoon chopped parsley
- 1 tablespoon chopped shallots
- ⅓ cup bourbon

Cover sirloin with salt, hickory-smoked salt, and a generous layer of freshly ground pepper in advance of cooking.

While grilling steak, place a sturdy oval flaming pan over coals until it is very hot. Just before steak is done, melt butter in pan with parsley and shallots. Place steak in pan and cover both sides with butter mixture. Pour warmed bourbon and blaze. Serves 4.

Mignons of Tenderloins Flared in Bourbon

- 2 well-trimmed slices filet mignon
- 2 tablespoons butter
- salt and pepper
- ½ cup rich brown gravy
- 1½ oz. bourbon

For each serving, allow two slices filet mignon (about 8 oz.). Sauté beef slices quickly in the butter, cooking to desired degree of doneness. Sprinkle slices with salt and freshly ground pepper. Transfer beef to heated serving platter. Blend the gravy into the pan drippings. Heat mixture thoroughly.

In another small saucepan, gently heat the bourbon. Ignite. Stir into the sauce. Pour the blazing sauce over beef slices. Serve at once. If desired, accompany with wild rice. Serves 1.

Beef Tenderloin with Rice and Chicken Livers

    4 *well-trimmed tenderloins (3 oz. each)*
    ½ *stick of butter*
       salt, freshly ground black pepper
    ⅔ *cup brown sauce*
    2 *oz. bourbon*
    2 *cups brown rice*
    2 *teaspoons pine nuts, toasted*
    4 *whole sautéed chicken livers*

In heavy skillet, melt butter. Add filets and sauté quickly to desired degree of doneness (3 minutes on each side for medium rare). Season to taste with salt and pepper and transfer to heated serving plate. Stir gravy into pan drippings; bring to boil. In small saucepan, heat bourbon slightly; ignite and stir into gravy. Arrange tenderloins on a bed of brown rice with pine nuts. Top with the chicken livers. Pour sauce over and serve at once.

Brown Rice

  ½ *cup butter*
  ½ *cup celery, chopped*
  1 *small onion, chopped*
  2 *cups brown rice*
  1 *teaspoon salt*
  ¼ *teaspoon pepper*
  1 *10½-oz. can condensed beef consommé*

Preheat oven to 350 degrees. Grease a 1-quart casserole.

Melt butter in skillet; sauté onion, celery, and rice over medium heat until rice is browned.

Stir in salt, pepper, and consommé and pour into casserole. Cover and bake for 1 hour.

Sautéed Chicken Livers

- 4 *whole chicken livers*
- *salt*
- 2-3 *twists of black pepper*
- 1 *tablespoon butter*

Wash livers under running hot water and pat dry.
Heat butter in sauté pan; add the livers and sauté on both sides.
Season with salt and 2-3 twists of black pepper.
Do not overcook the livers. Serves 4.

(The Presidents Restaurant, Chicago)

Steak au Poivre Flambé

- 1 *2-lb. sirloin steak*
- 1 *tablespoon whole peppercorns*
- *salt*
- 1 *tablespoon lemon juice*
- ¼ *teaspoon Tabasco*
- 1 *teaspoon worcestershire sauce*
- 1 *oz. butter*
- 2 *oz. bourbon*

An hour before you plan to broil, take steak out of refrigerator to bring to room temperature. Crack peppercorns. (They should be coarsely cracked with the flat of a cleaver or a whirl in blender.) With the heel of your hand or the flat of cleaver, press pepper firmly into both sides of steak. Let stand till ready to broil; then salt the bottom of a heavy skillet and heat very hot.

Lay in meat and sear on both sides. Reduce heat; cook to desired doneness.

Remove to a hot platter, pour off fat, and add to the pan lemon juice, Tabasco, and worcestershire. Return meat to pan; add butter and bourbon and light it.

When flames have died down, remove steak to warmed platter. Stir and dissolve meat essences on the pan; then pour the resulting sauce over the steak. Serves 4.

Steak au Poivre Vert

> 1   1- to 1½-inch-thick sirloin steak, about 3 lb.
>   salt
> 1   tablespoon bourbon
> 1   tablespoon drained green peppercorns, coarsely crushed in a mortar with a pestle
> ¼   cup heavy cream
> ½   teaspoon dijon mustard

Cut off a piece of fat from the steak and render it in a heavy skillet. Pan-fry the steak to desired degree of doneness. Transfer to a warm platter, season with salt to taste, and keep warm.

Remove any excess fat from the skillet. Add the bourbon and heat, stirring. Add the crushed green peppercorns and cream. Bring to a simmer, stirring. Stir in the mustard and pour sauce over the steak. Serves 3.

Broiled Top Round

> 1   cup cooking oil
> 1   cup bourbon
> ½   teaspoon pepper
> 1   tablespoon seasoned salt
> 1   teaspoon unseasoned meat tenderizer
> 1   2-inch cut top round
> 2   tablespoons flour
> 2   tablespoons marsala wine
> 2   tablespoons dry vermouth

Put the first 5 items into a shallow baking pan, stir, then turn the meat over lightly in the marinade and let marinate for 4 hours at room temperature, turning every 30 minutes.

Blend the last 3 items in a small saucepan, and just before cooking the meat, pour and blend over low heat, stirring. When smooth, reduce heat to the lowest simmer and let cook 30 minutes, stirring from time to time.

The meat may be broiled over good charcoal or under direct

broiler heat, 3½ to 4 inches from the heat. Cook each side 12 minutes, turning once.

Serve the meat sliced very thin, with the sauce alongside. Serves 2-3.

Steak Bourbon

> 1 lb. (16 oz.) top sirloin
> 1 clove fresh garlic
>   salt and pepper to taste
> 6 oz. bourbon
> 6 mushroom caps
> 1 oz. butter
> 2 oz. dry white wine

Take sirloin and let marinate in bourbon for 30 minutes.

Remove steak from bourbon; take garlic and rub steak on both sides very generously and thoroughly. Salt and pepper and put over hot charcoals. Several times during the broiling process, baste the steak with the bourbon. Cook to individual taste—rare, medium rare, or medium. Place mushroom caps that have been sautéed in a mixture of warm butter and white wine on top of steak. Serves 2.

Bourbon Skewered Steak

> 1 cup oil
> 1 cup vinegar
> 1 cup bourbon
>   salt, pepper, celery salt, and monosodium
>   glutamate to taste
> 1½ lb. sirloin, cut into 1-inch cubes

Combine oil, vinegar, bourbon, and seasonings. Marinate beef in mixture for at least 4 hours, stirring occasionally. Skewer and cook on hibachi, turning as necessary. Serves 4 as a snack.

Flank Steak, Bourbon County Style

    4 *lb. flank steak*
    8 *tablespoons soy sauce*
    4 *tablespoons bourbon*
  ¼ *teaspoon ground ginger*
    1 *clove garlic (finely minced or crushed)*
  ½ *cup hot water*
  ¼ *teaspoon black pepper*
    4 *butter pats, coated with minced parsley (optional)*

Place flank steak in large flat pan or dish. In a bowl, blend together soy sauce, bourbon, ginger, garlic, hot water, and pepper. Pour over flank steak and marinate for 1-2 hours, depending on intensity of flavor desired. Place on preheated broiler approximately 4 inches from heat and broil to desired degree of doneness.

Remove from broiler and top with pats of parsley-coated butter, if desired.

This steak is ideal for outdoor cooking also. Place over moderately hot coals and cook until one side is browned and juices are sealed in; turn and repeat process, basting with left-over marinade while steak is cooking.

Any extra sauce is delicious when warmed and passed to guests with steak. Serves 6.

Roast Beef Oriental

    3 *lb. roast beef (eye round or sirloin tip)*
  ½ *cup soy sauce*
    2 *teaspoons ground ginger*
    3 *large cloves garlic, cut in half*
    1 *medium onion, cut in thick slices*
    1 *teaspoon sugar*
    2 *oz. bourbon*

Place roast beef in large bowl. Mix other ingredients and pour over. Marinate for 24 hours, turning meat occasionally. Take out of marinade 2 hours before roasting. Pat dry and rub oil over roast.

Place on rack and roast in 300-degree oven at 20 minutes to the pound for medium rare. (It is best to use a meat thermometer and cook to desired degree of doneness as indicated on thermometer.) Serves 6.

Bourbon Stroganoff

   1½ *lb. ground lean beef*
    ¼ *cup bourbon*
    1 *teaspoon salt*
    ⅛ *teaspoon pepper*
    1 *egg, slightly beaten*
    ⅓ *cup fine dry bread crumbs*
    2 *tablespoons salad oil*
    ¼ *lb. mushrooms, sliced*
    1 *medium onion, sliced*
    1 *medium-sized green pepper, sliced*
    ½ *cup boiling water*
    1 *beef bouillon cube*
    1 *cup sour cream*

Combine beef, bourbon, salt, pepper, egg, and crumbs; mix well. Shape into 1½-inch balls. Heat oil; add meat balls and brown on all sides. Add mushrooms, onion, and green pepper and cook 5 minutes. Combine boiling water and bouillon cube; stir well. Add to beef mixture in pan. Cover and cook over low heat for 20 minutes. Remove from heat. Stir in cream. If necessary, reheat over low flame. Serve at once over rice or noodles. Serves 6.

London Broil

    2 *8-oz. cans tomato sauce*
    ¼ *cup chopped chives*
    ½ *teaspoon salt*
    ¼ *teaspoon pepper*
    ½ *teaspoon celery salt*
    ¼ *teaspoon garlic powder*

¼ cup bourbon
2 medium flank steaks (about 3 lb. together)
¼ lb. sliced mushrooms

Combine tomato sauce, chives, salt, pepper, celery salt, garlic powder, and bourbon; mix well. Add steaks and mushrooms and marinate for 2 hours, turning meat occasionally. Drain steaks and pat dry; reserve mushroom-bourbon mixture. Broil steaks 4 to 5 minutes on each side for medium rare. While steak is broiling, heat bourbon mixture to serving temperature. Slice steak across grain (on the diagonal), and serve with bourbon sauce. Serves 6.

Beef Bourbon Supreme

1 lb. sirloin of beef, cut in thin strips
1 small onion, sliced thin
1 green pepper, sliced thin
2 tablespoons butter
dash of salt and pepper
¼ cup bourbon
1 10-oz. can mushroom gravy

Sauté beef, onion, and pepper in butter until tender. Mix gravy and bourbon well and stir into meat mixture. Simmer a few minutes to blend. Add salt and pepper to taste. Serve with a bowl of fluffy rice and tossed salad. Serves 4.

Beef Bourbonnaise

¼ cup bacon fat, oil, or butter
6 small onions
½ lb. fresh mushrooms, trimmed and sliced
1 lb. lean round steak, cut in ¾-inch cubes
1 tablespoon flour
½ teaspoon salt
¼ teaspoon crumbled marjoram or rosemary
⅛ teaspoon freshly ground pepper

⅛ teaspoon crumbled thyme
1 10½-oz. can condensed beef broth
½ cup wine vinegar
½ cup bourbon

Melt fat in deep skillet or heavy pot. Add onions and mushrooms and cook, turning, until lightly browned. Remove to separate dish. Add round steak. Cook, turning frequently, over moderate heat, until meat is well browned. Sprinkle with flour, salt, pepper, marjoram, and thyme. Stir to coat meat. Combine 1 cup of the beef broth, 3 tablespoons of the wine vinegar, and ¼ cup of the bourbon and add to the meat, stirring. Bring to a boil; then reduce heat to keep mixture barely simmering. Simmer without cover for 2 hours, keeping beef barely covered with liquid, adding the remainder of the beef broth, vinegar, and bourbon, and up to ½ cup of water if needed. Return onions to pan and cook, covered, 40 minutes longer. Ten minutes before serving time, add sautéed mushrooms. The sauce will be brown and thick. Serves 2.

Polynesian Beef

2½ lb. chuck roast, 2 inches thick
   meat tenderizer
1 5-oz. bottle soy sauce
¼ cup brown sugar, packed
1 tablespoon lemon juice
¼ cup bourbon
1 teaspoon worcestershire sauce
1½ cups water

Mix ingredients together and marinate roast in them, 2-3 hours.
Remove, pat dry, place the roast on barbecue grill, and cook on hot coals to desired doneness. Serves 4-6.

Bourbon Beef Roast Flambé

boned rump roast, 4-6 lb.
flour

    salt, pepper
2 *onions, sliced*
2 *carrots, sliced*
½ *cup bourbon*
1 *8-oz. can tomato puree*
1 *cup beef bouillon*
½ *cup water*
    pinch of ginger
    salt, pepper, cayenne
¼ *cup bourbon for flaming*

Rub the meat well with flour seasoned with salt and pepper and brown it on all sides over high heat, the fat side first. Drain off extra fat.

Add onions and carrots, lower heat, and cook until onions are golden. Add remaining ingredients (except the last), cover, and braise in a moderate oven (350 degrees) until tender, about 3½ hours. Add more beef bouillon as needed. Remove meat.

Strain the gravy, forcing the vegetables through the sieve. Add salt and pepper to taste. Heat well; pour into hot gravy boat. Heat the ¼ cup bourbon, set it aflame, and pour it flaming over the roast. When the flames burn out, carve and serve. Spoon sauce over each serving. Serves 6-8.

Picnic Roast

1 *round boned roast, 2 inches thick, about 5 lb.*
    meat tenderizer
½ *cup plus 2 tablespoons soy sauce*
1 *tablespoon lemon juice*
¼ *cup bourbon*
¼ *cup brown sugar*

Sprinkle meat tenderizer on both sides of roast according to tenderizer directions; let stand for 1 hour.

Mix soy sauce with lemon juice, bourbon, and brown sugar; pour over meat. Marinate in refrigerator 6 hours or overnight. Turn occasionally. Drain off marinade; charcoal broil as you would any steak. Serves 8.

Gourmet Roast Beef Bourbon

 1 *beef round roast, 4-5 lb. (top or bottom round, eye of round, or rump)*
½ *cup bourbon*
 1 *tablespoon brown sugar*
 2 *tablespoons lemon juice*
 3 *cloves garlic, minced*
 3 *dashes bitters*
½ *cup oil*
 2 *tablespoons flour*
 1 *tablespoon salt*
 1 *teaspoon pepper*
 2 *cups hot water*
 2 *bouillon cubes*

Pierce beef deeply with a long skewer and marinate for several hours or overnight in a mixture of bourbon, sugar, lemon juice, garlic, bitters, and oil. Turn occasionally to season evenly. Remove from marinade, and coat with flour mixed with salt and pepper. Lay on a rack in a moderate oven (325 degrees) and roast about 34 minutes per pound, to the rare or medium rare stage. Baste with marinade from time to time. Remove meat to serving platter. To the pan juices add water and bouillon cubes and cook, stirring in the brown bits until the sauce is smooth and slightly thickened. Strain into heated sauceboat. Serves 6.

Mount Vernon Pot Roast

 1 *3-lb. chuck roast, tied*
  Bourbon Marinade (see below)
 3 *large onions, sliced*
 1 *tablespoon brown sugar*
¼ *cup bourbon*
 1 *tablespoon salt*

Bourbon Marinade
¼ *cup bourbon*
 2 *tablespoons brown sugar*

1 tablespoon worcestershire sauce
1 clove garlic, crushed
½ teaspoon allspice

Soak meat in bourbon marinade overnight. Remove meat from marinade. Dry on paper towels. Brown well in dutch oven. Remove meat and pour off all but two tablespoons fat. Brown onions in fat. Return roast to dutch oven. Pour remaining marinade over all, cover, and simmer over very low flame or place in 325-degree oven for 2½ hours. Add brown sugar, bourbon, and salt and simmer 1½ hours longer.

Bourbon Burgers

2 lb. ground beef, preferably round
½ teaspoon salt
½ teaspoon each, pepper and turmeric
1 small onion, grated
½ cup chopped peanuts
4 tablespoons bourbon

Put the meat on a large platter (not on a board because that would soak up and waste the beef juice) or on a sheet of waxed paper, and flatten the beef with the heels of hands until the meat is spread out in a wide, thin layer.

The sprinkle the meat with salt, pepper, turmeric, onion, and peanuts. Form it into a ball again, and squeeze and press until everything is thoroughly mixed in. Form the meat into 4 large balls, shaped like hamburgers, and broil them 3 inches from source of heat, on a lightly oiled pan, until they reach the state of doneness you prefer.

When the hamburgers are done, put the bourbon into a large ladle, warm it up, ignite it, and pour over the hamburgers. Serves 4.

Beef-Eggplant Casserole

1 eggplant, medium size
2 tablespoons olive oil

1 lb. ground beef
1 medium onion, chopped
¼ teaspoon garlic powder (or 1 clove garlic, minced)
2 teaspoons rosemary
1 teaspoon oregano
1 oz. butter
2 oz. (about ⅓ cup) chopped ripe olives
½ lb. mozzarella cheese, sliced
2 cups beef stock
1 tablespoon prepared mustard
2 teaspoons seasoning salt
½ teaspoon Accent
¼ cup bourbon

Peel, slice eggplant in ½-inch slices, and sauté lightly in olive oil. Set aside. Sauté meat, onion, herbs, and garlic in butter. In greased casserole, place layer of eggplant, layer of meat (about half), layers of cheese, and a layer of chopped olives. Repeat layers.

In saucepan, combine and bring to boil the stock, mustard, seasoning salt, and Accent. Pour half of hot stock, plus the bourbon, over the casserole contents. (At this point you can either continue cooking or place in refrigerator until desired.) Cover casserole and bake in medium oven (375 degrees) for 45 minutes.

Remove cover and continue baking 15 minutes, using remaining stock to keep moist as required. Serve over thick toasted bread. Serves 4.

Beef Slivers on Toast

1 each, medium onion, stalk of celery, and green pepper, chopped
½ stick butter or margarine
1 teaspoon worcestershire sauce
3 tablespoons flour
2 cups milk
½ teaspoon salt
1 tablespoon brown gravy coloring

1 lb. flank steak, broiled and sliced into thin slivers
¼ cup bourbon
¼ teaspoon paprika or cayenne
toast

Broil flank steak, with just a thin film of butter or oil on the pan, allow it to cool, and then cut into small, thin slivers.

In a large skillet or a saucepan, cook celery with onion and pepper in hot butter until they are soft, stirring over medium heat. Sprinkle with flour, stirring, for 2 minutes; then add the worcestershire sauce and the milk slowly, then the salt and gravy coloring, stirring over low heat.

Stir the beef into the mixture on the stove, raise the heat, add the bourbon and paprika, and cook, stirring, until the mixture comes to a boil and becomes slightly thickened. Pour over slices of toast. Serves 4.

Beef and Bourbon Aspic

1 envelope or 3 rounded teaspoons gelatine
¼ cup hot water
1 tablespoon butter
¼ lb. mushrooms, sliced
1 small onion, sliced
1 16-oz. can beef bouillon
¼ teaspoon mixed spices
½ cup bourbon

Sauté mushrooms and onion in butter until lightly brown. Dissolve gelatine in hot water; add to bouillon together with other ingredients. Thoroughly blend.

Pour into a mold and refrigerate until set. Serve with mixed bean salad and lettuce.

Roast Beef with Bourbon Sauce

¼ cup soy sauce
½ teaspoon ginger

¼ cup bourbon
¼ cup firmly packed brown sugar
¼ cup vinegar
2 tablespoons molasses
¾ cup orange juice
1 large clove garlic, crushed
1 medium-sized onion, chopped
1 4-lb. rolled beef rib roast
¼ cup all-purpose flour
½ cup water

Combine soy sauce, ginger, bourbon, brown sugar, vinegar, molasses, and orange juice; mix well. Add garlic, onion, and beef. Chill 3-4 hours, turning frequently. Remove beef; reserve bourbon mixture. Place beef on rack in shallow roasting pan.

Bake in slow oven (325 degrees) 2¼ to 2¾ hours, or until meat thermometer registers 140-170 degrees (depending on desired degree of doneness). Remove beef to heated serving platter. Reserve ½ cup beef drippings. Add flour; blend. Gradually add reserved bourbon mixture and water and cook over low heat, stirring constantly, until thickened. Serve bourbon sauce with beef roast. Serves 6.

Bourbon Burgers with Confetti Rice

Bourbon Burgers

1 cup soft bread crumbs
½ cup bourbon
1 lb. ground beef chuck
½ cup grated cheddar cheese
2 tablespoons chopped chives
½ teaspoon basil
1 teaspoon salt
⅛ teaspoon pepper

Combine crumbs and bourbon; mix well and let stand 5 minutes.

Combine bourbon-bread mixture, beef, cheese, chives, basil, salt and pepper. Shape into 8 patties, about 4 inches in diameter. Broil 3-4 inches from source of heat 4-5 minutes on each side,

Roast Beef with Bourbon Sauce

depending upon desired degree of doneness. Serve with Confetti Rice. Serves 4.

Confetti Rice

1 *cup rice*
2 *cups cold water*
1 *tablespoon butter*
2 *beef bouillon cubes*
2 *tablespoons chopped canned pimientos*

Combine all ingredients. Heat to boiling point over medium heat. Stir lightly with fork. Cover and cook over low heat 12-14 minutes, or until rice is tender.

Bourbon Stew

2½ *lb. lean beef*
¼ *cup flour*
⅛ *teaspoon pepper*
2 *tablespoons cooking oil*
½ *cup onion, chopped*
½ *cup green pepper, chopped*
1 *clove garlic, crushed*
1 *cup tomato sauce*
½ *cup diced celery*
½ *cup water*
¼ *cup bourbon*
1 *teaspoon salt*
½ *teaspoon sugar*
½ *teaspoon dried basil*

Cut the beef into 2-inch cubes. Dredge the cubes in a mixture of the flour and pepper.

Heat the oil in a dutch oven or deep skillet. Add the meat cubes and brown them on all sides over medium heat.

Remove browned meat from the pan and set aside.

Add onion, green pepper, celery, and crushed garlic to the same cooking pan; cook and stir until soft.

Return browned meat cubes to the pan.

Add tomato sauce and water. You can use an 8-ounce can of tomato sauce if you wish or some that you have made yourself.

Stir in the bourbon, salt, sugar, and basil. Rub the basil between the palms to release the flavor.

Mix all together well. Cover the pan and place over low heat to barely simmer for about 2 hours or until the meat is tender. Serves 6.

Bourbon Chili No. 1

    2 *lb. beef (preferably round), cut into small cubes*
    4 *tablespoons vegetable oil*
    1 *cup chopped tomatoes*
    2 *teaspoons cumin*
    2 *tablespoons chili powder*
    ¼ *cup bourbon*
    1 *clove garlic (on a toothpick, to be removed)*
  1¼ *cups hot water*
    2 *cups pinto beans, cooked*

Cut beef shoulder in very small cubes. In heavy skillet, brown meat in oil all around, turning until it is crusty brown. Add tomatoes. Mix seasonings with bourbon and pour over the meat, stirring well. Add garlic, but remove after 30 minutes. Stir in hot water. Bring to boil and cut heat to simmer immediately. Cook about 1 hour and add 2 cups cooked pinto beans. Simmer together until well blended, about 20 minutes longer. If needed, add more liquid.

Bourbon Chili No. 2

    ¼ *cup butter or margarine*
    ½ *cup chopped green pepper*
    1 *large onion, sliced*
  1½ *lb. ground beef round*
    2 *1-lb. cans kidney beans*
    2 *8-oz. cans tomato sauce*

¼ cup tomato catsup
2 tablespoons chili powder (or to taste)
1 square (1 oz.) unsweetened chocolate, grated
1 teaspoon salt
⅛ teaspoon pepper
1 tablespoon sugar
⅔ cup bourbon
   hot cooked rice

Melt butter or margarine; add green pepper, onion, and beef and cook over low heat, stirring occasionally, until meat is lightly browned. Add undrained kidney beans, tomato sauce, catsup, chili powder, chocolate, salt, pepper, and sugar. Cover and cook over low heat, stirring occasionally, 30 minutes. Add bourbon and heat to serving temperature. Serve over rice. Garnish with parsley, as desired. Serves 6.

Lamb

Butterflied Leg of Lamb

  1 *leg of lamb, about 6 lb.*
½ *cup oil*
¼ *cup bourbon*
¼ *cup lime juice*
  1 *small onion, finely chopped*
½ *teaspoon chopped parsley*
  1 *large clove garlic, crushed*
  1 *teaspoon salt*
  1 *teaspoon sugar*
  1 *teaspoon paprika*
  1 *teaspoon dried rosemary*
  1 *teaspoon oregano*
½ *teaspoon pepper*

Have butcher bone leg of lamb and cut "butterfly" fashion so that it is flattened for broiling. Secure any loose flaps of meat with small skewers. Combine remaining ingredients and pour over lamb.

Marinate 1 or 2 hours. Remove from marinade and pat dry. Reserve marinade. Broil 4 inches from heat about 1 hour, turning every 15 minutes and basting with marinade. This gives pieces well done on outside, medium rare inside. Serves 8.

Lamb Racks with Bourbon

- 2 *racks lamb, trimmed, about 2 lb. each*
- ¼ *cup soy sauce*
- ¼ *cup honey*
- ¼ *cup vinegar*
- 2 *oz. bourbon*
- 1 *garlic clove, crushed*
- ¼ *teaspoon ginger, powdered*
- 1¼ *cups beef bouillon*
- 1 *pineapple, peeled and sliced into rings*

Place lamb racks in a large enamel or glass pan. Combine remaining ingredients, except pineapple; pour over lamb, turning to coat all sides. Let stand about an hour. Dip pineapple into marinade; use to garnish racks on skewers. Broil lamb 6 inches from heat about 45 minutes, turning every 15 minutes and basting with marinade. Serves 4.

Crown Roast of Lamb

- 1 *crown roast of lamb (14-18 ribs, tied in a circle)*
- 2 *teaspoons salt*
- ½ *teaspoon pepper*
- ½ *teaspoon paprika*
- 1 *teaspoon dried rosemary*
- 1 *teaspoon dried mint*
- 3 *oz. bourbon*
- 1 *lb. ground lamb*

Season ground meat with 1 teaspoon salt, ¼ teaspoon pepper, ¼ teaspoon paprika, and 1 ounce bourbon; reserve.

Set oven at 325 degrees. Combine 1 teaspoon salt, rosemary, mint, ¼ teaspoon pepper, and ¼ teaspoon paprika. Rub into roast. Fold a long strip of aluminum foil in three, lengthwise, and grease lightly. Wrap around outside of the rib bones and fasten with a paper clip to make a collar rising about 2 inches above the rib ends. This will protect the bones from burning.

Roast for 45 minutes. Remove from oven and flame with 2 oz. bourbon. Spoon seasoned ground lamb trimmings into center of cavity. Return roast to oven for 15 minutes to set ground meat. Remove from oven; pour off fat from pan.

Roast 40 minutes longer or until meat stuffing is puffed and set. Put roast on a heated platter and gently remove foil collar. Serve with rice seasoned with saffron, dash of cayenne, bourbon, raisins, and pecans. Serves 6-8.

Crown Roast of Lamb au Bourbon

- 1 lb. ground lamb shoulder
- 1 cup fine dry bread crumbs
- 2 oz. bourbon
- 1 cup finely chopped onions
- ⅓ cup chopped parsley
- 1 teaspoon salt
- ½ teaspoon allspice
- ¼ teaspoon pepper
- 1 5- to 6-lb. crown roast (containing 2 racks)
- ¾ cup mint jelly
- 2 tablespoons lemon juice

Combine lamb, crumbs, bourbon, onions, parsley, salt, allspice, and pepper. Mix well. Fill crown roast center with lamb mix. Place on rack in shallow roasting pan. Roast in preheated 325-degree oven 2½ hours or till meat thermometer registers 175-180 degrees, depending on desired degree of doneness. Meanwhile, combine jelly and lemon juice. Cook over low heat, stirring occasionally, till smooth. Serve with lamb roast. Serves 6-8.

Lamb Kebabs Hoisin

    2 *lb. boneless lamb*
    1 *lb. mushroom caps*
    6 *oz. bourbon*

Cut meat into 1½-inch cubes and marinate in Hoisin-Bourbon Marinade* for 1 hour in refrigerator.

Thread meat and mushrooms alternately on skewers and broil in a preheated broiler or over charcoal 10-15 minutes, turning once. Remove from broiler, sprinkle warmed bourbon over each lamb-and-mushroom skewer, and ignite. Serves 6.

Julep Lamb Chops

    4 *double loin lamb chops (2 lb.)*
    2 *teaspoons dried mint*
      salt and pepper to taste
    2 *teaspoons butter*
    4 *slices pineapple*
    ⅓ *cup bourbon*

Preheat broiler. Press mint leaves into surface of lamb chops. Season with salt and pepper. Broil 4 inches from heat source, about 10 minutes for first side, 6 minutes for second, or until crusty brown, yet still pink within.

During the last 5 minutes of cooking, heat butter in electric skillet or large chafing dish. Add pineapple slices and sauté lightly on both sides. Place 1 lamb chop on each pineapple slice. Sprinkle with bourbon. Ignite and serve flaming. Serves 4.

Lamb Teriyaki

    2 *lb. thin-sliced lamb shoulder*
    ¼ *cup soy sauce*
    2 *oz. maple syrup*

---
*See Marinades and Sauces.

¼ cup vinegar
1 oz. bourbon
2 garlic cloves, crushed
¼ teaspoon nutmeg, powdered
1½ cups chicken broth

Cut lamb slices into strips about ½ by 3 inches across the grain. Combine remaining ingredients and pour over strips, turning them to coat well. Let stand 1 hour at room temperature. Turn occasionally to season evenly. Moisten bamboo skewers and weave strips onto skewers. Broil about 4 inches from heat about 2 minutes each side. Serves 6.

Lamb Chops with Sauce

6 shoulder lamb chops
flour, salt, pepper
1 oz. bourbon
½ cup currant jelly
1 tablespoon mustard
1 teaspoon lemon juice

Trim chops, season, and broil 5 inches from heat about 6 minutes on each side. Stir remaining ingredients over low heat till jelly melts and sauce is well blended. Brush chops with sauce on both sides. Serves 6.

Lamb Stroganoff

1½ lb. boneless lamb shoulder, thinly sliced
seasoned flour
3 oz. butter
1 clove garlic, finely chopped
2 oz. chopped onion
1 lb. mushrooms, sliced
salt and pepper to taste
1½ cups sour cream
2 oz. bourbon

Coat lamb with flour. Melt butter; add lamb, garlic, and onion and cook till lamb is lightly brown on all sides. Add mushrooms, salt and pepper. Cover and cook over low heat 20 minutes, stirring occasionally. Add cream and bourbon and mix well, simmering another 10 minutes. Serve with cooked rice as desired. Serves 6.

Lamb and Vegetable Jumble

    4 *or more neck slices, about 1 inch thick*
    1 *cup water*
  ½ *cup bourbon*
    2 *beef bouillon cubes*
    4 *small potatoes, pared*
  ¾ *teaspoon salt*
  ¼ *teaspoon pepper*
    4 *small carrots, diced*
  ½ *cup chopped celery*
    1 *medium onion, chopped*
  ¼ *lb. sliced mushrooms*
    2 *medium tomatoes, cut in wedges (or equivalent in canned tomatoes)*
  ¼ *cup chopped parsley*

Cook lamb over low heat till browned. Add water, bourbon, bouillon cubes, potatoes, salt and pepper. Cover and continue cooking for 20 minutes. Add remaining ingredients; cover and cook another 15 minutes, or till lamb and vegetables are tender. Serves 4.

Lamb Steaks with Bourbon Sauce

    6 *lamb steaks (sirloin or round leg), cut 1 inch thick*
  ¾ *cup butter or margarine*
    4 *teaspoons dry mustard*
    1 *tablespoon worcestershire sauce*
  ½ *cup bourbon*
     chopped parsley

Broil steaks 3 to 4 inches from source of heat for 4 to 6 minutes on each side or till desired degree of doneness. Melt butter in skillet and stir in mustard and worcestershire. Stir in bourbon, heat slightly, and ignite. Arrange steaks on platter and pour some sauce over them. Sprinkle steaks with parsley and serve with remaining sauce. Serves 6.

Lamb Scallopini

2 lb. thin slices from lamb leg
flour, salt, pepper, ginger
¼ cup vegetable oil
1 clove garlic
½ lb. mushrooms, sliced
4 oz. bourbon
4 oz. water
1 tablespoon tomato paste
chopped parsley

Pound slices of lamb. Dust with seasoned flour. Heat oil in skillet with garlic. Brown lamb scallopini on both sides. Add mushrooms to pan and brown. Add bourbon, water, and tomato paste. Spoon sauce over lamb and simmer gently for a few minutes, blending and thickening. Sprinkle with parsley. Serve lamb in sauce with rice. Serves 8. Good with burgundy.

Lamb Sesame

1 lb. thin-sliced lamb shoulder
4 tablespoons sesame seeds
2 tablespoons salad oil
½ onion, grated
2 tablespoons soy sauce
1 oz. bourbon

Cut lamb into thin strips. Spread sesame seeds in a small skillet and stir over moderate heat till seeds are brown. Transfer seeds to a board and pound with hammer wrapped in cloth, or whirl in blender. Add to oil and remaining ingredients. Coat meat with sauce and let stand 30 minutes, turning often. Weave strips onto skewers; grill close to heat about 4 minutes, till done to taste. Serves 4.

Pork and Ham

Mincemeat Pork Savories

    2 9- to 11-oz. packages piecrust mix
    2 9-oz. packages instant condensed mincemeat
    1 lb. ground pork
  ¼ teaspoon chopped parsley
    1 cup minced onions
       dash mace
    8 oz. bourbon

    Make piecrust according to directions. On lightly floured surface, roll out to ⅛ inch thickness. Cut in 4-inch circles and press into 3-inch fluted tart pans.
    Preheat oven to 350 degrees. In large bowl, combine mincemeat, ground pork, minced onions, parsley, mace, and bourbon. Mix well; then spoon into tart shells, filling to within ¼ inch of top.

Place tart pans on large cooky sheet so that you can handle easily.

Bake at 350 degrees for 40 minutes. Let cool in pans till lukewarm. Loosen around edge with tip of sharp knife; then remove tarts. Serve while warm. Makes 30 tarts.

Country-Style Spareribs

    3 *lb. country-style spareribs*
    1 *medium onion, quartered*
    2 *teaspoons salt*
    ¼ *teaspoon pepper*
      water

Barbecue Sauce

    ¼ *cup oil*
    ½ *cup bourbon*
    1 *small onion, chopped*
    2 *tablespoons tomato catsup*
    ½ *teaspoon salt*
    1 *teaspoon worcestershire sauce*
    1 *tablespoon brown sugar*
    1 *clove garlic, crushed*
      dash Tabasco

Place ribs, onion, salt and pepper in large pan. Cover with water and bring to boil. Cover and simmer over low heat 40 minutes. Simmer sauce ingredients 20 minutes, stirring frequently, and serve with ribs. Serves 6-8.

Roast Pork with Wild Rice

    1 *pork loin roast, about 5 lb.*
    1 *teaspoon salt*
    ½ *cup brown sugar*
    ¼ *cup bourbon*
    ½ *cup lime marmalade*

1 *teaspoon mustard*
dash ground cloves
dash nutmeg
1 *package (6 oz.) long-grain wild rice*
½ *cup chopped pecans*
¼ *cup quartered, pitted prunes*
1 *teaspoon grated lemon rind*
1 *tablespoon sugar*

    Place pork on rack in shallow roasting pan. Sprinkle with salt and roast 2½ hours in 325-degree oven or till roast reaches internal temperature of 170 degrees. Combine brown sugar, bourbon, marmalade, mustard, cloves, and nutmeg in small saucepan. Heat just to dissolve sugar. Brush roast with glaze several times during last 30 minutes of cooking.

    About 30 minutes before serving, cook contents of wild rice package according to directions. Stir pecans, prunes, lemon rind, and sugar into hot rice. Heat through. Serve pork with rice, spooning any remaining glaze over meat.

Tipsy Ribs

6 *lb. spareribs*
2 *oz. bourbon*
4 *tablespoons soy sauce*
dash worcestershire sauce
dash cayenne
¼ *teaspoon ginger*
4 *tablespoons brown sugar*
4 *tablespoons dijon mustard*

    Mix all ingredients, except ribs, together well and let stand 1 hour in refrigerator. Spread sauce thickly over both sides of ribs. Roast in 325-degree oven for about 2 hours or till brown and crisp. Turn once during roasting and baste frequently with sauce. Serves 6.

Ribs 'n' Bourbon

    2 lb. meaty spareribs
       salt, pepper, cayenne to taste
       dash Tabasco
½ cup apple cider
2 oz. bourbon

Sprinkle ribs with salt, pepper, and cayenne and place on rack in shallow roasting pan. Roast in 325-degree oven for about 1¼ hours. Set ribs under broiler few minutes till crisp. Discard fat in pan and put pan over direct heat. Add cider and Tabasco. Put ribs in pan and reduce cider slightly. Heat bourbon, pour over ribs, and ignite. Serves 2.

Bourbon-Orange Pork Loin

6 lb. pork loin
   salt and pepper to taste
1 cup orange marmalade
¼ teaspoon mace
¼ teaspoon nutmeg
2 oz. bourbon

Season pork with salt and pepper to taste and roast in 350-degree oven, allowing 30 minutes per pound. During the last hour, baste often with mixture of mace, nutmeg, marmalade, and bourbon. Serve with a garnish of bourbon-marinated fruits.

Fruit Garnish

2 oranges, peeled and thinly sliced
1 lemon, peeled and thinly sliced
¼ cup butter
¼ cup brown sugar
1 cup dried prunes
½ cup raisins
½ cup dried apricots
6 oz. bourbon

Brown orange and lemon slices lightly in butter, sprinkling with sugar. Place in shallow bowl with dried fruits; pour bourbon over the fruit, cover, and soak overnight. Place citrus slices around platter and tuck remaining fruits into curve of pork loin.

Whiskey Pork Chops

    6 *large center-cut pork chops*
1½ *teaspoons dry mustard*
      dash worcestershire sauce
 ¼ *teaspoon horseradish*
    3 *oz. bourbon*
 ¾ *cup cream*
      salt and pepper to taste

Slowly brown pork chops on both sides in large skillet until they are well done. Remove chops. To juices in pan add bourbon, mustard, worcestershire, horseradish, and cream. Slowly bring to boiling point. Add salt and pepper to taste. Arrange chops on platter and spoon on sauce, adding a little paprika, if desired. Garnish with parsley.

Ham Pie

    2 *9- to 11-oz. packages piecrust mix*
    3 *cups diced, lean ham, cooked*
    2 *tablespoons freshly chopped parsley*
 ½ *teaspoon salt*
 ⅛ *teaspoon ground black pepper*
 ⅛ *teaspoon paprika*
 ½ *teaspoon lemon juice*
 ⅛ *teaspoon thyme*
    2 *oz. bourbon*
    3 *hard-cooked eggs*

Make piecrust according to directions and use one crust to line a 9-inch pie pan. Combine ham and seasonings with whiskey. Cut eggs into thick slices. Fill pastry shell with alternate layers of ham and egg slices. Cover with other crust and make slits in top crust for air. Bake in 350-degree oven for 1 hour. Cool before unmolding. Chill before serving. Serve with pickles and potato salad.

Ham au Poivre Vert

    1 *3½-oz. jar green peppercorns in vinegar*
    1 *1-inch-thick center slice cooked, smoked ham*
    2 *tablespoons butter*
    2 *cups sauerkraut, cooked, rinsed, and drained*
      dash of mace
      dash of paprika
    1 *oz. bourbon*
    6 *oz. dry white wine*
    2 *teaspoons juniper berries, crushed*

Remove six peppercorns from jar and set aside. Place remainder of peppercorns with liquid in electric blender and chop fine. Spread both sides of ham with crushed peppercorns and set aside for an hour to season. Melt butter in skillet, and sauté ham slice, turning once. Add bourbon, mace, and paprika to ham slice. Transfer to warm platter with as many crushed peppercorns as desired.

Reheat sauerkraut with wine, reserved peppercorns, and crushed juniper berries. Simmer 10 minutes. Add sauerkraut to ham platter. Serves 2.

Sugared Ham

    1 *ham, 6-8 lb.*
    2 *cups light brown sugar*
    1 *cup bourbon*
  2½ *cups water*
    1 *tablespoon dry mustard*
   ¼ *teaspoon ginger*
   ¼ *teaspoon nutmeg*
    1 *cup dark brown sugar*
    2 *oz. bourbon (optional)*

Scrub ham and soak it overnight. Drain. Spread a double thickness of aluminum foil and put the ham in the center. Cover with 2 cups light brown sugar, water, and 1 cup bourbon and fold foil well to hold. Let cool in foil. Unwrap, remove rind. Sprinkle with dry mustard, ginger, dark brown sugar, and nutmeg mixed. Bake at 375 degrees for about 50 minutes. If desired, you may baste the ham with 2 oz. bourbon shortly before it is ready to remove from the oven.

Glazed Ham Steak

    1 *lb. center-cut slice of ham, cooked*
    2 *tablespoons vegetable oil*
  ¼ *cup brown sugar*
       dash cinnamon
       dash mace
    2 *oz. bourbon*
    2 *tablespoons bread crumbs*
       sprig parsley

Slash edge of ham steak in several places to prevent curling during cooking. Preheat oven to 400 degrees. Heat oil in large frying pan till hot. Place ham slice in skillet and cook over moderate flame, turning once till medium brown on both sides. Transfer to shallow pan or large metal pie pan. Mix sugar, spices, whiskey, and breadcrumbs till you have a paste. Spread paste over top of ham and place under broiler about 4 inches from flame. Broil till glaze is medium brown. Garnish with parsley and serve. Serves 2.

Baked Ham with Apricots

       ham steak, 1 inch thick, about 1 lb.
    1 *teaspoon dry mustard*
    1 *oz. molasses*
    1 *medium can apricots*
    2 *oz. bourbon*
    2 *tablespoons butter*

Rub ham with dry mustard and molasses mixed. Place in pan which has tight lid. Drain apricots, mixing juice with the bourbon, and pour liquid over ham. Cover pan and bake ham at medium heat about 30 minutes. Remove lid and arrange apricots, rounded sides up, atop ham. Dot apricots with butter and place pan under broiler long enough to brown them and fat edge of ham. Serves 2.

Canned Ham with Home Glaze

    1 *canned ham (about 5 lb.)*
    1 *cup bourbon*
    1 *cup brown sugar*
  ¼ *teaspoon powdered cloves*
    1 *teaspoon grated lemon rind*

Mix all ingredients except ham. Let stand, stirring frequently till sugar dissolves, while ham is cooking in oven (about 90 minutes). About 30 minutes before ham is removed from oven, spread about half the bourbon mixture over it. Baste ham with remainder of mixture during the final half-hour of cooking.

Breaded Country Ham

    1 *10-lb. country ham*
 2½ *cups water*
    4 *oz. bourbon*
    2 *cups brown sugar*
  ¼ *teaspoon cinnamon*
  ¼ *teaspoon nutmeg*
  ½ *cup coarse, water-ground cornmeal*
  ½ *cup brown sugar*

Scrub ham and soak it in water 24 hours. Cover a large pan with aluminum foil, making sure you have enough to wrap the ham. Place ham on foil and pour over it the water, bourbon, and sugar mixed with spices. Wrap foil around the ham and place in a slow oven of around 275 degrees. After 5 or 6 hours, when it feels

Canned Ham with Home Glaze

tender to the fork, the ham is done. Glaze top of ham with cornmeal mixed with brown sugar and place in 400-degree oven till sugar bubbles and crust forms.

Veal

Veal Amandine Flambé

    1 *pound veal scallops, cut very thin*
    ½ *cup sliced almonds*
    1 *cup flour*
       salt, garlic powder, and crushed basil to taste
    2 *oz. butter*
    ⅓ *cup bourbon*

Dip veal scallops in flour seasoned with the salt, garlic powder, and basil. Sauté quickly in butter. Add almonds and shake pan well till warmed. Add heated bourbon, ignite, and serve when flame subsides. Good with buttered noodles.

(Peter J. Robotti, owner-host of Le Chateau Richelieu)

Veal Cutlets with Bourbon

    2 veal cutlets, cut thin
       medium apple, cored, peeled, and diced
    2 oz. lemon juice
       salt and pepper to taste
       pinch paprika
       pinch nutmeg
    3 tablespoons butter
    1 oz. bourbon
    ½ cup heavy cream
    ½ cup raisins

Brush apple cubes with lemon juice to keep from turning dark. Season veal with salt, pepper, paprika, nutmeg, and lemon juice. Melt butter in heavy frying pan. When it starts to foam, put in veal and let it turn color on both sides. Add apples.

Heat bourbon in a ladle and ignite. Pour flaming over meat and at same time turn up heat slightly under pan. Rotate pan till flames die down. Pour in cream and add raisins. Lower heat. Cook gently about two minutes, stirring sauce and scraping up juices. As soon as cream has thickened, transfer meat to serving dish. Arrange apple cubes on top and pour sauce all around. Serves 2.

Veal Scallopini au Bourbon

   18 small slices veal
    1 tablespoon shallots, minced fine
    1 pinch oregano
    1 teaspoon Italian parsley, minced
    4 oz. bourbon
    2 tablespoons butter
    2 tablespoons vegetable oil
    ½ teaspoon salt
    2 tablespoons flour
    ½ teaspoon sugar

Mix salt, flour, and sugar and dredge meat with the mixture. Lay veal slices next to each other on absorbent paper, but do not overlap. In heavy skillet, sauté the shallots with the shortening till they are limp and translucent. Increase heat and add veal slices all at once. Keep turning fast with a spatula. As color changes, pour bourbon on the side of the meat (not over it). Using spatula, lift the pieces slightly and let bourbon flow under veal. Reduce heat to medium. Carefully turn all pieces of veal over. Sprinkle them with oregano and parsley. Turn meat once more, and then serve. Serves 4.

(Ala Moana Hotel, Honolulu)

Flamed Veal Scallopini

>   6½   oz. scallopini of veal
>   salt, pepper, dash lemon juice
>   4 oz. butter
>   ½   cup heavy cream
>   ½   cup brown gravy (prepared canned beef gravy will do)
>   3 oz. bourbon
>   pinch curry powder

Season veal with salt, pepper, lemon juice. Melt butter in skillet. Flour veal lightly and place in skillet. Color fast on both sides. Flame with bourbon, add gravy, and cook 1 minute. Add cream. Remove veal from skillet and set on platter. Let sauce simmer till it thickens. Add pinch curry powder and pour over veal. Serve with rice or egg noodles. Serves 2.

(Americana Hotel, New York City)

Mixed Meats

In Kentucky, the burgoo is practically an official dish, prepared in vast quantities over roaring outdoor fires. It is served traditionally on Derby Day or at auctions or horse sales. In the old days, the basic ingredients of burgoo stew included squirrels and rabbits, since such small game was the most plentiful meat available. Today, however, beef, pork, chicken, and veal are usually used.

Here are several versions of Kentucky's famed burgoo.

Kentucky Burgoo No. 1

    1 *lb. lean diced stewing beef*
    1 *lb. lean diced pork shoulder*
    3 *quarts water*
    3½ *lb. chicken, cut into pieces*

Mixed Meats

 2½ *cups canned tomatoes*
 1 *cup fresh or frozen lima beans*
 4 *diced small peppers*
 1 *small red pepper pod*
 ¾ *cup diced onion*
 2 *medium carrots, diced*
 1 *cup diced potatoes*
 1 *bay leaf*
 1 *tablespoon worcestershire sauce*
 4 *oz. bourbon*
 2 *cups whole kernel corn*
   salt and pepper

Place beef, pork, and water in heavy kettle; bring slowly to boil and simmer 2½ hours.

Cover chicken with water in another kettle, bring to boil, and simmer 1 hour till meat is tender.

Pour chicken liquid into first kettle; remove chicken from bones, and add to kettle. Add tomatoes, beans, peppers, red pepper pod, onion, carrots, potatoes, bay leaf, worcestershire, and bourbon. Add salt and pepper to taste.

Simmer mixture 30 minutes; then add corn and continue cooking till all vegetables are soft. Remove bay leaf, correct seasonings, and serve in deep bowls. Serves 12.

Kentucky Burgoo No. 2

 1 *frying chicken, cut up*
 1 *lb. round steak, cut in cubes*
 ½ *cup chopped onion*
 3 *tablespoons shortening*
 2 *oz. chili mix*
 ¾ *teaspoon garlic salt*
 1 *1-lb. can tomatoes*
 ¼ *cup water*
 4 *oz. bourbon*
 10 *oz. frozen mixed vegetables*
 10 *oz. frozen okra*

Brown chicken, steak, and onion in shortening in big skillet. Stir in chili mix, garlic salt, tomatoes, water, and bourbon and cover. Simmer one hour. Add mixed vegetables and okra. Cover again and simmer 10 minutes or till vegetables are tender. Serves 4.

Kentucky Burgoo No. 3

   2 *lb. lean pork*
   2 *lb. lean veal*
   2 *lb. lean beef*
   6 *lamb shanks*
   1 *4-lb. stewing chicken, cut up*
   3 *quarts water*
   1 *cup bourbon*
   2 *lb. canned tomatoes*
   3 *12-oz. cans corn*
   4 *cups diced carrots*
   4 *cups sliced onions*
   3 *cups diced potatoes*
   2 *lb. canned lima beans, drained*
   3 *tablespoons salt*
   1 *tablespoon black pepper*
   2 *teaspoons chopped parsley*
   2 *teaspoons marjoram leaves*
   2 *teaspoons sage*
   2 *green peppers, seeded and diced*
   ¼ *cup worcestershire sauce*

Dice up pork, veal, and beef. Add with lamb shanks, chicken, and bourbon to boiling water and simmer till tender. Remove chicken and lamb shanks from liquid, cool, and remove meat from bones. Return meat to liquid. Add vegetables, except potatoes and lima beans, and simmer 2 hours. Add remaining ingredients and cook another hour till all vegetables are tender. Burgoo should be very thick; so add 2 tablespoons cornstarch mixed with water, if necessary, and cook till clear and thickened. Serves 25.

Mixed Meats

Kentucky Burgoo No. 4

   2 lb. pork shank
   2 lb. veal shank
   2 lb. beef shank
   2 lb. breast of lamb
   1 4-lb. chicken
   8 quarts water
1½ lb. potatoes
1½ lb. onions
   1 bunch carrots
   2 green peppers
   2 cups chopped cabbage
   1 quart tomato puree
   2 cups whole corn, fresh or canned
   2 pods red pepper
   2 cups diced okra
      chopped parsley
   2 cups lima beans
   1 cup diced celery
   6 oz. bourbon
      salt, pepper to taste
      Tabasco to taste
      A-1 and worcestershire sauces to taste

Put all meat into cold water and bring slowly to boil. Simmer till meat is tender enough to fall from bones. Lift meat out of stock. Cool, remove from bones and chop up. Return meat to stock. Pare potatoes and onions and dice. Add all vegetables with the bourbon to the meat and stock. Allow to simmer till very thick. Season to taste. Serves 12-14.

Kentucky Burgoo No. 5

2 lb. lamb
3 lb. stewing beef
2 lb. pork shank
1 5-lb. stewing chicken

1 cup bourbon
8 quarts water
3 cups potatoes
1½ cups diced onions
1½ cups diced carrots
1 cup diced celery
½ cup diced green pepper
4 cups tomato puree
2 cups whole kernel corn
1 cup lima beans
1 small red pepper
½ clove garlic
1 cup red beans, canned
salt and pepper to taste

Cook meat in water and bourbon till it falls off bones. Remove all bones. Add vegetables and seasoning to broth and simmer, 4-6 hours, stirring every half-hour. Serves 30.

Meat Loaf en Croûte

2¼ lb. meat loaf mixture (pork, veal, and beef)
2 eggs
½ cup bread crumbs
¼ cup bourbon
juice of ½ lemon
1¼ teaspoons salt
pepper
pinch of oregano
¼ cup chopped parsley
¼ can solid part of solid pack tomatoes
1 1-lb. loaf sourdough French bread
2 slices Monterey Jack cheese
butter

Mixed Meats

Mix above ingredients well with two forks (mixture is heavy otherwise).

Take a round or oval 1-pound loaf of sourdough French bread. Slice off the top and reserve. Scoop out the loaf. Pack meat loaf mixture firmly into bread. Place 2 slices of Monterey Jack cheese over meat (this holds top on). Replace top tightly. Rub loaf well with butter. Wrap in aluminum foil. Bake 2¼ hours at 350 degrees.

Remove from oven and loosen foil (to prevent loaf from becoming soggy). Let cool. Rewrap until serving time. Slice thinly. Serves 10.

Game

Charcoal Venison

    4 *1-inch rib steaks*
    2 *oz. bourbon*
    2 *oz. red wine*
    1 *medium onion, chopped*
  ½ *cup honey*
  ½ *teaspoon ground nutmeg*

Marinate venison steaks at least 6 hours in mixture of the bourbon and other ingredients. Remove from marinade, sprinkle with salt and pepper, and cook over charcoal to desired degree of doneness. Serves 4.

Venison Ragout

    2 *lb. boneless venison stew meat, cut into 1½-inch pieces*
      flour
    4 *oz. butter*
      salt, pepper
    1 *cup red wine*
    2 *cups beef bouillon*
    4 *oz. bourbon*
    1 *bay leaf*
    2 *stalks celery, chopped*
    ½ *teaspoon dried, crushed rosemary*
    6 *whole small onions, peeled*
    3 *cloves, stuck into 3 of the onions*
    3 *medium carrots, cut into 2-inch chunks*
  12 *small new potatoes, scrubbed*
    ¼ *lb. whole button mushrooms*

Roll venison in flour. Melt butter in heavy pot and quickly brown meat on all sides. Sprinkle with salt and pepper. Add wine and bourbon; cook 10 minutes. Add bouillon, bay leaf, celery, and rosemary. Cover tightly and cook over low heat 1 hour. Add onions, carrots, potatoes, and mushrooms. Cover and simmer another 30 minutes, till meat is tender and vegetables done. If liquid becomes too thick, add more bouillon. When meat is done, put in a tureen or covered casserole. Serves 4-6.

Bourbon Squirrel

    2 *squirrels, 1 lb. each, cut in serving pieces*
      flour
      salt, pepper
    ¼ *cup diced bacon*
      dash Tabasco
    1 *cup bourbon*
    3 *tablespoons butter*

6 oz. cream, warmed
2 teaspoons flour

Wipe meat dry; then dust with flour, salt, and pepper. In large skillet, fry bacon till it is golden. Add meat and brown. Pour in bourbon and Tabasco, cover, and simmer till meat is tender and the liquid almost evaporated. Add 2 tablespoons butter and stir. Remove meat to platter. Add cream to pan. Stir in remaining butter. Sprinkle with flour. Continue to heat, stirring till thickened. Pour over meat. Serves 4.

Bourbon-Flamed Quail

8 quail, each about 8 oz.
1½ cups bourbon
½ teaspoon powdered cloves
1 cup seedless raisins
1 cup chopped pecans
2 cups cooked rice
¼ lb. butter
¼ teaspoon each, salt and pepper
½ cup orange juice
1 tablespoon cornstarch

Pour 1 cup of bourbon into a bowl; add powdered cloves, raisins, pecans, and rice. Let it soak in a warm place for 1 hour.

Strain the bourbon-rice mixture (reserve bourbon) and stuff each bird with the raisin-nut-rice mixture. Sew them up and rub each one with a little salt and pepper.

Over direct heat on top of oven, melt the stick of butter in a roasting pan large enough to hold the birds, and roll them around in it, until well coated. Pour the bourbon in which the raisins, etc. were soaked over the birds, then pour ¼ cup orange juice over them. Roast the birds for 5 minutes at 400 degrees; then lower heat to 300 degrees and roast for an additional 25 to 30 minutes, basting frequently, and turning birds. In the last 5 minutes of roasting, stir the tablespoon of cornstarch into the remaining ¼ cup orange juice, to dissolve it. Take the birds out of roasting pan, place them on a serving platter, and put them into oven, with the door open and heat off. Put roasting pan on top of stove and stir in the cornstarch-orange juice mix; cook, stirring until mixture thickens, scraping the pan with a spatula or spoon. Bring the birds to the table, garnished with watercress or parsley.

Pour the remaining ½ cup of bourbon into a large ladle, warm it up by heating bottom of ladle with a lighted match, set the bourbon aflame, and pour it over the birds. Put gravy into a bowl and serve with birds.

Partridge Casserole

    4 *small partridge*
      salt and freshly ground pepper
    8 *juniper berries*
    8 *slices bacon*
    2 *tablespoons bourbon*
    ⅓ *cup game stock made by boiling partridge giblets with water, seasoning, and onion*
    ⅓ *cup champagne*
  1½ *cups sliced mushrooms*

    Wash and pat dry the birds. Season the cavity and outside of birds with salt and pepper. Put 2 juniper berries in each cavity. Wrap the bacon over breasts and legs; secure with string while trussing the birds.

    Brown the birds on all sides in a heavy heatproof casserole, turning with wooden spoons. This takes about 25 minutes. Add the bourbon and set aflame.

    When the flame dies down, add the game stock and champagne. Cover and cook gently, 15 to 20 minutes longer, or until the birds are tender.

    Remove the birds to a warm platter. Remove trussing. Add the mushrooms to the casserole and cook, stirring, 3 minutes. Pour drippings and mushrooms over birds. Serves 4.

Pheasant au Crème Bourbon

> 4 whole pheasant breasts
> 4 oz. butter
> ¾ cup sliced mushrooms
> 1 teaspoon minced onion
> 1 cup bread crumbs
> ½ teaspoon dried parsley
>   salt, pepper, and cayenne
> 1 tablespoon cream
> 4 slices bacon
> 1 cup condensed chicken broth
> 1 can cream of celery soup
> ½ can milk
> 1 oz. bourbon

Melt butter in a heavy skillet. Sauté mushrooms for 5 minutes together with the onion. Add bread crumbs and stir over medium heat till lightly browned. Add parsley, salt, pepper, and cayenne to taste and the tablespoon of cream. Dry breasts. Spread with stuffing, wrap each in bacon slice, and secure edges with picks. Place in skillet to accommodate snugly and pour in stock. Cover tightly and simmer 30 minutes or till tender, turning twice. Remove bacon and picks and transfer to heated platter. Heat soup and milk together. Slowly add bourbon and stir in. Pour over pheasant breasts. Serves 4.

Brace of Wild Ducks

> 2 wild ducks, 2½-3 lb. each
> 2 small apples, cored and quartered
> 2 large sprigs parsley
> 2 small shallots, peeled
> 2 celery stalks
> 4 juniper berries
> 2 tablespoons butter
>   black pepper
> 6 oz. dry vermouth

1 stick butter
½ cup bourbon, heated
¾ cup grape jelly
1 tablespoon butter

Wipe birds dry inside and out. Stuff each with 1 apple, 1 tablespoon butter, 1 sprig parsley, 1 shallot, 1 celery stalk, and 2 juniper berries. Sew up cavities. Place birds on spit close together. Rub with butter and sprinkle with pepper. Heat vermouth and a stick of butter to use as a basting sauce. Roast ducks on rotary spit 30 minutes, basting often. Place birds on heated platter, pour bourbon over, and ignite. As soon as the flames die, start carving birds. Serve in slices with sauce made from the jelly and 1 tablespoon butter heated together. Serves 4.

Vegetables

Carrots Newburg

   4 cups raw carrots, diced
   1 inch boiling water
   1 teaspoon salt
 ½ teaspoon sugar
   2 tablespoons butter or margarine
   2 tablespoons flour
 ¾ cup chicken stock
 ¼ cup heavy cream
   1 oz. bourbon
 ½ teaspoon chopped fresh parsley
 ¾ teaspoon finely chopped onion
   2 teaspoons finely chopped green pepper
 ¼ teaspoon salt

Place carrots, 1 inch of boiling water, 1 teaspoon salt, and sugar in saucepan. Cover and cook 12 minutes or till crisp-tender. Melt butter or margarine in a saucepan. Blend with flour. Add chicken stock and rest of ingredients. Stir and cook about 10 minutes or till medium thick. Add carrots and serve. Serves 6.

Onion Casserole

    2 *lb. small white onions, boiled*
    4 *oz. condensed mushroom soup*
    4 *oz. shredded Swiss cheese*
    1 *oz. bourbon*
    2 *oz. chopped pecans*
    1 *tablespoon butter*

Drain onions after boiling and place in greased 1-quart casserole. In a pan, combine mushroom soup, cheese, and bourbon. Heat till cheese melts. Pour over onions in casserole. Toast the pecans in a small pan with the butter till lightly browned and sprinkle over the onions. Bake uncovered in a 350-degree oven for 25-30 minutes or till bubbling. Serves about 6.

Cepes à la Bordelaise

    1 *15-oz. can cepes (wild French mushrooms)*
    4 *tablespoons butter*
    ½ *teaspoon salt*
    ¼ *teaspoon fresh ground pepper*
    2 *medium green onions, chopped*
    1 *clove garlic, minced*
    2 *tablespoons dried bread crumbs*
    1 *oz. bourbon*

Drain cepes. Leave small ones whole; cut up larger ones. Sauté in butter till brown. Add remaining ingredients, except bourbon. Cook briefly, soaking pan till crumbs are brown. Warm bourbon in ladle, ignite, and pour over mushrooms. Serve when flames subside. As side dish, serves 4-6.

Mushrooms Flamed with Bourbon

    1 *lb. fresh mushrooms*
    2 *oz. butter*
    1 *teaspoon minced onion*
    2 *teaspoons lemon juice*
       dash Tabasco
       salt and pepper to taste
    3 *tablespoons heavy cream*
    1 *oz. bourbon*
       chopped parsley

If mushrooms are large, slice caps. Heat butter in heavy pan. Add mushrooms and onion; sprinkle with lemon juice, Tabasco, salt and pepper. Cook 3 minutes over moderate heat. Warm bourbon in a ladle, ignite, and pour flaming over the mushrooms. After flame subsides, pour in cream and simmer gently for 2 minutes. Place in a hot serving dish, sprinkle with parsley, and serve. Serves 4 to 6 persons.

Broccoli Egg Divan

    1 *bunch broccoli*
    4 *hard-cooked eggs*
   ½ *teaspoon salt, divided*
   ¼ *teaspoon pepper*
    1 *10½-oz. can condensed cheddar cheese soup*
   ⅓ *cup milk*
    1 *oz. bourbon*
   ¼ *cup dry bread crumbs*
    2 *tablespoons melted butter*

To prepare broccoli, cut off large leaves and bottom of stalk. Wash well. If stalk is more than ½ inch in diameter, make 2 lengthwise slits almost to flowerets. Cook broccoli, uncovered, in boiling salted water to cover till tender, or about 15 minutes. Drain. Arrange broccoli, stems toward center, in a 10-inch pie plate. Slice eggs crosswise and lay in layers over broccoli. Sprinkle with ¼ teaspoon salt and pepper. Mix undiluted soup with milk and bourbon till smooth. Pour over the broccoli and eggs in pie plate. Mix together bread crumbs, melted butter, and remaining ¼ teaspoon salt. Sprinkle over the cheese sauce. Bake in 375-degree oven 20 minutes till cheese sauce bubbles and bread crumbs are lightly browned. Serves 4.

Bourbon Mushrooms with Peas

    8 *oz. sliced mushrooms*
    2 *tablespoons butter*
    ¼ *teaspoon marjoram leaves*
    ⅛ *teaspoon ground mace*
      dash almond extract
    1 *oz. bourbon*
    2 *10-oz. packages frozen small peas*

Drain mushrooms, reserving liquid. In frying pan heat mushrooms in melted butter till sizzling; then stir in marjoram, mace, almond extract, and bourbon. Break up peas and pour into pan with mushrooms. Turn off heat and let stand. Just before serving, add 2 tablespoons of reserved mushroom liquid to peas and bring to a boil, stirring occasionally. Serves 6.

Carrots Bourbonade

    1 *bunch carrots, scraped*
    2 *tablespoons butter*
    2 *tablespoons maple syrup*
    ½ *teaspoon nutmeg*
      pinch salt
    ½ *teaspoon lemon juice*
    1 *oz. bourbon*
    1 *teaspoon fresh dill, chopped*

Slice carrots crosswise at angle. Place in saucepan with butter, maple syrup, nutmeg, salt, and lemon juice. Simmer over low flame; cover till tender-crisp. Add bourbon; simmer uncovered 1 minute more. Serve sprinkled with dill. Serves 4.

Bourbon Mushrooms on Toast

    2 3-oz. cans sliced mushrooms
    4 tablespoons butter
    2 teaspoons minced chives
    ¼ teaspoon paprika
      pinch onion powder
    2 tablespoons tomato catsup
    ½ cup light cream
    1 oz. bourbon
    2 slices toast

Drain mushrooms. Melt butter in small skillet. Add mushrooms, chives, paprika, and onion powder. Cook gently till crowned. Stir in catsup and cream. When heated through, add bourbon and serve on toast. Serves 2.

Bourbon Sweet Potatoes

    8 medium sweet potatoes
    2 oz. orange juice
    ⅔ cup brown sugar
    ¼ cup water
    ¼ cup butter
    ¼ cup bourbon
    1 teaspoon cinnamon

Cook sweet potatoes in jackets till tender. Cool, peel, and cut into uniform thirds or quarters. Arrange in buttered baking dish. Bring orange juice, sugar, water, and butter to boil in small saucepan. Add bourbon. Pour syrup over potatoes and bake in moderate oven (350 degrees) about half an hour till brown and candied. Baste often with syrup and sprinkle cinnamon atop. Serves 4.

Kentucky Sweets

    2 no. 2½ cans sweet potatoes
    1 cup sugar

¼ teaspoon nutmeg
¼ lb. butter
¼ teaspoon lemon extract
   marshmallow topping
2 oz. bourbon

Heat potatoes till hot, drain off water, and mash well. Add sugar, nutmeg, butter, lemon extract, and bourbon. Beat well and spoon into baking pan. Top with marshmallow and cook about half an hour in a 350-degree oven. Serves 8.

Bourbon Squash

1 acorn squash
   salt
2 teaspoons butter
2 tablespoons granulated brown sugar
½ teaspoon mace
¼ teaspoon vanilla
1 oz. bourbon

Wash squash and cut in half. Put in each half a sprinkling of salt and half the butter, sugar, mace, and vanilla. Place squash halves on a cooky sheet and bake 30 minutes in 350-degree oven. Pour half the bourbon in each squash half and pierce flesh with a knife, not cutting through skin. Cover cooky sheet with foil and bake for another 15 to 30 minutes, depending on size. Serves 2.

Baked Kidney Beans

3 1-lb. cans kidney beans
3 medium onions, sliced thin
¼ cup wheat germ
1 cooking apple, peeled, cored, and sliced
3 oz. unsulphured molasses
3 oz. bourbon
3 cloves minced garlic

1 teaspoon dry mustard
1 teaspoon salt
dash worcestershire sauce
¼ teaspoon pepper
pinch of paprika
⅛ teaspoon thyme
⅛ teaspoon marjoram
3 whole cloves
1 bay leaf
dash Tabasco
3 slices lean bacon, cut into thirds

Drain beans, reserving liquid. Cover bottom of greased 2½-quart casserole or bean pot with one-third of the beans. Top with one-third of sliced onions sprinkled with one-third of the wheat germ. Repeat this layering process, ending with wheat germ. Arrange apple slices over the mixture. Combine molasses, bourbon, garlic, and seasonings and pour over bean mixture. Top with bacon pieces. Bake, covered at 350 degrees for 1 hour. Then bake at 300 degrees, uncovered, 1 more hour. If mixture becomes dry during baking, add some of reserve bean liquid. Serves 8.

Beans for Barbecues

1 large onion, chopped (about 2 cups)
1 cup diced green pepper
1 stalk celery, chopped
3 tablespoons vegetable oil
2 24-oz. cans pinto beans, well drained
1 1-lb. can lima beans, well drained
1 15-oz. can small red beans, well drained
1 19-oz. can pork and beans, well drained
1 cup stewed tomatoes, chopped
1 teaspoon monosodium glutamate
2 teaspoons garlic salt
2 tablespoons cornmeal
½ cup tomato catsup
4 teaspoons brown sugar
1 cup bourbon

Chop onion, green pepper, and celery and cook in oil till onions and celery are soft. Dump beans into large pot or casserole dish. Mix in onion, celery, and green pepper. Add monosodium glutamate, tomatoes, garlic salt, cornmeal, catsup, brown sugar, and bourbon. Mix well. Place in 325-degree oven and bake, uncovered, 2 hours, stirring occasionally. Serve with barbecued meat. Serves 6-8.

Spanish Baked Beans

3 1-lb. cans baked beans
1 small onion, chopped
2 oz. bourbon
1 oz. lemon juice
¼ cup strong black coffee
½ cup sliced pineapple (20-oz. can)
cold sour cream

Three or four hours before serving time, empty the canned beans into a baking dish. Stir in chopped onion, bourbon, lemon juice, and coffee and let stand at room temperature for half an hour. Remove cover and bake 1 hour in a 375-degree oven. Cut pineapple slices in halves, stand around edge of beans, and bake another 15 minutes. Serve with chilled sour cream placed in dollops on the pineapple pieces.

Coffee Baked Beans

4 1-lb. cans Boston-style baked beans
½ teaspoon dry mustard
¼ teaspoon Tabasco
¼ teaspoon paprika
3 oz. bourbon
⅓ cup strong black coffee
brown sugar

Mix all ingredients except brown sugar. Place in large casserole or bean pot. Sprinkle lightly with sugar. Let stand at room temperature for 1 hour so beans will soak up added flavor. Bake, covered at 375 degrees for 90 minutes. Serves 10-12.

Chili Bourbon Beans

    3 *1-lb. cans baked beans*
    1 *teaspoon dry mustard*
  ½ *teaspoon horseradish*
    1 *teaspoon lemon juice*
    1 *tablespoon grated lemon rind*
  ½ *cup chili sauce*
    1 *tablespoon molasses*
  ½ *cup bourbon*
  ½ *cup strong black coffee*
      orange slices
      brown sugar

Combine all ingredients except orange and brown sugar. Add little brown sugar. Cover and let stand overnight. Bake at 375 degrees for 40 minutes, covered. Take lid off, put on orange slices and sprinkling of brown sugar, and bake 55 minutes without the cover.

Fiery Bean Pot

    4 *slices bacon, diced*
    1 *medium onion, thinly sliced*
  ½ *cup chopped celery*
  ½ *green pepper, diced*
  ¼ *lb. grated parmesan cheese*
    4 *cups red kidney beans, cooked*
    1 *cup tomatoes, diced*
  ¼ *cup tomato catsup*
    2 *oz. bourbon*
    1 *tablespoon chili powder*
    1 *teaspoon salt*
    1 *teaspoon worcestershire sauce*

Fry bacon. Add onion, celery, and pepper. Fry and stir ingredients for 5 minutes. Add cheese and rest of ingredients. Let simmer in skillet at least 30 minutes or bake in 350-degree oven 40 minutes. Serves 6.

Bourbon, Orange, and Beans

    4 *12-oz. cans baked beans*
    4 *oranges, sliced whole*
    1 *cup prunes, pitted and chopped*
    1 *cup raisins*
    1 *lemon, sliced whole*
    1 *cup molasses*
    1 *teaspoon fresh ginger*
  ¼ *teaspoon mace*
    1 *cup bourbon*

Add all ingredients except bourbon to the baked beans and put in large casserole. Mix thoroughly. Add bourbon gradually, making sure it is well blended. Bake in 300-degree oven for 1 hour. Serves 6-8.

Kentucky Cassoulet

    4 *13-oz. cans Boston baked beans*
    4 *baking apples, peeled, cored, and sliced*
    1 *large lime, sliced*
    4 *tablespoons grated orange rind*
    1 *cup raisins*
    1 *cup molasses*
    1 *teaspoon cinnamon*
  ¼ *teaspoon mace*
    4 *oz. bourbon*

In a shallow 3-quart baking dish, combine beans with apples, lime slices, orange rind, raisins, molasses, cinnamon, and mace. Mix well and bring to a boil on top of the stove. Remove from the heat and gradually add bourbon. Bake in a 350-degree oven about a half-hour, till slightly crusty. Serves 8.

Bourbon, Orange, and Beans

Marinades and Sauces

Bourbon Barbecue Sauce

    1 *cup tomato catsup*
⅓ *cup bourbon*
¼ *cup molasses*
¼ *cup vinegar*
    1 *tablespoon worcestershire sauce*
       dash Tabasco
    2 *teaspoons soy sauce*
½ *teaspoon dry mustard*
¼ *teaspoon pepper*
    2 *cloves garlic, mashed*
    1 *tablespoon lemon juice*

Blend all ingredients together thoroughly. Let stand for several hours. Use as a marinade, basting sauce, or to add to hamburgers, hot dogs, spareribs, or other meats before or after cooking.

All-Purpose Sauce

¼ cup salad oil
¼ cup bourbon
2 tablespoons soy sauce
dash Tabasco
1 teaspoon worcestershire sauce
dash cayenne
1 teaspoon garlic powder
pepper to taste

Blend all ingredients well. Pour over meat or fish and marinate in refrigerator (turn when you think of it). Marinate roasts for 24 to 48 hours; steak, 4 hours; salmon or fowl, 2 hours. Also used as a basting sauce during broiling or roasting.

Economy Roast Marinade

4 oz. bourbon
1 tablespoon white sugar
1 tablespoon salt
2 tablespoons lemon juice
4 oz. salad oil
clove garlic, minced
dash Tabasco

Mix ingredients and place a round or rump roast of beef in the mixture. The marinade will both season and tenderize the meat.

Marinade for Beef Roast

2 oz. A-1 sauce
2 oz. butter
2 oz. bourbon
1 teaspoon lemon juice
dash Tabasco

Mix ingredients and bring to a boil. Baste the roast during last 30 minutes of cooking with this sauce piping hot.

Hoisin-Bourbon Marinade

    1 *cup Hoisin Sauce**
    1 *cup honey*
    1 *cup tomato puree*
    1 *cup bourbon*
    1 *clove garlic, mashed*
    1 *tablespoon chopped fresh ginger* or
  ½ *teaspoon powdered ginger*
      dash worcestershire sauce
      dash soy sauce

Thoroughly mix all ingredients and refrigerate in glass jar.

Piquant Steak Marinade

    2 *oz. bourbon*
    2 *oz. soy sauce*
      dash bitters
      dash Tabasco
    1 *clove garlic, crushed*
  ¼ *teaspoon ginger*

Mix ingredients and set a porterhouse or T-bone steak 1½ inches thick in the mixture; let it set for 4 hours.

Marinade for Steak

    9 *tablespoons bourbon*
    6 *tablespoons soy sauce*
    2 *tablespoons garlic vinegar*

---

*This comes from Hong Kong and may be purchased in any oriental specialty shop.

2 tablespoons olive oil
½ teaspoon salt
½ teaspoon any herb, to your taste
½ teaspoon monosodium glutamate
½ teaspoon freshly ground pepper

Marinate steak for 3 hours; then grill to suit your taste.

Bourbon Marinade for Roast

1 cup soy sauce
1 tablespoon ground ginger
3 large garlic cloves, cut in half
1 medium onion, cut in thick slices
2 oz. bourbon
1 teaspoon sugar

Place all ingredients in large bowl and soak roast for 48 hours, turning occasionally. Take out of marinade 2 hours before roasting. Rub oil over roast. Place on rack in pan and roast in 300-degree oven at 20 minutes to the pound.

Barbecue Sauce for Venison

1 cup bourbon
1 medium onion
1 clove garlic
1 oz. melted butter
1 cup water

Blend all ingredients in blender at high speed. Place venison roast on rotisserie spit and baste with sauce every 15 minutes until roast is done.

Hot Dog Cocktail Sauce

16 oz. tomato catsup
¾ cup bourbon
¾ cup brown sugar, packed

Marinades and Sauces

These 3 ingredients are combined in a small saucepan and simmered gently for at least 2 hours, or until the sauce is thick enough so as almost to hold its shape.

Liquor Butter

    ½ *cup butter*
    ⅛ *teaspoon garlic powder*
    ⅛ *teaspoon pepper*
    1 *tablespoon minced parsley*
    1 *tablespoon bourbon*

Cream butter till fluffy. Beat in garlic powder, pepper, and parsley. Very slowly add liquor and mix to combine well. If sweet butter is used, add salt to taste. Makes about ½ cup.

All-Purpose Barbecue Sauce

    ¼ *cup olive oil*
    2 *oz. bourbon*
    2 *tablespoons soy sauce*
       dash Tabasco
    1 *teaspoon worcestershire sauce*
       dash cayenne
    1 *teaspoon garlic powder*
    ¼ *teaspoon white pepper*

Combine all ingredients with the meat in a plastic bag. Tie securely and place in a pan in case bag leaks. Marinate a roast in refrigerator at least 24 hours; steaks marinate 4 hours and fish or chicken about 2 hours.

Spicy Bourbon Sauce

    16 *oz. chutney*
    12 *oz. chili sauce*
    16 *oz. tomato catsup*

8 oz. steak sauce
dash Tabasco
1 teaspoon worcestershire sauce
2 tablespoons lemon juice
2 oz. bourbon

Put chutney through food grinder. Combine remaining ingredients and blend thoroughly.

Bourbon Sauce for Turkey

3 oz. bourbon
2 tablespoons honey
1 teaspoon lemon juice
1 teaspoon dry mustard
2 tablespoons flour
½ teaspoon nutmeg
2 cups turkey stock
salt and pepper to taste

Half an hour before the turkey is finished roasting, blend whiskey, lemon juice, honey, and mustard and brush bird as with a glaze. Continue roasting, brushing several more times. Remove bird to serving platter and keep warm. Pour off all but two tablespoons fat in roasting pan.

Stir in flour and nutmeg and cook 2 minutes. Add stock and continue to cook, scraping brown bits that cling to pan, till sauce is smooth and thick. Add any remaining glaze and adjust seasoning with salt and pepper to taste. Strain into heated sauceboat and serve with turkey.

Spaghetti Sauce

¼ cup salad oil
1 lb. chicken livers, cut in quarters
1 medium onion, chopped
2 8-oz. cans tomato sauce
1 tablespoon sugar

2 teaspoons worcestershire sauce
salt and pepper to taste
⅓ cup bourbon
8 oz. spaghetti

Heat oil; add chicken livers and onion. Cook over low heat, stirring occasionally until livers are browned. Stir in tomato sauce, sugar, and worcestershire sauce; add salt and pepper. Cook, uncovered, over low heat for 20 minutes, stirring occasionally. Add bourbon during last 2 minutes of cooking. Meanwhile, prepare spaghetti according to package directions. Drain and arrange on serving platter. Remove sauce from heat and pour over spaghetti. Serves 2-3.

Bourbonnaise Sauce

2 tablespoons butter
2 shallots, chopped
2 onion slices
1 rib celery, chopped
2 cloves
2 bay leaves
2 tablespoons flour
1 cup condensed beef bouillon
3 tablespoons bourbon
dash salt and pepper

Melt butter. Add shallots, onion, celery, cloves, and bay leaves. Sauté about 5 minutes till onions and shallots are golden. Take from fire and add flour. Stir till smooth. Place over low flame and stir till flour is browned. Take from heat and gradually stir in bouillon. Put back over medium heat and bring to boiling point, stirring constantly. Reduce heat and simmer, stirring occasionally about 15 minutes. Strain sauce and discard vegetables. Add salt and pepper and bourbon. Warm up.

Bourbon Glaze for Ham

    1 *cup bourbon*
    1 *cup brown sugar*
    ¼ *teaspoon nutmeg*
    6 *whole cloves*
    1 *tablespoon grated lemon rind*

Mix all ingredients. Let stand till sugar has dissolved in bourbon, stirring occasionally. Half an hour before taking ham from oven, spread half of mixture over meat. Baste periodically during remainder of baking process with rest of glaze mixture.

Bourbon Seafood Sauce

    ⅔ *cup chili sauce*
    ⅔ *cup tomato catsup*
    1 *teaspoon worcestershire sauce*
      dash Tabasco
    ½ *teaspoon dry mustard*
    ½ *teaspoon salt*
    1 *tablespoon horseradish*
    2 *tablespoons wine vinegar*
    ¼ *teaspoon black pepper*
    3 *tablespoons bourbon*

Mix first 9 ingredients together well. Stir in bourbon. Chill and serve with seafood.

Crème Anglaise

    ¾ *cup sugar*
    6 *egg yolks*
    ¼ *teaspoon salt*
    2 *cups milk*
      dash nutmeg
      dash mace

Marinades and Sauces

    2 *tablespoons finely chopped, crystallized ginger*
    1 *teaspoon bourbon*

Combine sugar, yolks, and salt in saucepan and beat with wire whisk. Bring milk to boil, blend in nutmeg and mace, and add very gradually yolk mixture, beating constantly. Place saucepan over flame on asbestos mat and cook sauce, stirring steadily with wooden spoon. When sauce is done it will coat back of spoon. Stir in ginger and bourbon and serve hot or cold over fruit cakes or puddings. Makes about 2¾ cups sauce.

Bourbon Sauce

    4 *eggs, separated*
  1⅓ *cups powdered sugar*
      dash vanilla
      dash mace
    2 *oz. bourbon*

Beat yolks till thick. Add ⅔ cup sugar slowly. Beat egg whites till they form peaks. Add ⅔ cup sugar to whites and combine with yolks, adding vanilla and mace. Add bourbon very slowly, stirring constantly. Serve on any pudding or cake.

Tipsy Bourbon Sauce

    1 *cup powdered sugar*
    2 *tablespoons soft butter*
  ½ *cup heavy cream*
      dash nutmeg
      dash vanilla
    3 *tablespoons chopped raisins*
    3 *tablespoons bourbon*

Blend sugar with butter, cream, nutmeg, and vanilla. Add raisins and whiskey and blend well. Good over cakes or puddings.

Dessert Sauce

    ½ cup heavy cream
    2 tablespoons sugar
    2 teaspoons bourbon
    dash mace
    dash almond extract

To the cream add the sugar, whiskey, and flavorings. Stir till sugar is dissolved and pour ice cold over the dessert you are serving. This is very good over rice pudding, Elberta peaches, or even baked apples. Serves 4.

Bourbon Dessert Sauce

    1 medium can unsweetened cherries with juice
    2 cups granulated sugar
    1 teaspoon vanilla
    dash nutmeg
    4 oz. bourbon
    2 tablespoons chocolate syrup
    1 tablespoon cognac

Cook cherries with juice and sugar till they reach temperature of 218 degrees. Remove from heat and add vanilla and nutmeg. Cool to room temperature and add bourbon, chocolate syrup, and cognac. Mix in blender and put up in jars.

Flaming Cherry Sauce

    1 medium can pitted bing cherries (reserving syrup)
    2 oz. bourbon
    dash mace
    dash lemon extract

Boil down cherry syrup for a few minutes in the top pan of a chafing dish. Add cherries to syrup along with mace and lemon extract. Warm bourbon, ignite, and pour flaming over the cherries.

When the flame subsides, serve the sauce on pudding, cake, or ice cream.

Whiskey Sauce for Pudding

    1 *cup sugar*
      dash lemon extract
  ½ *cup butter*
    2 *beaten eggs*
      dash cinnamon
    1 *cup light cream*
    1 *tablespoon bourbon*

Cook and stir together in top of double boiler the sugar, lemon extract, butter, eggs, cinnamon, and cream, stirring constantly. When thickened, add the bourbon.

Apricot-Raisin Sauce

    ½ *cup dried apricots*
    ¼ *cup sugar*
  1½ *cups water*
    2 *tablespoons bourbon*
    2 *oz. raisins*
    1 *tablespoon lemon juice*

In small saucepan, combine apricots and sugar with 1½ cups water and lemon juice and bring to boil. Reduce heat and simmer, covered, 20 minutes or till apricots are tender. Press apricots and liquid through sieve or blend at high speed in electric blender for 30 seconds. Add raisins. Refrigerate and chill 1 hour. Just before serving, stir in bourbon. Good with dessert soufflés and puddings. Serves 6.

Strawberry Bourbon Sauce

    1 *quart strawberries*
    2 *oz. orange juice*
    2 *cups sugar*
      dash lemon extract
    4 *oz. bourbon*

Wash and hull strawberries. Add sugar, orange juice, and lemon extract and let mixture stand half an hour. Bring to a boil and cook, stirring from time to time till sugar dissolves. Add bourbon and chill. Keep in refrigerator. Good over ice cream.

Cherry-Bourbon Sauce

    2 *cups canned sour cherries, drained*
    2 *cups sugar*
    1 *tablespoon lemon juice*
      dash vanilla
    2 *oz. bourbon*

Stir cherries, sugar, lemon juice, vanilla, and whiskey over low heat till sugar dissolves. Chill. Use over pudding or ice cream.

Raspberry-Bourbon Sauce

    2 *cups raspberries, cleaned*
    ½ *cup sugar*
    2 *tablespoons orange juice*
      dash almond extract
    1 *tablespoon cornstarch*
    2 *oz. bourbon*

Cook berries and sugar with almond extract till sugar dissolves. Stir orange juice and cornstarch together and add to fruit. Cook, stirring steadily, till sauce is clear. Add whiskey. Chill. Serve over ice cream, puddings, or cake.

Bourbon Custard Sauce

    1 *cup light cream*
    ¼ *cup sugar*
       dash almond extract
       dash mace
    3 *egg yolks*
    1 *oz. bourbon*

In saucepan, combine cream, sugar, almond extract, and mace. Bring mixture to a boil and simmer, stirring steadily for 15 minutes. In a bowl, beat egg yolks till they are light. Pour in cream mixture slowly, stirring all the time. Transfer mixture to a heavy saucepan and cook over moderate heat, stirring with wooden spatula till it thickens and coats the spatula. Do not let it boil. Add bourbon and strain custard into a bowl. Cover with buttered round of wax paper and chill. Makes about 1 cup. Good over sponge cake or jelly roll.

Crepe Sauce

    ¼ *lb. butter*
      juice 2 oranges
    1 *tablespoon lemon juice*
      grated rind 1 orange
    2 *tablespoons bourbon*
      dash nutmeg

Combine all ingredients in skillet and stir over low heat till sauce thickens. Chill. Makes about 1 cup sauce.

Bourbon Hard Sauce

    ½ *cup butter*
      dash vanilla
      dash mace

3 cups confectioner's sugar
⅓ cup bourbon

Gradually add sugar and bourbon alternately to butter, with vanilla and mace, and beat till smooth. Chill. Serve with steamed pudding.

Hot-Sweet Sauce

½ cup butter
1 cup granulated sugar
dash vanilla
¼ cup bourbon
dash mace

Cream butter, sugar, and vanilla and stir mixture over heat, bringing to boiling point, stirring steadily and removing immediately. Add bourbon and mace.

Serve the sauce hot. Serve on holidays over plum pudding or mince pie. Makes about 1½ cups.

Fruit Desserts

Fruit Tart

Pastry
2 cups flour
2 tablespoons sugar
¼ teaspoon salt
2 egg yolks
1 cup butter
grated rind of 1 orange
2 tablespoons bourbon
¼ teaspoon lemon extract

Fruit
3 apricots
1 apple
1 pear
lime juice
large black grapes

Cream

¼ cup sugar
¼ teaspoon mace
2 tablespoons cornstarch
3 egg yolks, beaten lightly
1 cup milk
2 tablespoons bourbon

Glaze

1 cup apricot preserves
¼ cup bourbon
½ teaspoon lemon juice

To make pastry: toss flour, sugar, and salt to mix. Make a well in center; drop in remaining ingredients. Blend with fingers or knife, working from the center ingredients outward. Press out on a double-thick sheet of heavy aluminum foil to make a uniform oval 11 inches long and about 9 inches wide across the center. Trim the foil ½ inch from the oval and turn up the pastry and foil together to make a 1-inch edge. Prick with a fork and bake in a hot oven (about 450 degrees) until firm and golden, or about 15 minutes. Cool before filling.

To make cream: mix sugar, mace, cornstarch, and egg yolks in a small saucepan. Gradually add the milk, stirring rapidly with a wire whisk. Cook over low heat, stirring continually, till the mixture thickens. Do not let it boil. Cool slightly, beat in bourbon, and continue to cool.

To prepare fruit: dip apricots into boiling water and slip off skins. Cut in half and remove stones. Peel, core, and slice thinly apple and pear. Dip into lime juice. Remove seeds from grapes.

To make glaze: melt apricot preserves over low heat and force through sieve. Add lemon juice and bourbon and stir.

To assemble: spread cooled baked tart shell with cream. Arrange apricots at ends of oval, pear and apple next, and row of grapes down center. Brush fruit with warm glaze. Serves 16.

Watermelon Cheer

    1 *medium-sized watermelon*
    2 *cups bourbon*
    ½ *cup peach cordial*

Make lengthwise slashes, about 2 inches apart, on watermelon, through the rind, just to the meat. With a sharp, slender blade, cut a circle, about 2 inches in diameter, at top center (long dimension of melon) through the rind and meat to a depth of about 6 inches. Remove this plug. Place watermelon in large pan and refrigerate several hours. Drain any juice which has accumulated in the cavity. Mix bourbon and cordial. Pour about 1 cup of liquor mixture into cavity. Continue to chill. Add remaining liquor, ½ cup at a time, at 1-hour intervals. Refrigerate several hours longer. Serve in half-moon slices. serves 10.

Bourbon Watermelon

    1 *medium-sized watermelon*
    1 *cup apricot brandy*
    1 *pt. bourbon*

On two sides of the watermelon, cut several parallel diagonal gashes, cutting through the rind to the meat.

With a sharp knife, cut a circle approximately 2 inches in diameter at top center of horizontal watermelon.

Cut through the rind and meat to a depth of about 6 inches; remove core. Place melon in a deep container and let stand in refrigerator 1 hour.

Pour off any moisture in cavity. Fill center with 1 cup bourbon-apricot blend. Chill several hours, adding ½ cup liquor every hour. Garnish slices with coconut. Serves 10.

Drunken Figs

    1 *12-oz. package dried figs*
    1 *teaspoon lemon juice*
    1 *teaspoon lemon rind*
  ¼ *cup bourbon*
  ½ *cup heavy cream*

Add water, lemon juice, and rind to cover figs and simmer 45 minutes. Add bourbon and chill 3-4 hours. To serve, add whipped cream on each portion. Serves 6.

Poached Apricots in Bourbon

    6 *cups water*
  ½ *teaspoon nutmeg*
       dash vanilla
    3 *cups sugar*
  ½ *cup bourbon*
    1 *sprig fresh mint*
    2 *lb. fresh apricots*

In a heavy kettle, bring water, nutmeg, vanilla, sugar, whiskey, and mint to a boil over medium-high heat.

With a spoon drop apricots into the boiling liquid. Boil apricots until they are tender but still hold their shape (this will vary according to ripeness of fruit).

Remove apricots with slotted spoon and slip off skins. Chill in some of the poaching liquid until ready to serve. Serves 6.

Flaming Peaches

  ½ *cup butter*
  ½ *cup honey*
    2 *teaspoons grated lemon rind*
    2 *30-oz. cans cling peach halves, drained*
  ⅔ *cup bourbon*

Fruit Desserts

½ teaspoon nutmeg
1 quart vanilla ice cream
1 cup finely chopped walnuts

Melt butter in chafing dish over direct canned heat flame; stir in honey and lemon rind. Add peaches and heat, basting frequently. Sprinkle fruit with bourbon and nutmeg, heat, and ignite by holding a match to liquid in dish (or start with liquor heated in spoon). Spoon flaming liquid over peaches until flame burns out. Serve immediately with ice cream topped with chopped walnuts. Serves 12.

Bourbon-cured Peaches

9 lb. (about 80 good-size) ripe peaches
9 lb. sugar
1 quart water
1 cup lemon juice
4 sticks cinnamon, broken
1 teaspoon nutmeg
2 tablespoons whole cloves
2 fifths bourbon

Scald the fruit, a few at a time, and peel.
Dissolve the sugar with lemon juice in the water; add cinnamon, nutmeg, and cloves tied in a muslin bag. Bring to a boil. When clear, add the fruit a few at a time and simmer until barely tender. Drain fruit on a platter and repeat until all fruit is cooked.
Boil the syrup until it is slightly thickened or registers 222 degrees on a candy thermometer. Cool slightly. Stir in the bourbon.
Place the fruit as it drains in hot sterilized jars. Cover with bourbon syrup; seal. Yield: 9-12 quarts, depending on size of fruit.

Bananas Flamed with Bourbon

4 tablespoons sweet butter
6 large ripe bananas
¼ cup dark brown sugar

2 tablespoons orange juice
¼ cup bourbon

Preheat oven to 450 degrees. In a shallow casserole, melt 4 tablespoons butter. Cut bananas in half and dunk into butter, coating all around.

Place in casserole and bake 15 minutes. Sprinkle with brown sugar and orange juice. Return to oven 3-4 minutes to melt sugar. Take from hot oven and pour ¼ cup warmed bourbon over the surface. Light the bourbon and carry flaming to table.

Spoon flaming sauce over bananas until flames die down. Serves 4.

Bananas Flambé

6 *firm bananas*
¼ *cup melted butter*
1 *tablespoon lemon juice*
¼ *cup brown sugar, packed*
⅓ *teaspoon cinnamon*
⅓ *cup bourbon*
1 *tablespoon crème de cacao*

Peel and slice bananas in half lengthwise and horizontally. In a chafing dish, melt butter, add sugar and cinnamon, and stir until blended. Add bananas and turn in the butter-sugar mixture until golden brown. Add lemon juice and crème de cacao.

Just before serving, heat bourbon and pour over bananas. Flame and serve over ice cream. Serves 6.

(Hotel Americana, New York City)

Hot Fruit Compote

1 *8-oz. can pineapple slices*
1 *16-oz. can peach slices*
1 *11-oz. package mixed dried fruit*
3 *cinnamon sticks*

12 whole cloves
½ teaspoon vanilla
¾ cup bourbon
1 1-lb. can pitted cherries, drained
1 cup seedless green grapes
sour cream (optional)

Drain pineapple and peach slices, reserving syrups. Place dried fruit in large saucepan; add syrups, cinnamon sticks, cloves, vanilla, and bourbon. Simmer for 15 minutes, stirring occasionally. Add pineapple and peach slices, cherries, and grapes; then simmer 5 more minutes. Serve warm, topped with a dollop of sour cream, if desired. Serves 12.

Cherries Jubilee

2 cups pitted bing cherries
1 tablespoon lemon juice
dash mace
2 oz. bourbon

Drain syrup from cherries and boil it down in the top pan of a chafing dish for a few minutes. Add the cherries with lemon juice and mace and heat them through.

Warm ¼ cup bourbon, ignite it with a match, and pour over the fruit. Serve as soon as the flame burns out, over hard-frozen ice cream, if you like.

Bourbon Molds

1 package strawberry-flavored gelatine
1 cup hot water
½ cup bourbon
1 teaspoon lemon juice
1 1-lb. can jellied cranberry sauce
½ cup chopped pecans

Dissolve gelatine in hot water. Add bourbon and lemon juice. Chill until slightly thickened. Crush cranberry sauce with a fork and add to gelatine. Add nuts. Pour into 6 individual molds or into a 1-quart mold. Chill until firm. Serves 6.

Burning Apples

4 *baking apples*
½ *cup mincemeat*
½ *cup brown sugar*
¼ *teaspoon mace*
2 *tablespoons butter*
2 *tablespoons water*

Core and remove peel from top half of apples. Place in baking dish and fill centers with mincemeat. Sprinkle sugar and mace over apples, dot with butter, and pour water in bottom of dish. Bake in 375-degree oven for 30-40 minutes or until apples are tender. Do not refrigerate apples.

Sauce
⅓ *cup bourbon*
3 *tablespoons sugar*
2 *tablespoons orange juice*
¼ *cup warm bourbon*

Pour juice from baking apples into blazer pan; add ⅓ cup bourbon, sugar, and orange juice and place over moderate heat. Stir until sugar is dissolved; then add baked apples. Baste apples with liquid and heat until apples are warm. Pour ½ cup warm bourbon over apples and ignite. Serves 4.

Gourmet Baked Apples

1 *cup raisins*
¼ *cup honey*

¼ teaspoon cinnamon
¼ teaspoon ground cloves
¼ cup bourbon
6 baking apples
¾ cup water
1 oz. lemon juice
1 cup sugar
red food coloring

Core apples, removing top and a circle of peel around fruit. Place in baking dish and stuff apples with mixture of raisins, cinnamon, honey, and cloves. Boil water, lemon juice, and sugar together about 5 minutes. Remove from heat and add enough food coloring to give it a pink glow. Pour syrup over apples. Bake apples in 350-degree oven 45 minutes to 1 hour, or till tender. Spoon syrup over apples frequently while baking. When ready, remove apples and sprinkle lightly with sugar.

To flame, hold large serving spoon full of bourbon over apples and light a kitchen match; after a second, hold match to liquor to ignite. Pour flaming bourbon over apples and carry blazing to table. Spoon sauce over apples gradually till flames subside. Serves 6.

Mousses

Frozen Lee

    1½ *cups whipping cream*
    1 *oz. ground nuts*
    1 *tablespoon granulated sugar*
    4 *oz. bourbon*

Mix above ingredients in a metal dish. Add to this liquid nitrogen or liquid air from one of the flasks dermatologists use, stir vigorously, and freeze. When frozen, you have a golden brown ice cream.

Festival Freeze

    1½ cups milk
    ½ cup heavy cream
    1 package chocolate instant pudding
    2 tablespoons sugar
    ⅓ cup chopped toasted pecans
    ⅓ cup chopped raisins
    2-3 tablespoons bourbon

Add pudding mix and sugar to cream and milk; beat as directed on package. Pour into shallow pan and freeze 1 hour or until ice crystals form 1 inch in from edge.

Spoon mixture into bowl and beat until smooth, but not melted. Fold in nuts and raisins. Freeze 30 minutes longer. Stir in bourbon and freeze firm. Serves 6.

Mocha Parfait

    1 6-oz. package semisweet chocolate bits
    1 tablespoon butter
    ⅓ cup honey
    ½ teaspoon vanilla
    ¼ cup bourbon
    1½ pt. coffee ice cream

Combine chocolate bits, butter, and honey and stir over hot (not boiling) water until chocolate is melted. Add vanilla and bourbon. Mix well. Let sauce cool to room temperature.

Alternate layers of chocolate sauce and ice cream in parfait glasses, starting and finishing with sauce. Place glasses in freezer until ready to serve. About 10 minutes before serving, transfer parfaits from freezer to refrigerator. Serves 6.

Snowball Ice Cream Mold

    3 pt. vanilla ice cream
    ½ cup crushed, stale macaroons

½ cup minced, candied fruit soaked in ¼ cup bourbon
1 cup heavy cream, whipped
2 tablespoons sugar
candied violets, roses, or large raisins plumped up in bourbon
1 melon mold

Line melon mold with a narrow strip of waxed paper, long enough to hang over at each end.

Leave the ice cream out long enough to soften sufficiently to mix it with the crushed macaroons and candied fruit.

Pack this in the mold, fold the strips of wax paper over the ice cream, and freeze for at least 2 hours. (This can be done weeks ahead.) The day that you plan to use it, unmold the ice cream onto a chilled serving dish. You will find the strips of wax paper help the unmolding.

Frost the ice cream with sweetened whipped cream, piped through a pastry bag, or do it with a spatula as you would a cake. Decorate with candied flowers or raisins. Replace dessert in the freezer until serving time.

Peppermint Bourbon Mousse

3 egg whites
2 tablespoons granulated sugar
3 egg yolks
¼ cup granulated sugar
½ cup heavy cream
½ cup milk
½ cup straight bourbon
½ cup cold water
1 envelope gelatine
2 tablespoons granulated sugar
⅛ teaspoon salt
½ teaspoon oil of peppermint
½ cup heavy cream
green food coloring

Beat egg whites until they form peaks but are not dry. Beat in 2 tablespoons sugar. In separate bowl, beat egg yolks well; add ¼ cup sugar. Add cream and milk to egg yolk mixture. Fold in egg whites. Dribble in bourbon. Set aside.

Put ½ cup water into top of double boiler. Sprinkle gelatine over water. Add 2 tablespoons sugar and salt. Blend. Place pan over barely simmering water. Stir constantly until gelatine is thoroughly dissolved (about 4 minutes). Remove from heat; stir in eggnog mixture. Add oil of peppermint. Chill until mixture is slightly thicker than the consistency of unbeaten egg white. Fold in whipped cream and coloring. Turn into large mold or individual molds. Serves 8.

(Bourbon Institute)

Bourbon Angel

> 1 *pt. vanilla ice cream*
> 1 *cup bourbon*
> 1 *cup heavy cream, whipped*
> *grated orange rind*
> *toasted chopped almonds*

Soften ice cream slightly. Beat in bourbon; fold in whipped cream. Or combine first 3 ingredients in a blender and whirl until foamy. Spoon into glasses and sprinkle top with grated orange rind and toasted chopped nuts. Serves 8-10 in 4-ounce glasses.

Daily Double
(Ice Cream and Bourbon Sugar Sauce)

> 1 *cup dark brown sugar, packed*
> ½ *cup bourbon*
> 4 *tablespoons cornstarch*
> 3 *tablespoons heavy cream*
> 1 *tablespoon butter*
> 1 *teaspoon vanilla extract*

Sift together brown sugar and cornstarch into saucepan. Slowly add bourbon, blending to a smooth paste. Bring to boiling over a medium flame; boil for 2 minutes, stirring frequently. Add cream, butter, and vanilla extract.

Cool to room temperature and serve over coffee ice cream.

Chocolate Parfait American

> 8 tablespoons cocoa
> ⅔ cup hot water
> 1 tablespoon butter
> ½ cup honey
> ⅓ cup white corn syrup
> ½ teaspoon vanilla
> ¼ cup bourbon
> 1 quart vanilla ice cream
> whipped cream

Blend cocoa, water, butter, honey, and corn syrup in a saucepan and cook until boiling. Remove from heat; stir in vanilla and bourbon. Place alternate layers of ice cream and chocolate sauce in parfait glasses. Place in freezer until ready to serve. Top with whipped cream. Serves 8.

Bourbon Cloud

> ¾ cup granulated sugar
> 1 envelope unflavored gelatine
> 3 eggs, separated
> ¾ cup bourbon
> ½ cup chopped pecans
> 1 cup heavy cream
> lady fingers (optional)

In top of double boiler, blend the gelatine and half of the sugar thoroughly. Add and blend egg yolks.

Trickle in bourbon. (Too speedy addition of bourbon tends to "cook" eggs; blend thoroughly, adding slowly.)

Place over simmering (not boiling) water and cook, stirring constantly, until mixture thickens slightly and coats a metal spoon (about 10 minutes).

Beat egg whites until foamy. Continue beating while adding remaining sugar. Beat until stiff, shiny peaks form.

Gradually fold in yolk mixture. Let stand in refrigerator until cool (about 20 minutes).

Beat cream until soft peaks form. Fold into pudding mixture and fold in chopped nuts.

Pour into mold, which may be lined with lady fingers, cut side out. Chill at least 6 hours or overnight. Serves 8.

Fig Fancy

>   1 *pint vanilla ice cream*
>   1 *can figs*
>   1 *oz. bourbon*
>   1 *oz. fig syrup (from can)*

Chill 4 dessert dishes. Drain figs. Place 2 or 3 in each dish. Top with ice cream. Mix bourbon and fig syrup and pour a tablespoon over each portion.

Macaroon Delight

>   2 *dozen macaroons*
>   3 *oz. bourbon*
>   1 *quart coffee ice cream*
>   1 *can toasted slivered almonds*
>   1 *pint whipped cream*

Soak macaroons in bourbon. When crumbly, mix with softened ice cream and almonds.

Place in silver bowl and harden in deep freeze for 30-40 minutes. Before serving, pile whipped cream on top. Serves 8.

Eggnog Mousse

>   1 *envelope unflavored gelatine*
>   ½ *cup cold water*
>   4 *eggs, separated*

¼ cup sugar
½ cup bourbon
1½ cups heavy cream, whipped

Sprinkle gelatine on cold water to soften; dissolve over low heat. Beat egg yolks with sugar until thick and light. Beat in bourbon. Add gelatine and fold in whipped cream. Chill until mixture will mount on a spoon.

Beat egg whites stiff; fold in. Pile in 6-cup serving compote; shape hollow in center with back of large spoon. Chill 1-2 hours, until firmly set. Fill with fruit salad.

Serves 6.

Pumpkin Mousse

2 tablespoons gelatine
½ cup cold water
1 cup bourbon
½ cup sugar
1 tablespoon lemon juice
1½ cups cooked pumpkin
1 cup sour cream
1 cup heavy cream, whipped
1½ teaspoons cinnamon
1 teaspoon ginger
½ teaspoon mace
chopped walnuts

Soften gelatine in cold water and dissolve it over hot water. Add bourbon, sugar, and lemon juice. Stir the mixture until it is well blended and chill it until it is slightly thickened. Combine cooked pumpkin, rubbed through a fine sieve or pureed in a blender, with sour cream and whipped cream. Add cinnamon, ginger, and mace and combine the mixture with the slightly thickened gelatine, blending well. Turn the mixture into a 5½-cup mold, rinsed in cold water, and chill it until it is firm. Unmold the mousse on a chilled platter; garnish it with chopped walnuts.

Pies

Chocolate Walnut Pie

    1 *9-inch unbaked pastry shell*
    2 *eggs*
    1 *cup sugar*
  ½ *cup butter, melted*
    3 *tablespoons bourbon*
    1 *teaspoon almond extract*
  ¼ *cup cornstarch*
    1 *cup finely chopped walnuts*
    1 *cup semisweet chocolate chips*

In a small mixer bowl, beat eggs slightly and gradually add sugar. Add melted butter, bourbon, and almond extract and mix well. Blend in cornstarch. Stir in nuts and chocolate chips; pour into unbaked pastry shell. Bake at 350 degrees for 50 minutes. Cool one hour and serve with a dollop of whipped cream. Serves 8-10.

Bourbon Delight Pie No. 1

    4 *eggs, separated*
½ *cup dark brown sugar*
¼ *teaspoon nutmeg*
1½ *tablespoons cornstarch*
1½ *cups milk*
    5 *oz. bourbon*
    2 *squares bitter chocolate*
½ *teaspoon almond extract*
    1 *envelope plain gelatine*
½ *cup granulated sugar*
¼ *teaspoon cream of tartar*
½ *cup heavy cream, whipped*

Combine in double boiler egg yolks, nutmeg, cornstarch, and brown sugar; beat till light and fluffy. Gradually stir in 1½ cups milk and 6 tablespoons bourbon. Place in double boiler over hot water and stir constantly till custard is thick and smooth. Remove from heat, take out 1 cup custard, and stir in 1½ squares bitter chocolate (melted) and ½ teaspoon almond extract. Cool. Pour into baked pie shell. To the rest of the custard, add envelope gelatine and 4 tablespoons bourbon. Cool slightly. Beat 4 egg whites with cream of tartar till stiff; then beat in ½ cup granulated sugar. Combine with custard and pour into pie shell onto chocolate layer. Chill several hours. Pipe or spoon on a border of whipped cream. Sprinkle remaining ½ cube bitter chocolate, grated, over center of pie.

Bourbon Delight Pie No. 2

    1 *cooled graham cracker crust*
½ *cup sugar*
    3 *oz. bourbon*
    3 *egg whites, stiffly beaten*
    3 *egg yolks*
       dash vanilla
       dash mace

½ pint whipping cream
½ package semisweet chocolate chips

Cream egg yolks with vanilla, mace, sugar, and bourbon. Cook in double boiler till mixture thickens. Cool; then add stiffly beaten egg whites and whipped cream. Pour into cool crust. Sprinkle with chocolate chips. Freeze at least 3 hours.

Bourbon-Marshmallow Pie

21 *marshmallows*
1 *13-oz. can evaporated milk*
½ *pint whipping cream*
3 *tablespoons bourbon*
1 *box chocolate snap cookies (to make about 2 cups crumbs)*
½ *cup melted margarine*

Melt marshmallows in evaporated milk in saucepan, but do not boil. Chill. Whip cream and fold it in with bourbon. Fold whipped cream and bourbon into marshmallow-milk mixture. Pour into cooled crumb crust. Refrigerate about 4 hours or till set. When ready to serve, top with added whipped cream and chocolate crumbs.

For crust: Crush chocolate snaps with rolling pin. Mix with melted margarine. Pat into 9-inch pie pan. Bake in 350-degree oven about 10 minutes, till crust hardens. Cool crust thoroughly before pouring in filling.

(Weidmann's Restaurant, Meridian, Mississippi)

Brownie-Bottomed Bourbon Pie

5 *egg yolks*
¾ *cup honey*
1 *envelope unflavored gelatine*
¼ *cup cold water*

½ cup bourbon
¼ teaspoon vanilla
1½ cups heavy cream
1 10-inch brownie, baked in a pie pan from a mix or your favorite recipe
2 tablespoons shaved bittersweet chocolate

Beat egg yolks in electric mixer or by hand till thick and lemon-colored. Slowly beat in honey.

Soften gelatine in water, and add one-third of the bourbon. Heat gelatine over boiling water till it dissolves. Pour into egg yolks slowly while stirring briskly. Stir in rest of bourbon and vanilla. Whip 1 cup of the cream and fold into mixture. Pour into pie pan over the brownie and chill 4 hours. Whip remaining cream and use to decorate top of pie. Sprinkle shaved chocolate on top.

Whiskey Pie

1 tablespoon plus ½ teaspoon gelatine
½ cup water
salt
¼ cup milk
2 squares unsweetened chocolate
¼ teaspoon almond extract
4 egg yolks
½ cup sugar
2 egg whites
1¼ cups heavy cream, whipped
¼ cup chopped walnuts
2 tablespoons bourbon
1 9-inch baked pie shell
toasted, sliced almonds

Dissolve gelatine in cold water. Melt over hot water in double boiler till hot and clear. Mix pinch of salt with milk, chocolate, almond extract, egg yolks, and ¼ cup plus 2 tablespoons sugar. Cook till chocolate and sugar are dissolved. Put in bowl and add gelatine mix. Chill over crushed ice till syrupy.

Beat egg whites till stiff, adding 2 tablespoons sugar gradually. Fold chocolate mix and ¾ cup whipped cream into beaten egg whites. Add walnuts and whiskey. Fold till smooth. Pour into baked pie shell. Top with remaining whipped cream and sliced almonds.

Bourbon Pie

    ½ *package chocolate wafers*
    3 *tablespoons butter*
    1 *tablespoon honey*
        dash vanilla
    ½ *pint whipping cream*
    1 *small can evaporated milk*
  21 *marshmallows*
    4 *oz. raisins*
    3 *tablespoons bourbon*

Roll wafers into crumbs and mix with melted butter. Save ½ cup crumbs for top. Spread balance of crumbs evenly in pie pan and bake 5 minutes in 350-degree oven. Cool. Mix evaporated milk with marshmallows, honey, vanilla, and raisins in double boiler and heat over hot, but not boiling water, till smooth, stirring till mixed. Cool. Whip cream and add bourbon. Fold into cooled marshmallow-raisin mixture and pour into pie shell. Sprinkle with reserved crumbs on top. Chill thoroughly.

Bourbon Graham Cracker Pie

    1 *9½-inch graham cracker pie shell, cooled*
    4 *egg yolks*
 1¼ *cups granulated sugar*
    1 *envelope unflavored gelatine*
    2 *tablespoons warm water*
  ⅓ *cup bourbon*
    1 *pint heavy cream*
    2 *oz. chopped pecans*

In mixing bowl, beat egg yolks with sugar (will be very stiff). Add gelatine, melted in the warm water and bourbon. Beat in well. Fold in half the cream, whipped. Put in refrigerator overnight. When ready to serve, spoon mixture into pie shell, whip rest of cream, and spread over pie. Sprinkle chopped nuts on top.

Bourbon Cream Pie

- ¾ cup honey
- ¼ cup cornstarch
- ½ teaspoon salt
- ¼ cup bourbon
- 2¼ cups milk
- dash cinnamon
- 3 egg yolks, slightly beaten
- 1 tablespoon butter
- 1 teaspoon almond extract
- 1 9-inch baked pie shell, cooled
- 1 1-oz. square semisweet chocolate, kept at room temperature
- 1 cup heavy cream, whipped

Combine honey, cornstarch, and salt in saucepan. Gradually stir in bourbon, milk, and cinnamon, mixing till smooth. Bring to boil over medium heat, stirring. Boil 1 minute, stirring constantly. Remove from heat.

Stir half of hot mixture into egg yolks, mixing well, and pour back into saucepan. Bring back to boil, stirring constantly. Boil 1 minute and remove from heat. Stir in butter and almond extract and pour at once into pie shell. Chill. Shave chocolate curls off semisweet chocolate square, using vegetable parer. Cover top of chilled pie with whipped cream and sprinkle chocolate curls atop. Chill before serving.

Eggnog Pie No. 1

- 3 beaten egg yolks
- ½ cup sugar

2 cups light cream
dash salt
dash mace
dash cinnamon
1 teaspoon bourbon
3 egg whites, beaten stiff
1 recipe piecrust

Beat egg yolks, sugar, and cream. Add salt, mace, cinnamon, and bourbon. Fold in beaten egg whites. Pour into 9-inch pastry-lined pie pan. Bake in 400-degree oven for half-hour. Chill in refrigerator and serve.

Eggnog Pie No. 2

¾ cup sugar
3 tablespoons flour
4 beaten egg yolks
1 teaspoon almond extract
¼ teaspoon mace
1½ cups milk
2 oz. bourbon

Mix above ingredients and simmer in double boiler, stirring constantly till thick. Cool. Pour mixture in graham cracker-lined pan and let stand overnight. Top with whipped cream and sprinkle with chopped almonds.

Eggnog Walnut Pie

1 envelope unflavored gelatine
¼ cup milk
3 eggs, separated
½ cup granulated sugar
¼ teaspoon mace
⅛ teaspoon salt
dash vanilla

3 *oz. bourbon*
½ *cup whipping cream, whipped*
1 *9-inch Walnut Crumb Crust (see below)*

Soften gelatine in milk. In top of double boiler beat egg yolks together with mace, salt, and half of the sugar. Cook and stir over hot water till mixture thickens and coats a spoon. Add softened gelatine and stir till gelatine is dissolved. Cool. Add vanilla and bourbon. Beat egg whites till stiff and gradually beat in remaining sugar. Fold into gelatine mixture. Fold in whipped cream. Pour into chilled shell and chill till firm. Serve garnished with a wreath of whipped cream decorated with walnut halves. Makes one 9-inch pie.

Walnut Crumb Crust
1 *cup fine graham cracker crumbs*
½ *cup finely chopped walnuts*
¼ *cup granulated sugar*
¼ *cup soft butter*

Mix all ingredients. Press into 9-inch pie pan. Chill and bake at 375 degrees for about 7 minutes.

Chiffon Pie

1 *3¼ -oz. package vanilla pudding mix (not instant)*
1 *envelope unflavored gelatine*
2 *cups dairy eggnog*
¼ *teaspoon nutmeg*
2 *tablespoons bourbon*
2 *cups whipping cream*
1 *cup diced glacé fruits*
1 *9-inch baked pie shell*
2 *oz. raisins*
glacé cherries for garnish

Combine pudding mix and gelatine in saucepan. Gradually blend in eggnog and nutmeg. Cook over medium heat, stirring constantly till mixture comes to full boil. Remove from heat and stir in bourbon. Pour into bowl and cover with plastic film. Chill till almost set. Whip 1½ cups of the cream; fold into eggnog mixture with raisins and glacé fruits. Spoon into pie shell. Chill till firm. When ready to serve, whip remaining ½ cup cream and place atop pie. Garnish with cherries.

Walnut Cream Pie

>   1 *envelope gelatine, unflavored*
>   ½ *cup hot water*
>   3 *eggs, separated*
>   ½ *cup honey*
>   ¼ *teaspoon mace*
>   1 *cup milk*
>   ⅛ *teaspoon salt*
>   ⅓ *cup bourbon*
>   ½ *cup cream, whipped*
>   *Walnut Pie Shell (see below)*

Beat egg yolks and ¼ cup honey till lemon-colored. Dissolve gelatine in hot water and add to egg mixture, stirring constantly. Add milk, salt, mace, and bourbon, beating constantly till well blended. Beat egg whites, gradually adding remainder of honey till thick. Fold egg whites and gelatine mixture together and pour into prepared pie shell. Chill till set. Garnish with whipped cream and walnut halves.

>   **Walnut Pie Shell**
>   1 *cup biscuit crumbs*
>   ½ *cup finely chopped walnuts*
>   ¼ *cup sugar*
>   ¼ *cup butter*

Mix ingredients, line pie tin, and chill.

Bourbon Nut Pie

>   2 *eggs, well beaten*
>   1 *large can evaporated milk*

1 cup sugar
1 tablespoon flour
8 oz. pitted dates, chopped
2 oz. raisins
1 cup chopped walnuts
1 teaspoon vanilla
6 oz. bourbon

Make custard of first 4 ingredients and cook till thick. Add dates and raisins to custard, set aside, and cool. Add nuts, vanilla, and bourbon. Pour filling into baked pie shell and top with whipped cream.

Coffee Pie

1 envelope unflavored gelatine
2/3 cup sugar
1½ teaspoons instant coffee powder
¼ teaspoon salt
3 eggs, separated
1 cup homogenized milk
¼ cup bourbon
1 teaspoon lemon extract
1½ cups heavy cream
1 baked 9-inch pie shell with fluted rim
candied lemon peel

Combine gelatine, ⅓ cup sugar, coffee powder, and salt in top of double boiler and mix well. Beat egg yolks with homogenized milk. Add to gelatine mixture; set over boiling water. Cook 10 minutes, stirring, till mixture thickens slightly and coats spoon. Remove from heat and stir in bourbon and lemon extract. Cool till mixture begins to jell. Beat egg whites till stiff. Gradually beat in remaining ⅓ cup sugar to make a stiff meringue. With same beater, beat 1 cup cream till it peaks. Fold meringue and cream into gelatine mixture and turn into baked pie shell. Chill several hours before cutting. When ready to serve, whip remaining ½ cup cream and dollop on top of pie. Sprinkle top with candied lemon peel. Makes 1 9-inch pie.

Bourbon Mincemeat Pie

    1 *quart prepared mincemeat*
    1 *teaspoon grated orange rind*
  ½ *oz. lemon juice*
    4 *cooking apples*
  ¼ *teaspoon salt*
    1 *cup bourbon*
    2 *unbaked pie shells*

Peel, quarter, and grate apples; add prepared mincemeat, orange rind, lemon juice, salt, and bourbon. Pour into two unbaked pie shells; cover with top shells or lattice crust if preferred. Bake at 425 degrees for 45 minutes, or till crust is brown. Serve hot or cold.

Frozen Mincemeat Pie

    1 *18-oz. jar mincemeat*
    1 *pint vanilla ice cream*
      dash vanilla
      dash nutmeg
    2 *oz. bourbon*
 1¼ *cups graham cracker crumbs*
  ½ *cup melted butter*
    2 *tablespoons sugar*
      whipped cream

Blend graham cracker crumbs with butter and sugar. Line 9-inch pie pan with mixture. Bake at 300 degrees for 15 minutes. Set aside and cool. Mix mincemeat with softened ice cream, vanilla, nutmeg, and bourbon. Turn into shell and freeze. Serve with dollop of whipped cream atop. Serves 6-8.

Pumpkin-Bourbon Pie

    1 *cup canned pumpkin*
    1 *cup honey*

1½ cups evaporated milk
2 oz. bourbon
3 egg yolks, beaten slightly
1 teaspoon cinnamon
1 teaspoon mace
  dash vanilla
1 9-inch unbaked pie shell

Mix pumpkin meat and other ingredients well; pour into 9-inch unbaked pie shell and sprinkle a few pecans atop. Bake for 15 minutes at 450 degrees.

Sweet Potato Pie

1 cup sweet potatoes, cooked and mashed
2 eggs
¾ cup sugar
¼ teaspoon nutmeg
  dash vanilla
1 cup evaporated milk
1 tablespoon butter
¼ cup bourbon

Mash potatoes till soft and creamy. Add eggs, sugar, nutmeg, vanilla, milk, and melted butter. Add bourbon and mix well. Pour into 10-inch pastry-lined pie pan. Bake at 375 degrees for 50 minutes. Serve warm with whipped cream atop.

Flaming Pecan-Pumpkin Pie

1 9-inch unbaked pie shell

Filling
1 1-lb. can pumpkin
3 tablespoons bourbon
2 eggs, slightly beaten

    ¾ cup brown sugar
1½ cups light cream
    ½ teaspoon nutmeg
    ½ teaspoon mace
    1 teaspoon lemon juice
    ½ teaspoon salt

Topping

    2 tablespoons butter
    ¼ cup brown sugar
    ¼ cup bourbon
    1 cup pecan halves

Prepare 9-inch shell with piecrust mix or favorite recipe. Chill.

Combine pumpkin with bourbon. Add eggs, brown sugar, cream, spices, lemon juice, and salt. Pour into pie shell. Bake in preheated 425-degree oven for 10 minutes. Reduce heat to 350 degrees and bake 50 minutes longer, or till knife inserted in center comes out clean. Remove from oven and cool.

For topping: Combine butter and brown sugar in saucepan; heat, stirring till sugar is dissolved. Stir in 2 tablespoons bourbon. Add pecans and stir to glaze. Spoon nuts around edge of pie. At serving time, warm remaining bourbon, ignite, and pour flaming onto pecan border. Serve when flames subside. Serves 8-10.

Chocolate Icebox Pie

    6 lady finger
    8 macaroons
    2 oz. bourbon
    3 packages semisweet chocolate bits
    6 tablespoons confectioner's sugar
    4 tablespoons water
    8 egg yolks
    2 teaspoons vanilla
      dash mace
      dash cinnamon
    8 beaten egg whites
1½ cups whipping cream

Line a spring mold with lady fingers. Line bottom with macaroons soaked in bourbon.

Take chocolate bits, sugar, and water and melt in double boiler. Let cool. Add egg yolks, vanilla, mace, cinnamon, egg whites, and 1 cup cream. Pour into spring mold and chill overnight in refrigerator. Cover top of mold with ½ cup cream, whipped, and shave bitter chocolate over top.

Tipsy Apple Pie

pastry for 1 9-inch crust
6 *large winesap apples, sliced*
1 *oz. bourbon*
1 *cup honey*
2 *tablespoons cornstarch*
½ *teaspoon nutmeg*
½ *cup sliced dates*
2 *tablespoons butter*

Peel, core, and slice apples; place in bowl and sprinkle with bourbon. Combine honey, cornstarch, and nutmeg and add to apples along with sliced dates, mixing gently till apple slices are coated. Grease sides and bottom of 1½-quart casserole with butter. Place apple mix in casserole about 2 inches deep. Roll pastry to fit top of casserole, allowing extra inch on all sides. Place pastry over apple mix, tuck overhand down around edge of apples, and crimp molded edge. Do not cut steam vents in crust if pie is to be frozen, but wrap and freeze at once. Do not thaw before time to bake. At baking time, cut slits in top crust and bake at 400 degrees for 20 minutes; then lower heat to 350 degrees and bake about 50 minutes. Serves 6.

Cranberry-Apple Pie

1 *package (2-crust size) piecrust mix*
1 *oz. bourbon*
1 *tablespoon lemon juice*

>   water
> 2 cups cranberries
> 4 large green apples, cored, peeled, and sliced
> 1½ cups sugar
> ¼ teaspoon mace
> 1 tablespoon flour
> 2 tablespoons butter
> ¼ cup bourbon

Make pie dough as directed on package, using 1 oz. bourbon for part of required liquid and lemon juice and water for rest. Divide dough in half, roll out one-half, and line a 9-inch pie plate. Fill with half the fruit. Mix sugar, mace, and flour, and sprinkle half on fruit. Add remaining fruit and remaining sugar, mace, and flour. Dot with butter.

Roll out second half of crust mixture and cut into ½-inch strips with pastry cutter. Twist strips and crisscross pie to make lattice crust. Bake in 450-degree oven for 10 minutes. Reduce heat to 350 degrees and bake 30 minutes longer or till crust is browned and apples are tender. Spoon the ¼ cup bourbon through openings in crust, shaking pie gently to distribute it. Sprinkle pie with nutmeg. Serve warm.

Mince-Apple Deep Dish Pie

> 3 lb. tart cooking apples
> ½ cup sugar
> ½ teaspoon ground cinnamon
> ¼ teaspoon ground mace
> 2 teaspoons lemon juice
> ½ cup mincemeat
> ½ cup bourbon
> ⅓ cup corn syrup
> 1 cup chopped pecans
> ¼ cup butter, softened
> ½ cup light brown sugar
> ¾ cup sifted flour
> 1 cup heavy cream, whipped

Preheat oven to 375 degrees. Peel and core apples and slice 8 cups. Combine sugar with cinnamon and mace. Mix apples with sugar-spice mixture and lemon juice in large bowl. Set aside. Stir mincemeat, bourbon, and corn syrup together. Add one-half cup of the nuts. Set aside. To make topping, cream the butter with brown sugar; add flour and remaining one-half cup of nuts. Mix well till mixture is crumbly.

Butter a 1½-quart shallow casserole. Arrange layer of apples in bottom; add layer of mincemeat mixture. Repeat layers till dish is full, ending with apples. Sprinkle sugar-nut mixture over top. Bake about 50 minutes till apples are tender when tested with toothpick and syrup begins to bubble. Serve with whipped cream.

Fruit-Bourbon Kuchen

1 *10-oz. package piecrust mix*
1 *lb. purple plums, halved and pitted*
1 *tablespoon sugar*
1 *cup lemon marmalade*
2 *tablespoons bourbon*

Prepare piecrust mix according to directions. Roll into 10-inch circle. Fit into 9-inch flan ring which has been set on a baking sheet. Cut plums in half and cut each half into thirds. Sprinkle with sugar. Arrange wedges evenly over pastry. Heat marmalade till softened and spoon over fruit. Bake 30 minutes at 425 degrees. Let stand 15 minutes. Warm bourbon, set aflame, and pour over the pie. Serves 6.

Puddings

Black Gold Bourbon

Bottom Layer in Mold
- 1 *package lime jello*
- 1 *tablespoon lime juice*
- ¾ *cup white wine*
- 2 *oz. bourbon*
- 1 *cup water*

Bring water and lime juice to a simmer. Dissolve jello. Chill 20 minutes in refrigerator. Mix wine, bourbon, and jello and pour into 3-quart mold. Put back in refrigerator to jell.

Top Layer in Mold

¾ cup sugar
1 envelope plus 1 teaspoon unflavored gelatine
3 eggs, separated
7 oz. bourbon
1 cup chopped pecans
1 cup whipping cream
2 oz. unsweetened chocolate
1 tablespoon butter

Combine 6 tablespoons sugar and gelatine. Mix well. Beat egg yolks till lemon yellow. Gradually add bourbon (too quickly will cook the yolks). Add yolk and bourbon mixture to gelatine. Cook over hot but not boiling water for several minutes. Add chocolate and butter which have been melted over hot water and continue cooking till mixture coats a metal spoon (about 10 minutes). Set aside. Beat egg whites till foamy. Gradually add remaining 6 tablespoons of sugar and beat till stiff and glossy. Fold whites into first mixture. Chill 20 minutes in refrigerator. Whip heavy cream. Fold in cream and chopped nuts. Chill 4 hours. Unmold and decorate with 1 cup whipped cream flavored with bourbon and powdered sugar.

Plum Pudding

½ lb. currants
3 oz. bourbon
hot water
½ lb. dark raisins
¼ lb. glazed orange rind, chopped fine
¼ lb. glazed lemon rind, chopped fine
¼ lb. citron peel, chopped fine
½ lb. pecans, ground fine
1 cup flour
1 teaspoon baking soda
1 teaspoon salt
1 teaspoon cinnamon
¼ teaspoon nutmeg

½ lb. *ground suet*
3 *thinly sliced bread slices*
   apple juice
1 *cup brown sugar*
3 *eggs, beaten lightly*
⅓ *cup black currant jam preserves*

Place currants in bowl. Sprinkle with 1 oz. of the bourbon and add enough water to cover fruit. Set aside while chopping peel. Place raisins, orange and lemon rinds, and citron peel in large bowl. Sift together flour, baking soda, salt, cinnamon, and nutmeg and add to the bowl. Stir in soaked currants and suet. Tear bread slices into small pieces, place in small bowl, and dampen with apple juice. Add to fruit mixture.

Stir in remaining ingredients and beat well. Turn into well-oiled, 2-quart pudding mold that has a cover. Secure cover with string and cover that with aluminum foil. Set on rack with boiling water coming halfway up mold, or steam in top of a steamer for 6 hours. Uncover and pour remaining bourbon over mixture. Place fresh piece of wax paper next to pudding and cover with lid or foil. Store in a cool place about 3 weeks to ripen. Steam 3 more hours before serving. If desired, warm 4 oz. bourbon with teaspoon sugar, ignite, and pour over pudding before serving. Serves 12-15. Good with a hard sauce.

Hard Sauce
½ lb. *whipped sweet butter, softened*
⅓ *teaspoon salt*
⅛ *teaspoon nutmeg*
2 *cups sifted confectioner's sugar*
1 *egg yolk*
¼ *cup heavy cream*
2 *oz. bourbon*

Place half ingredients in electric blender and blend at medium speed till smooth. Add remaining ingredients and continue blending till smooth and creamy. Refrigerate, but remove at least 1 hour before serving.

Old-Fashioned Steamed Pudding

- 2 quarts fine bread crumbs
- 2 cups bourbon
- 8 eggs, beaten
- 2 cups orange juice
- 2 oz. lemon juice
- 1 cup molasses
- 1 cup melted butter
- 2 teaspoons baking soda
- 2 cups currants
- 1 lb. diced candied pineapple
- ½ cup all-purpose flour
- 4 teaspoons cinnamon
- ½ teaspoon mace
- ½ teaspoon cloves

Combine crumbs and 1 cup bourbon. Mix well and let stand 15 minutes. Add eggs, orange and lemon juice, molasses, butter, and baking soda and beat well. Combine currants and pineapple. Add spices to flour and sprinkle over combined fruits. Add fruits to molasses mixture and mix well. Turn into 4 greased 1-quart molds. Cover tightly. Steam 90 minutes or till pudding tests done. Turn the puddings onto a large, flameproof serving platter. Garnish with sprays of holly. Heat and pour ¼ cup bourbon over each pudding and ignite. Serve each portion with dab of hard sauce.

Bourbon Hard Sauce

Cream 12 oz. butter till smooth. Add 5 cups sifted confectioner's sugar gradually; then add 3 oz. bourbon. Beat till fluffy and chill.

Bread Pudding with Fruit

- 2 tablespoons soft butter
- 12 oz. day-old French bread
- 1 quart milk

4 eggs
2 cups sugar
4 oz. raisins
½ teaspoon mace
1 17-oz. can fruit cocktail
1 tablespoon vanilla extract

Preheat oven to 350 degrees. Grease 13 x 9 x 2-inch baking dish with butter and set aside. Break bread into 1-inch pieces, pour milk over it, and soak till milk is absorbed. Beat eggs and sugar together till mixture is smooth and thick. Add raisins, mace, drained fruit cocktail, and vanilla. Pour mixture over bread and toss to blend. Turn into buttered baking dish. Place dish in large, shallow roasting pan, set on middle shelf of oven, and pour boiling water into pan to depth of 1 inch. Bake 1 hour or till knife inserted in center comes out clean.

Whiskey Sauce
1 stick butter
1 cup sugar
1 egg
4 oz. bourbon

Melt butter into top of double boiler over hot but not boiling water. Stir sugar and egg together and add mix to butter. Stir till sugar dissolves. Do not let sauce come to boil or egg will curdle. Cool to room temperature before adding bourbon. Serve pudding warm with the sauce. Serves 8-10.

Bourbon Pudding

2 boxes pitted dates
½ cup raisins
1¾ cups sugar
2 cups chopped walnuts
1 cup bourbon
6 eggs, separated

6 tablespoons flour
2 teaspoons baking powder
¼ teaspoon salt

Cut and mash dates into bourbon and add raisins. Allow to set till dates and raisins have absorbed most of the whiskey (about 2 hours). Add the sugar, nuts, and egg yolks; then add the flour sifted with baking powder and salt. Mix well; then add egg whites, beaten till stiff. Pour into buttered ring mold and bake at 350 degrees for 1 hour. Unmold and serve with whipped cream.

Kentucky Bourbon Pudding

¾ cup milk
1 egg yolk
¼ cup sugar
1 tablespoon flour
pinch of salt
½ teaspoon almond extract
1 teaspoon lemon juice
1 oz. bourbon
¼ cup raisins
¼ cup candied cherries
½ cup chopped pecans
¼ cup well-drained, crushed pineapple
2 cups whipping cream

Heat milk in double boiler top. Blend sugar, flour, and salt together. Beat egg yolk slightly and blend sugar mixture into egg. Add spoon or two of hot milk and blend thoroughly. Working slowly, blend egg mixture into hot milk and cook mixture over boiling water till thick, stirring constantly. Remove from heat and cool.

Add almond extract, lemon juice, and bourbon to custard and chill 1 hour. Place 2-quart mixing bowl and beater blades from mixer in refrigerator and chill. Mix raisins, cherries, nuts, and pineapple together and chill. Whip cream in the chilled 2-quart bowl till stiff and slowly stir in custard. Divide mixture in half and pour into two ice cube trays. Freeze till mixture is a frozen mush. Remove one tray at a time, add half fruit mixture to each tray, and blend thoroughly. Return to refrigerator freezing section and freeze at least 3 hours.

After pudding is frozen, allow trays to remain in freezer section till time to serve. Makes about 1 quart.

Eggnog, Russian Style

   2 *cups milk*
   4 *eggs, separated*
  ¾ *cup sugar*
   2 *envelopes unflavored gelatine*
  ¼ *cup bourbon*
  ½ *teaspoon salt*
  ½ *teaspoon mace*
    dash vanilla extract
   1 *3-oz. package lady fingers, split*
1½ *cups heavy whipping cream*
    semisweet chocolate, grated for garnish

Beat 1 cup milk and egg yolks with a fork in a double boiler till mixed. Sprinkle in ½ cup sugar and gelatine. Cook over hot, but not boiling water, stirring constantly till mixture thickens and coats spoon (about 30 minutes). Stir in remaining cup of milk, bourbon, salt, mace, and vanilla; cover surface with waxed paper. Meanwhile, line sides of 8-inch spring-form pan with lady fingers, split.

In small bowl with mixer at high speed, beat egg whites till soft peaks form. Do not scrape sides of bowl. Gradually sprinkle in ¼ cup sugar, 1 tablespoon at a time, beating at high speed till sugar dissolves and mixture stands in stiff, glossy peaks. Gently fold in gelatine mixture.

Wash bowl and beaters; then at medium speed beat 1 cup heavy cream till soft peaks form. Fold gently into gelatine mixture. Spoon mixture into lined pan and refrigerate at least 4 hours till set. Carefully remove sides of spring-form pan. In small mixer bowl at medium speed beat remaining ½ cup heavy cream and use to garnish top. Sprinkle top with grated chocolate. Serves 12.

Tipsy Pudding

    1 *quart your favorite recipe for boiled custard*
1½ *cups cream, whipped*
    2 *layers sponge cake*
       bourbon, about 2 oz.
       grape jelly
    1 *cup chopped walnuts*

Make custard day before dessert is to be eaten, since it must set about 8 hours. Sprinkle layers of sponge cake with bourbon. In large bowl, place 1 layer of cake and cover with layer of custard. Dot custard with jelly and sprinkle nuts over it. Repeat these layers and top with whipped cream, sweetened and flavored with a little bourbon. Sprinkle with chopped nuts and chill thoroughly for 8 hours in refrigerator.

Charlotte Russe

    1 *package plain gelatine, dissolved in 2 oz. cold water*
    6 *egg yolks*
    8 *oz. scalded milk*
      dash vanilla
    2 *cups raisins and chopped prunes, mixed and soaked in 2 oz. bourbon*
    2 *oz. chopped pecans*
  ½ *lb. powdered sugar*
    1 *quart whipping cream*

Beat egg yolks with sugar. Stir milk into softened gelatine; then boil till gelatine dissolves. Add egg mixture to gelatine mix and flavor with a little vanilla. Cool. Whip cream and add to cooled custard along with fruit-nut mixture. Spoon into bowl and garnish top with nuts and cherries. Chill and serve.

Baked Carrot Pudding

  ½ *cup shortening*
  ½ *cup dark brown sugar*

Puddings

  2 *eggs, slightly beaten*
  1 *cup grated raw carrots*
  2 *tablespoons candied lemon peel*
½ *cup seedless raisins*
  1 *cup currants*
¼ *cup bourbon*
1¼ *cups flour*
  1 *teaspoon baking powder*
½ *teaspoon mace*
    dash lemon extract
½ *teaspoon cinnamon*
½ *teaspoon baking soda*

Set oven at 350 degrees and butter a 1-quart pudding mold. Sift together dry ingredients. Cream together shortening and brown sugar; add beaten eggs, carrots, fruit, bourbon, and lemon extract. Stir in sifted dry ingredients and put in mold. Bake about 35 minutes. Cool 15 minutes and serve with Bourbon Sauce.

Bourbon Sauce
4 *eggs, separated*
1 *cup powdered sugar*
¼ *cup bourbon*

Beat egg yolks till thick and add ½ cup sugar slowly. Beat egg whites. Add ½ cup sugar to whites. Combine. Add bourbon slowly. Serve on pudding.

Booze Pudding

2½ *cups milk*
  3 *medium-sized yams*
  3 *eggs*
  2 *cups sugar*
  2 *teaspoons cinnamon*
½ *cup chopped pecans*
  2 *oz. raisins*
  2 *tablespoons butter*
½ *cup bourbon*

Put milk in 2-quart casserole. Grate yams, adding to milk as grated to prevent them from turning dark. Beat eggs and add sugar gradually. Add cinnamon, nuts, and raisins, and mix with yams. Dot generously with butter and bake in 300-degree oven for 2 hours. Just before serving, pour bourbon over the pudding.

Cups of Gold, Flambé

>   6 *navel oranges*
>   1 *lb. cooked yams*
>   4 *tablespoons butter, melted*
>   *dash mace*
>   1 *oz. grated orange rind*
>   ¼ *teaspoon salt*
>   3 *oz. bourbon*

Halve oranges, scoop out meat, squeeze, and reserve juice. Mash yams. Add melted butter, orange juice, mace, orange rind, salt, and 1 ounce bourbon. Mound mixture into orange cups.

Place orange cups in shallow baking pan. Heat at 350 degrees about 20 minutes, or till heated through. Place cups in flameproof tray, pour remaining bourbon over, and ignite. Serve flaming. Serves 6.

Sweet Potato Pudding

>   4 *medium sweet potatoes*
>   ½ *cup light brown sugar*
>   ½ *teaspoon mace*
>   ½ *teaspoon cinnamon*
>   ½ *cup raisins soaked in port*
>   1 *stick (¼ lb.) melted butter*
>   2 *oz. bourbon*

Mash potatoes with above ingredients. Place in greased casserole; sprinkle with a little sugar-and-spice mixture. Bake in 400-degree oven about 15 minutes or till golden-brown crust forms. Serves 6.

Bourbon Custard

    4 egg yolks
¼ cup sugar
    pinch of salt
    dash nutmeg
    dash mace
1¾ cups scalded milk
½ teaspoon almond extract
¼ cup bourbon
    1 cup heavy cream
½ cup raspberry jam

Beat egg yolks, sugar, nutmeg, mace, and salt together. Stir in milk and cook over low heat, stirring constantly till mixture begins to thicken and coats the spoon. Stir in almond extract and bourbon and chill. While custard is cooling, beat heavy cream with little sugar added till soft peaks form. Spoon over top of the custard, placed in a bowl. Dot the top with teaspoonsful of raspberry jam.

Walnut Pudding

    1 large egg
½ cup light brown sugar
    2 oz. bourbon
    1 cup unsifted flour
    1 teaspoon baking soda
    1 teaspoon salt
½ teaspoon mace
½ cup granulated sugar
1½ cups thoroughly drained canned fruit cocktail
½ cup chopped walnuts

In medium mixing bowl, beat egg. Add brown sugar and beat till mixture is thick and there are no sugar lumps. Add bourbon and beat slightly to blend. Add flour, baking soda, salt, and mace, beating gently till smooth. Add granulated sugar, fruit cocktail, and nuts. Mix with spoon till fruit and nuts are well distributed. Then turn into buttered square baking dish 8 x 8 x 2 inches and spread evenly.

Bake in preheated 325-degree oven till a cake tester inserted in center comes out clean, top is browned, and pudding shrinks from sides of dish (about 45 minutes).

Serve warm. At serving time, cut in squares in baking dish and serve in separate dessert dishes topped with whipped cream.

Chocolate Bavaroise

    1 *envelope plain gelatine*
    ¼ *cup hot water*
    4 *oz. dark chocolate*
    1 *tablespoon confectioner's sugar*
       dash nutmeg
       dash vanilla extract
    4 *eggs*
    1 *tablespoon bourbon*
    ½ *pint heavy cream*

Separate egg yolks from whites. Chip chocolate and put into double saucepan with ¼ pint cream, reserving a little chocolate. Stir over hot water till melted. Remove from heat. Beat in sugar, nutmeg, and vanilla, and blend in egg yolks one at a time. Beat till mixture is smooth. Dissolve gelatine in hot water and add to mixture. Whip egg whites till stiff and fold into mixture with the bourbon. Turn into parfait glasses till set and decorate with remaining cream, whipped, and shaving of remaining chocolate.

Derby Delight

    4 *eggs separated*
    ½ *cup dark brown sugar*
    1½ *tablespoons cornstarch*
    1½ *cups milk*
    5 *oz. bourbon*
    2 *squares bitter chocolate*

½ teaspoon almond extract
1 envelope gelatine
   dash of mace
½ cup granulated sugar
¼ teaspoon cream of tartar
½ cup heavy cream, whipped

In top of double boiler, combine egg yolks, brown sugar, and cornstarch. Beat till light and fluffy; then gradually stir in 1½ cups milk and 3 oz. of bourbon. Place over hot water and cool, stirring constantly till custard is thick and smooth. Remove from fire.

Take 1 cup of custard and stir in 1½ squares chocolate, melted, almond extract, and mace. Cool this custard and pour into pie shell. To rest of custard add 1 envelope gelatine dissolved in 2 ounces bourbon and cool slightly.

Beat 4 egg whites with cream of tartar till stiff; then beat in ½ cup granulated sugar. Combine with custard and pour into pie shell over chocolate layer. Chill several hours. Pipe border of whipped cream around edge of custard and sprinkle with remaining chocolate, grated.

Jellies and Jam

Cherry Jelly

    2 *1-lb. cans water-packed sour red cherries*
    1 *1¾-oz. package powdered pectin*
  2½ *cups sugar*
  ½ *cup bourbon*

Drain cherries; reserve fruit and 1½ cups juice. Combine juice with pectin; bring to boil. Add sugar; bring again to a rolling boil, and boil rapidly for 1 minute, stirring constantly. Add bourbon and cherries. Makes 3½ cups.

Berry Bourbon Jelly

  5 *cups sugar*
  2 *cups water*
  1 *6-oz. bottle liquid fruit pectin*
  1 *6-oz. can concentrate for fruit-berry punch*
  1 *cup bourbon*

Bring sugar and water to a full rolling boil; boil 1 minute. Stir in fruit pectin. Add concentrate for fruit-berry punch and bourbon. Mix well. Skim quickly. Pour into sterilized jars. Seal with ⅛-inch paraffin. Fills about 7 glasses, 8 ounces each.

Syllabub

  2 *teaspoons gelatine*
  2 *tablespoons hot water*
 ¼ *pint sherry*
  3 *tablespoons bourbon*
  2 *oz. sugar*
   juice of 1 lemon
 ½ *pint cream*
   wafer biscuits

Dissolve gelatine in hot water. Add sugar. Put wine, bourbon, and lemon juice into a large bowl with the gelatine-and-sugar solution. Add cream. Whip together until thick. Pour into small individual sweet glasses and chill. Serve with wafer biscuits.

Fruited Duo

  4 *teaspoons gelatine*
 ¼ *cup hot water*
  1 *15-oz. can apricots*
  1 *15-oz. can pineapple pieces*
   juice of 1 lemon

3 tablespoons bourbon
2 egg whites
cherries and angelica for decoration

Drain liquid from fruit and add lemon juice. Chop fruit into small pieces; over this pour the bourbon.

Dissolve gelatine in hot water and add to juices.

Allow to thicken slightly and fold in the chopped fruit and bourbon.

Beat egg whites until thick and fold through the fruit mixture.

Pile into small individual sweet glasses and decorate with cherries and angelica. Chill.

Bourbon Apple Jelly

1 cup apple juice
1 cup bourbon
3 cups sugar
½ bottle liquid pectin (3 oz.)

Combine apple juice, bourbon, and sugar in suacepan. Bring to boil, stirring constantly. Stir in pectin and continue stirring briskly till boiling; let boil 1 minute, still stirring. Remove from heat, skim off foam, and pour into 4 8-oz. jelly glasses. Cover while still hot with a thin layer of paraffin melted over hot water. After jelly cools, add another layer paraffin.

Peach Butter

1½ lb. ripe peaches
1 cup orange juice
2 cups white sugar
1 teaspoon cinnamon
½ teaspoon mace
4½ tablespoons bourbon

Pour boiling water over peaches to loosen skins and plunge peaches into cold water. Remove skins and pits and mash pulp into 1-quart measuring cup. Add orange juice. Put mixture in saucepan and simmer, covered, till pulp is tender. Add sugar, cinnamon, and mace and simmer, stirring constantly. Take 3 8-oz. hot sterilizing jars. Place 1½ tablespoons bourbon in bottom of each jar. Pour boiling butter into jars and seal at once.

Jellied Old-Fashioneds

1 8½-oz. can pineapple tidbits
1 8¾-oz. can pear halves
1 8¾-oz. can sliced peaches
water
1 orange, peeled and cut into bite-size pieces
1 8-oz. jar red maraschino cherries
2 3-oz. packages red raspberry gelatine
2 teaspoons grated lemon peel
1 tablespoon lemon juice
⅔ cup bourbon
thin orange slices
stemmed red maraschino cherries

Drain syrup from pineapple, pears, and peaches; add enough water to make 3 cups liquid. Set aside. Cut pears into bite-size pieces. Divide canned fruits and orange pieces evenly among 10 old-fashioned glasses. Drain cherries, reserving ¼ cup syrup. Halve the cherries and add to each glass.

Heat the 3 cups of fruit syrup and water with the gelatine in medium saucepan; stir constantly just until gelatine dissolves. Remove from heat; stir in the ¼ cup reserved cherry syrup, the lemon peel and juice, and bourbon. Pour over fruit in glasses. Chill 4 or more hours.

Serve in glasses garnished with orange slices and stemmed cherries. (May also be served as salad, if desired.) Serves 10.

Grapefruit-Orange Marmalade

2 medium-sized oranges
1 small grapefruit
1 cup water
2 oz. lemon juice
⅛ teaspoon baking soda

½ cup bourbon
5 cups sugar (about 2¼ lb.)
1 cup bourbon
½ bottle liquid pectin (3 oz.)

Remove orange and grapefruit peel in quarters. Remove about half of white membrane from peels. Slice peels in very fine strips. Combine peels, lemon juice, water, and baking soda; heat to boiling point. Cook, covered, over low heat, 20 minutes, stirring often. Meanwhile, section peeled fruits; remove seeds. Add fruit pulp, fruit juice, and ½ cup bourbon to fruit peel mixture. Cover and cook over low heat 10 minutes.

Combine prepared fruit and peel, sugar, and 1 cup bourbon in large saucepan. Heat to full rolling boil over high heat. Boil vigorously 1 minute, stirring constantly. Remove from heat; stir in pectin at once. Skim off foam with metal spoon; stir and skim about 7 minutes to allow slight cooling and prevent floating fruit. Fill scalded glasses or jars to within ½ inch of top. Cover at once with ⅛ inch hot paraffin. Cool and cover tightly. Makes about 5½ cups.

Bourbon Mold

3 rounded teaspoons gelatine
¼ cup hot water
¾ cup sugar
3 eggs, separated
¼ cup bourbon
½ cup chopped walnuts
½ pint cream, whipped
strawberries for decorating

Separate egg yolks and whites. Combine sugar and egg yolks in double boiler. Stir over low heat until the mixture coats the back of the spoon. Remove from heat.

Dissolve gelatine in hot water and add to egg mixture with bourbon. Be sure to add the whiskey slowly and stir constantly to keep egg from congealing. When cool, fold in the whipped cream. Beat egg whites until thick and add to mixture. Chill until mixture thickens slightly and fold in the walnuts.

Pour into a mold. Unmold when firm. Decorate with strawberries.

Candy

Tipsy Bits

    2½ *cups NBC vanilla wafers, crumbled*
    ½ *cup rum*
    ¼ *teaspoon almond extract*
    3 *tablespoons bourbon*
    1 *cup chopped walnuts*
    1 *cup powdered sugar*
    2 *level teaspoons cocoa*
    3 *tablespoons Karo syrup*

Crumb vanilla wafers and mix with dry ingredients. Add rum, almond extract, and bourbon and drip in the Karo. Mix thoroughly and roll into bite-sized balls. Roll in powdered sugar and store.

Tipsy Balls

    2 *cups finely rolled vanilla wafer crumbs*
  ½ *cup coarsely chopped pecans*
    2 *tablespoons ground sweet cooking chocolate*
  ¼ *teaspoon vanilla*
  ½ *cup chopped candied fruit*
    1 *cup powdered sugar*
      sifted confectioner's sugar
  ⅓ *cup bourbon*
    3 *tablespoons light corn syrup*

Combine first 6 ingredients. Combine liquor and syrup. Add to mixture and mix thoroughly. Form in 1-inch balls and roll in confectioner's sugar. Makes 3 dozen.

Bourbon Sugar Balls

    1 *6-oz. package (1 cup) semisweet chocolate pieces*
    3 *tablespoons light corn syrup*
  ¼ *teaspoon almond extract*
  ½ *cup bourbon*
  2½ *cups crushed vanilla wafers*
  1½ *cups powdered sugar*
    1 *cup walnuts, chopped*

Melt chocolate over hot, not boiling water; add corn syrup, almond extract, and bourbon. Combine crushed vanilla wafers, powdered sugar, and nuts. Add to chocolate mixture and mix well. Let stand about 30 minutes. Form into 1-inch balls. Roll in powdered sugar. Let remain in covered container several days. Makes 4½ dozen.

Bourbon Fudge Balls

    2 *cups finely crushed vanilla wafers*
  ¼ *cup bourbon*

2 6-oz. packages (2 cups) semisweet chocolate
    morsels
⅔ cup sweetened condensed milk
    finely chopped pecans

Combine crumbs and bourbon; mix until crumbs are moistened. Melt chocolate over hot (not boiling) water. Add condensed milk and stir just to blend.

Gradually stir chocolate mixture into crumb mixture. Shape into 1-inch balls. Roll in chopped pecans. Let stand until cool. Makes about 5½ dozen.

Cocoa Bourbon Balls

1 cup finely crushed vanilla wafers
1 cup sifted confectioner's sugar
¼ teaspoon vanilla
1 cup chopped walnuts
2 tablespoons cocoa
2 tablespoons light corn syrup
¼ cup bourbon
    fine granulated sugar and chopped walnuts

Combine wafer crumbs, confectioner's sugar, vanilla, walnuts, and cocoa. Add corn syrup and bourbon; mix well. Shape into 1-inch balls. Roll some in granulated sugar, others in chopped walnuts. Store in air-tight container. Makes 3 dozen.

Concord Grape Bourbon Balls

24 oz. Concord grape jam
⅔ cup bourbon
2 cups finely chopped walnuts
2 13½-oz. packages graham cracker crumbs or 28
    oz. vanilla wafer crumbs
1 cup granulated sugar
    blue and red food coloring

Combine all ingredients except sugar and food coloring in a 3-quart bowl. Mix until mixture is very thick. Pinch off pieces and roll into 1-inch balls. Color sugar a deep lavender, using 2 drops blue and 1 drop red food coloring. Roll each ball in sugar; let stand at room temperature. When ready to serve, place balls on a platter in the shape of a giant bunch of Concord grapes. Garnish with a stem and grape leaves. Makes about 100 balls.

(American Concord Grape Association)

Coffee Bourbon Balls

- 2 *cups fine vanilla wafer crumbs*
- ¼ *teaspoon nutmeg*
- 1 *cup confectioner's sugar*
- 1 *cup chopped pecans*
- ¼ *cup instant coffee powder*
- 3 *tablespoons corn syrup*
- ⅓ *cup bourbon*
  dash of salt
  additional confectioner's sugar

Combine all ingredients except additional sugar. Mix thoroughly. Roll into balls, using a rounded teaspoon of mixture for each. Store in tightly covered container for several days. Before serving, roll in confectioner's sugar. Makes about 50 balls.

Bourbon Drops

- 1 *6-oz. bottle liquid pectin*
- 2 *tablespoons water*
- ½ *teaspoon baking soda*
- 1 *cup granulated sugar*
- 1 *cup light corn syrup*
- ⅓ *cup bourbon*
- 1 *teaspoon sweet sherry*
  food coloring
  granulated sugar, plain or tinted

Combine pectin and water in 2-quart saucepan; stir in baking soda. Mix 1 cup sugar and corn syrup in another saucepan. Cook both mixtures over very high heat, stirring alternately, until foam disappears from pectin mixture and sugar mixture boils rapidly (about 3-5 minutes). Pour pectin mixture in slow, steady stream into boiling sugar mixture, stirring constantly. Boil and stir 1 minute.

Remove from heat. Add bourbon and sherry and tint with food coloring as desired. Pour at once into 8-inch round or square pan. Cool at room temperature until firm, about 3 hours. Cut into desired shapes with sharp aspic knife or with 1-inch aspic cutters. Roll in granulated sugar. Makes about 1¼ pounds.

Satin Fudge

    3 *cups granulated sugar*
    ¼ *cup light corn syrup*
    3 *tablespoons butter*
    ½ *teaspoon salt*
    1 *cup evaporated milk*
    1 *oz. bourbon*
    ½ *cup water*
    2 *teaspoons vanilla*
    1 *cup bleached, slivered almonds*

Combine sugar, corn syrup, butter, salt, evaporated milk, bourbon, and water in medium-sized heavy saucepan. Heat, stirring constantly, to boiling; then cook rapidly, stirring several times, to 238 degrees on a candy thermometer (a teaspoonful of syrup should form a soft ball when dropped in cold water). Remove from heat; add vanilla but do not stir. Cool mixture in pan to 110 degrees; beat 3 minutes till it starts to thicken and loses gloss. Spread in buttered pan 8 x 8 x 2 inches. Let stand 3 minutes till set, and cut into squares. Decorate each piece with almond sliver. Let stand till firm.

Bourbon Pralines

　　1 *cup granulated sugar*
　　2 *cups light brown sugar*
　¼ *cup light corn syrup*
　⅛ *teaspoon salt*
1¼ *cups milk*
　　1 *teaspoon almond extract*
　　1 *tablespoon bourbon*
1½ *cups pecan halves*

　Combine sugars, corn syrup, salt, milk, and bourbon in saucepan. Bring to boil and cook without stirring until mixture registers 236 degrees on candy thermometer (half a teaspoon of mixture dropped into cold water should form a soft ball). Add almond extract and pecans and beat with spoon till mixture begins to thicken and loses gloss. Drop from tablespoon onto wax paper and spread to form patties about 4 inches in diameter. Let stand till firm. Makes 12 pralines.

Cake

Mrs. Dean Rusk's Fruit Cake*

- 5 *cups flour, sifted before measuring*
- 1 *lb. white sugar*
- 1 *cup brown sugar*
- 6 *eggs, beaten separately*
- ¾ *lb. butter or margarine*
- 1 *pt. bourbon*
- 1 *lb. shelled pecans*
- ½ *lb. white raisins*
- 2 *teaspoons nutmeg*
- 1 *teaspoon baking powder*
- 1 *lb. candied red cherries, cut in pieces*

---

*This recipe was supplied by Mrs. Dean Rusk, wife of the former secretary of state.

Soak cherries and raisins in bourbon in covered bowl overnight. Cream sugar and butter until fluffy. Add yolks of eggs and beat well. Add soaked fruit and remaining liquid. Reserve a small amount of flour for nuts and add remainder to mixture. Add nutmeg and baking powder. Fold in beaten egg whites. Add lightly floured pecans last.

The recipe will make 5 small cakes, using loaf pans or empty fruit cans, dusted with flour. Fill each a scant ¾ full and place in a large roasting pan containing a few inches of water in the bottom. Steam, covered, for 2½ hours at 300 degrees.

Fruit Cake

- 1 *lb. seedless raisins*
- 1 *lb. shelled pecans*
- ½ *cup candied orange peel, cut fine*
- 4 *oz. candied cherries, cut fine*
- 4 *oz. lime peel, cut fine*
- 4 *oz. candied pineapple, cut fine*
- 1 *teaspoon nutmeg*
- 2¼ *cups flour*
- 1 *cup sugar*
- ¾ *cup butter (1½ sticks)*
- ¼ *cup syrup (white Karo)*
- ½ *teaspoon baking powder*
- ½ *cup bourbon*
- 3 *eggs, separated*

Cream butter and add sugar slowly. Beat egg yolks and add to creamed butter and sugar. Add syrup.

Sift 2 cups flour, baking powder, and nutmeg together and add mixture alternately with whiskey. Fold in stiffly beaten egg whites.

Chop nuts, raisins, orange peel, etc. Dust with 4 tablespoons flour and stir into mixture. Do not beat.

Pour into tube pan lined with greased paper and bake 3 hours at 275 degrees.

A Traditional Combination: Fruit Cake and Eggnog, Both Made with Bourbon

Tipsy Cake

    1   *small sponge or angel food cake*
    4   *oz. bourbon, divided*
1½   *cups milk*
    3   *egg yolks*
    1   *egg*
    2   *tablespoons sugar*
         pinch of salt
 ½   *pint (1 cup) heavy cream, whipped*
    1   *cup finely chopped blanched almonds*

Cut cake in slices; then sprinkle 2 ounces bourbon over. Top with chilled custard sauce.

To make custard sauce, scald milk in top of double boiler. Beat egg yolks, egg, sugar, and salt in a small bowl until just blended. Gradually add a small amount of hot milk to mixture, stirring constantly. Add mixture to rest of milk in double boiler while stirring constantly. Cook gently over hot, not boiling, water until mixture coats a metal spoon. Remove from heat and cool. Stir in 1 ounce bourbon; then chill. Makes about 1¾ cups.

Top cake with whipped cream flavored with the remaining ounce of bourbon. Sprinkle with finely chopped almonds. Serves 6-8.

Tipsy Christmas Kisses

2½   *cups seedless raisins*
 ¼   *lb. diced candied citron*
   2   *oz. diced orange peel*
 ¼   *lb. (2 cups) candied cherries, cut in half*
   1   *lb. pecan halves*
 ½   *cup bourbon*
 ¾   *cup granulated brown sugar*
 ½   *teaspoon salt*
 ¼   *cup butter or margarine*
   2   *eggs*
1½   *cups sifted all-purpose flour*
1½   *teaspoons baking soda*

1½ teaspoons cinnamon
1½ teaspoons nutmeg
½ teaspoon ground cloves

Toss fruits and nuts in bourbon in large mixing bowl. Cover mixture and let stand 15 minutes.

Combine sugar, salt, and butter in small mixing bowl; beat until well mixed. Beat eggs into sugar mixture until light and smooth. Sift together flour, soda, and spices. Gradually blend into creamed ingredients. Add batter to fruit mixture and mix thoroughly.

Drop from teaspoon onto ungreased cooky sheets. Bake in moderate oven (325 degrees) until lightly browned, about 15 minutes. Remove to cooling rack. Store in air-tight containers. Makes about 10 dozen small cakes.

Fruit Nuggets

½ cup brown sugar
¼ cup butter or margarine
2 eggs, well beaten
1½ cups sifted all-purpose flour
1½ teaspoons soda
1 teaspoon cinnamon
¼ teaspoon each, nutmeg and cloves
½ cup bourbon
1½ lb. mixed chopped candied fruit
1 lb. pecan halves
1 lb. candied cherries, halved or quartered

Cream sugar and butter until light and fluffy. Add eggs.

Sift together dry ingredients; add to creamed mixture. Add bourbon. Mix in chopped fruits and nuts.

Line tiny muffin pans, 1½ inches in diameter and ¾ inch deep, with tiny fluted paper cups. Press mixture into cups. Top each with tiny piece of candied cherry or candied pineapple, or a tiny pecan or slivered almond.

Bake at 325 degrees for 25 minutes, or until browned. Store in plastic boxes in layers separated by plastic wrap. Moisten occasionally with bourbon, using sterilized medicine dropper or teaspoon. Makes about 70 tiny cupcakes.

Flag Cake

Cake
1 cup butter
1⅔ cups sugar
5 eggs, beaten
¼ cup bourbon
2 cups sifted all-purpose flour
½ teaspoon salt

Frosting
½ cup butter
2 cups confectioner's sugar
1 egg yolk
1½ tablespoons milk
¼ cup bourbon

Decorations
2 pints strawberries, hulled
1 pint blueberries

Cake: Cream butter; gradually beat in the sugar and beat until light and creamy. Beat in eggs and bourbon. Gently fold in flour and salt. Turn batter into a greased and floured 13 x 9 x 2-inch cake pan. Bake in 350-degree oven 1-1¼ hours, until the cake tests done. Cool on a rack.

Frosting: Cream butter; gradually beat in sugar and egg yolk. Beat well. Add milk and bourbon; combine well. Chill until mixture will hold shape.

Decorations: Spread the top and sides of the cake with ⅔ of the frosting mixture. In the upper lefthand corner, mark off a rectangle 4 inches long by 3 inches deep, for the field of stars. Use a flag as a guide to placing blueberries on the field, to have 50 white spaces for the stars. Align seven rows of strawberries for stripes, and pipe remaining icing in bands between berries. Chill the cake.

Saint Patrick's Day Cake

 2½ cups sifted cake flour
 4 teaspoons baking powder
 ½ teaspoon salt
 ¼ teaspoon nutmeg
 ¾ teaspoon cinnamon
 ¾ cup shortening
 2 cups sugar
 2 eggs, separated
 3 1-oz. squares unsweetened chocolate, melted
 1 cup mashed potatoes
 1 teaspoon vanilla
 ¾ cup milk

Sift together flour, baking powder, salt, and spices. Cream shortening until light; gradually add sugar and cream until light and fluffy. Add egg yolks and beat well. Mix in chocolate, potatoes, and vanilla; blend well. Add sifted ingredients and milk alternately to chocolate mixture, beating well after each addition. Beat egg whites until stiff; fold into batter. Turn batter into 3 greased and floured 8-inch layer cake pans. Bake in a preheated 350-degree oven 35-40 minutes, or until cake tests done. Cool 5 minutes; remove from pans and cool thoroughly.

Filling

 3 tablespoons cornstarch
 ½ cup sugar
 1 cup orange juice
 ½ cup bourbon
 1 cup flaked coconut

Mix cornstarch and sugar. Slowly add orange juice and bourbon, stirring constantly. Cook over low heat, stirring, until thickened and clear. Remove from heat. Stir in coconut; cool. Spread filling over 2 cake layers; stack layers and top with plain layer.

Frosting

2 *cups heavy cream, whipped*
flaked coconut, tinted green

Frost top and sides of cake with whipped cream. Sprinkle coconut over top of cake in shamrock pattern. Serve immediately or chill until serving time.

Southern Yule Cake

1 *cup mashed potatoes, well whipped*
2 *cups sifted all-purpose flour*
4 *teaspoons double-acting baking powder*
1 *teaspoon ground cloves*
½ *teaspoon cinnamon*
1 *cup butter*
2 *cups sugar*
2 *egg yolks*
½ *cup milk*
½ *cup raisins*
1 *tablespoon bourbon*
2 *egg whites*

Butter and line the bottom of a 9 x 13-inch baking pan with waxed paper. Sift flour, baking powder, and spices together. Cream butter, add sugar, and blend well. Add egg yolks and beat until mixture is light and fluffy.

Blend in whipped potatoes. Add flour mixture alternately with milk, beating until smooth after each addition. Stir in raisins and bourbon. Beat egg whites stiff and gently fold into mixture. Turn into prepared pan and bake in a moderate oven about 40 minutes or until cake tests done. Serves 10-12.

Whiskey Cake

2-2½ *cups raisins*
1 *cup bourbon*

¾ cup butter
1½ cups sugar
1 teaspoon finely grated orange rind
4 eggs
4 cups sifted all-purpose flour
2 teaspoons baking powder
¾ teaspoon baking soda
¾ teaspoon salt
2 cups medium-fine chopped almonds
Browned Butter Frosting (see below)

Measure raisins into a bowl; pour bourbon over them, cover, and marinate overnight at room temperature, turning several times during marinating. Drain before using, reserving liquor. Butter 2 loaf pans 9½ x 5½ x 3 inches and line with buttered wax paper. Heat oven to 325 degrees. Cream butter; add sugar and continue creaming until very fluffy, using electric mixer. Beat in grated rind and eggs until mixture is light. If mixing by hand, beat eggs separately before adding to mixture. Add flour sifted with baking powder, baking soda, and salt alternately with liquor drained from raisins. Fold in marinated raisins and nuts. Turn into prepared pans and spread batter evenly. Bake in a 325-degree oven about 1 hour or until cake springs back when touched lightly in center with fingertip. Remove to rack to cool, loosen from pans with spatula, invert on rack and remove paper. Cover and let stand for 4 days to age before serving. Brush with bourbon several times, if desired. Served frosted with Browned Butter Frosting.

Browned Butter Frosting
¼ cup butter
2 tablespoons bourbon
¼ teaspoon salt
½ teaspoon vanilla
2-2½ cups sifted confectioner's sugar

Place butter in 1-1½-quart saucepan and melt over medium heat until light brown. Remove from heat. Add bourbon, salt, and vanilla. Beat in confectioner's sugar a little at a time until it forms a good spreading consistency.

Raisin Bourbon Fruit Cake

    1   15-oz. package dark or golden seedless raisins
1½   cups mixed candied fruits and peels
¾   cup whole candied cherries
¾   cup candied pineapple chunks
¾   cup citron chunks
1½   cups candied orange peel chunks
    1   cup pitted dates
½   cup bourbon
¾   cup brown sugar, packed
½   cup butter
    4   eggs
¼   cup golden molasses
    1   cup walnut halves
½   cup pecan halves
    1   cup sifted flour
¾   teaspoon salt
    1   teaspoon cinnamon
¼   teaspoon nutmeg
¼   teaspoon baking powder

    Combine raisins, candied fruits, peels, and dates with bourbon. Cover and let stand overnight. Beat brown sugar and butter until very light and fluffy. Beat eggs until thick and combine with sugar mixture. Blend in molasses. Stir in fruits and nuts.

    Resift flour with salt, spices, and baking powder into sugar mixture to form batter. Mix until well blended. Turn into greased 9- or 10-inch tube pan, lined with greased brown paper. Bake in slow oven (300 degrees) 3½ hours or until cake tests done. Makes 1 tube cake.

Bootlegger's Dream

5   cups sifted flour
1   lb. white sugar
1   cup brown sugar
3   sticks butter

6 *eggs, separated*
1 *pt. bourbon*
1 *lb. candied red cherries, halves*
1 *teaspoon cinnamon*
1 *lb. shelled walnuts*
½ *lb. golden raisins*
1 *teaspoon baking powder*

Soak cherries and raisins in bourbon overnight. Cream butter and sugar until fluffy; add yolks and beat well. Add soaked fruit and remaining liquid; add flour, except small amount to flour nuts. Add cinnamon and baking powder; fold in beaten egg whites and floured walnuts last. Bake in large tube pan, greased and lined with wax paper. Bake at 250-275 degrees for 3-4 hours. When thoroughly cool, place in tightly covered container. Stuff center hole with cheesecloth, soaked in whiskey. Wrap in heavy waxed paper; keep cold.

Bourbon Pecan Pound Cake

shortening
3½ *cups all-purpose flour*
2 *cups pecans*
½ *cup bourbon*
½ *teaspoon salt*
½ *teaspoon grated lemon rind*
½ *teaspoon ground cinnamon*
½ *teaspoon ground cloves*
1½ *teaspoons baking soda*
2 *cups (4 sticks) butter*
2½ *cups sugar*
8 *whole eggs*
2 *teaspoons bourbon*

Line the bottom of a 10-inch tube pan with heavy baking parchment. Grease the sides and tube with shortening; then coat lightly with flour. Set aside. Chop the nuts fine and combine with ½ cup bourbon and lemon rind. Set this aside, too. Combine the flour with salt, spices, and soda in a flour sifter.

Work the butter with electric beater or mixer until soft and fluffy. Add the sugar gradually, beating constantly. Add the eggs, one at a time, beating hard after each addition. Add nuts, bourbon, and lemon rind mixture. With a spatula, thoroughly stir in the flour mixture. Finally, stir in 2 teaspoons bourbon. Pour into the prepared pan and bake in a preheated 350-degree oven for 35 minutes. Reduce oven heat to 325 degrees and continue baking another 35 minutes (a total of 1 hour and 10 minutes). At this point, plunge a toothpick in the center. If it comes out dry, without any batter clinging to it, the cake is baked.

Remove from the oven to a cake rack and allow to stand for about 15-20 minutes. Then run a metal spatula around the edge and invert on the rack. Cool thoroughly.

Bourbon Walnut Cake

- 2 *cups whole red candied cherries*
- 2 *cups white seedless raisins*
- 1 *cup bourbon*
- 2 *cups softened butter*
- 3 *cups light brown sugar*
- 4 *cups sifted flour*
- 1 *teaspoon grated orange rind*
- 4 *cups walnut halves*
- 1½ *teaspoons baking powder*
- 1 *teaspoon salt*
- 1½ *teaspoons ground mace*
- 8 *eggs, separated*

Combine cherries, raisins, and bourbon in a large mixing bowl. Cover tightly and let stand in the refrigerator overnight. Drain fruits and reserve bourbon.

Place butter in the large bowl of electric mixer and beat at medium speed until softened. Add sugar slowly, stirring constantly. Add egg yolks, beating until well blended.

Combine ½ cup of the flour with orange rind and nuts. Sift remaining flour with the baking powder, salt, and mace.

Add 2 cups of the flour mixture to the creamed mixture and mix thoroughly. Add the reserved bourbon and the remainder of the flour mixture alternately, ending with flour. Beat well after each addition.

Beat egg whites until stiff but not dry; fold gently into cake batter. Add drained fruits and floured nuts to the cake batter; blend thoroughly. Grease a 10-inch tube cake pan; line with wax paper. Grease and lightly flour wax paper. Pour cake batter into pan to within 1 inch of the top. (Any remaining batter may be baked in a small loaf pan prepared in the same manner as the tube cake pan.)

Place in a 275-degree oven; bake tube cake 4½-5 hours and loaf cake 2 hours, or until a cake tester inserted in the center of cakes comes out clean. Cool cakes in pans on cake rack about 2-3 hours. Remove cakes from pans; peel off wax paper.

Wrap cakes tightly in aluminum foil or plastic wrap and store in a cool place or in the refrigerator until ready to serve. Cut into thin slices for serving.

Kentucky Pecan Bourbon Cake

  1 *lb. shelled pecans*
 ½ *cup butter*
  3 *eggs, separated*
 1½ *cups flour*
  1 *teaspoon baking powder*
  1 *cup plus 2 teaspoons sugar*
  2 *teaspoons mace*
 ½ *cup (4 oz.) bourbon*
 ½ *lb. seeded raisins*
   dash of salt

Break pecans and cut raisins in half. Measure sifted flour and sift twice more. Take ½ cup of flour and mix with nuts and raisins. To the rest of flour add the baking powder and sift again. Cream butter and sugar. Add yolks of eggs, one at a time, and beat until smooth and lemon-colored. Soak mace in bourbon for at least 10 minutes. Add flour and bourbon to butter mixture alternately, beating as batter is being blended. Slowly fold in raisins and nuts. Fold in stiffly beaten egg whites to which you have added a few grains of salt. Grease 9-inch tube cake pan; line with wax paper. Bake at 325 degrees for 1¼ hours. Let stand in pan 30 minutes before removing.

Chestnut-Almond Torte

  2 *cups Chestnut Puree (see below), or 1 15-oz. can unsweetened chestnut puree*
  6 *eggs, separated*
1½ *cups sugar*
  6 *tablespoons bourbon*
  1 *cup finely ground or grated blanched almonds*
  1 *pt. heavy cream*
  ¼ *cup confectioner's sugar*
  ½ *cup toasted chopped almonds*
    whole glazed chestnuts for garnish (optional)

Prepare puree from fresh chestnuts as described below. If canned puree is used, beat well to remove lumps. Preheat oven to 325 degrees. Grease 3 8-inch layer cake pans. Line bottoms with wax paper and grease again. Beat egg yolks with ¾ cup sugar until lemon-colored and very thick. Beat in 2 tablespoons bourbon. Gently stir in chestnut puree and ground almonds. Beat egg whites until soft peaks form. Gradually add remaining ¾ cup sugar, beating until stiff. Fold into chestnut mixture. Divide batter among 3 prepared pans. Bake about 50 minutes, until layers start to pull with a small knife.

As the layers cool, they will pull away from the sides of the pans a little more, and will fall a bit. Cool completely. Loosen layers again from sides of pans and carefully turn out. Combine heavy cream with remaining 4 tablespoons bourbon and beat until it starts to thicken. Gradually add confectioner's sugar, beating until stiff. Arrange layers on serving plate with whipped cream between them. Spread top and sides of torte with whipped cream. Cover sides with toasted almonds. Decorate top with whole glazed chestnuts, if desired. Serves 12.

Chestnut Puree

Wash about 1½ pounds chestnuts and cut a cross on the flat side of each nut. Place in saucepan, cover with cold water, bring to boil, and then boil for ½ hour, until chestnuts are tender. As soon as chestnuts are cool enough to handle, peel off shells and inner skins. Chestnuts can be pureed through a food mill, or in a blender. If a blender is used, divide chestnuts into 3 parts and puree each part with ¼ cup water. Makes about 2 cups puree.

Cherry Bourbon Cake

>   8 *oz. red maraschino cherries*
>   1 *lb. butter*
> 2½ *cups sugar*
>   ½ *teaspoon cinnamon*
>   3 *eggs, separated, at room temperature*
>   3 *cups sifted all-purpose flour*
>   ½ *cup chopped pecans*
>   ⅓ *cup bourbon*

Drain and chop cherries fine. In large bowl, cream butter with 2 cups of the sugar and cinnamon until light and fluffy. Add egg yolks one at a time, beating after each addition; then add cherries.

Combine flour and nuts; add to butter mixture alternately with bourbon. Beat egg whites until soft peaks form. Gradually add remaining sugar and beat until stiff, but not dry. Fold into batter. Turn into greased and floured 10-inch tube pan. Bake in 350-degree oven for 1 hour and 5 minutes or until cake tests done. Cool 1 hour, remove from pan, and finish cooling on rack.

Polish Pound Cake

> 1 *cup butter*
> 2 *cups sugar*
> 4 *eggs, beaten one at a time*
> 3 *cups regular flour*
> 1 *tablespoon baking powder*

1 tablespoon lemon extract
3 oz. bourbon
1 cup milk
1 cup walnuts, chopped
⅓ cup powdered sugar

Grease and flour tube pan. Cream butter. Add sugar and beat well. Add eggs, one at a time. Beat well after each addition. Add flour and baking powder that have been sifted together 4 or 5 times, alternating with milk. Add lemon extract. Add whiskey. Add ⅔ cup nuts, floured.

Mix ⅓ cup powdered sugar and ⅓ cup nutmeats together. Put on top of cake before baking. Bake in tube pan 1 hour in a 350-degree oven.

Bourbon Lemon Cake

1 cup butter
2 cups granulated sugar
2 tablespoons grated lemon rind
5 eggs
3 cups sifted cake flour
1 tablespoon baking powder
½ cup fresh lemon juice

Preheat oven to 350 degrees. Butter and flour a 10-inch tube pan. Cream butter and sugar till fluffy. Add grated lemon rind. Add eggs, one at a time, beating well after each addition. Sift together, twice, flour and baking powder. Add dry ingredients alternately with lemon juice, ending with juice, beating well after each addition. Spoon or pour into prepared pan. Bake 1 hour, or until cake springs back when touched.

Glaze

¼ cup butter
2-3 cups granulated sugar
½ cup bourbon

As soon as cake is taken out of the oven, combine glaze ingredients and heat till sugar is melted. Pour evenly over cake while it is hot, and leave in pan till thoroughly cooled.

Bourbon Cake

    1 *cup butter*
    1½ *cups sugar*
    2 *tablespoons bourbon*
    1 *teaspoon grated lemon rind*
    ½ *teaspoon nutmeg*
    4 *eggs*
    2 *cups sifted cake flour*
    ½ *teaspoon salt*
    1 *teaspoon double-acting baking powder*
    ¼ *cup milk*

Cream butter, sugar, bourbon, nutmeg, and lemon rind. Add eggs, one at a time, beating well after each addition. Combine flour, salt, and baking powder and add to butter mixture alternately with milk, mixing well until smooth.

Pour batter into greased loaf pan 9½ x 5 x 3 inches. Bake in preheated 325-degree oven for 1¼ to 1½ hours. Cool for 5 minutes. Remove from pan to cake rack to cool thoroughly. When cool, slice cake carefully lengthwise into five thin slices. Put slices together with Bourbon Butter Cream (see below); if desired, frost top and sides with Butter Cream. Chill before slicing. Serves 10-12.

Bourbon Butter Cream

    1 *cup sugar*
    ⅓ *cup water*
    ¼ *teaspoon cream of tartar*
    4 *egg yolks*
    5 *oz. semisweet chocolate*
    6 *tablespoons bourbon*
    1½ *cups sweet butter*

In saucepan combine sugar, water, and cream of tartar. Bring to a boil and boil rapidly until syrup spins a long thread.

Beat egg yolks until fluffy and gradually beat in syrup. Continue to beat until mixture is stiff.

Melt chocolate with 4 tablespoons of the bourbon over simmering water, or stirring over low heat.

Stir melted chocolate mixture into sugar-egg mixture. Beat in butter bit by bit. Stir in remaining 2 tablespoons bourbon. Chill until right consistency to spread.

Bourbon Ice Cream Cake

1 9½-oz. package yellow cake mix
1 teaspoon unflavored gelatine
¼ cup cold water
½ cup milk
¼ cup heavy cream
1 teaspoon vanilla
¼ cup sugar
⅓ cup bourbon
1 cup heavy cream, whipped
4 oz. mixed candied fruits (about ½ cup)
4 oz. candied cherries, chopped (about ½ cup)
¼ cup bourbon
1½ cups heavy cream, whipped

Prepare and bake cake as directed on package for 8-inch layer cake. Cool 5 minutes on cooling rack. Remove from pan and cool thoroughly.

Soften gelatine in cold water. Add milk, ¼ cup heavy cream, vanilla, and sugar. Cook over boiling water, stirring constantly, until gelatine is dissolved. Cool thoroughly; add ⅓ cup bourbon and chill until slightly thickened. Fold gelatine mixture into 1 cup heavy cream, whipped. Turn into 8-inch layer cake pan and freeze until mushy. Turn into bowl and beat until smooth. Fold in mixed candied fruits and cherries. Turn into 8-inch layer cake pan. Freeze until firm.

Unmold ice cream layer on top of cake layer. Gradually fold ¼ cup bourbon into 1½ cups heavy cream, whipped. Frost top and sides of ice cream cake with bourbon whipped cream. Serve immediately. Makes 1 8-inch layer cake.

Bourbon Cream Cake

    5 *egg yolks*
    1 *cup sugar*
    1 *teaspoon vanilla*
    ½ *cup milk*
    1 *tablespoon gelatine*
    ⅔ *cup bourbon*
    1 *tablespoon sherry*
    5 *egg whites*
    ½ *pint cream*
      pieces of angel or chiffon cake

Put gelatine into the whiskey to soften. Cook egg yolks, ½ cup sugar, vanilla, and milk over low heat until mixture coats spoon; cool slightly and add gelatine and whiskey mixture and the sherry.

Beat egg whites and rest of sugar and add to custard; whip cream and add. Line pan with wax paper and pour in layer of custard; add pieces of angel or chiffon cake and fill with custard. Let stand 8 hours in refrigerator.

Remove from pan and frost with 1½ cups whipped cream flavored with a dash of vanilla and 3 teaspoons powdered sugar (proportions may be varied to suit taste). This can be put in parfait glasses in the making and used as a less formal dessert.

Eggnog Squares

    1 *box white cake mix*
    ½ *teaspoon vanilla*
    ½ *teaspoon nutmeg*
    2 *lb. sifted confectioner's sugar*
    1¾ *sticks of butter*
    1 *cup bourbon*
    12 *oz. vanilla wafers*
    1½ *lb. pecans*

Bake cake and cut in 2-inch squares a day before icing. Cream vanilla, nutmeg, confectioner's sugar, and butter and add bourbon. Mix until smooth. Dip cake squares in mixture and roll in a blend of the vanilla wafers and pecans which have been ground together in food grinder. Let set out about 30 minutes before storing. Will keep 3 weeks or longer in refrigerator. Makes about 8 dozen squares.

Bourbon Petits Fours

1 *17-oz. package pound cake mix*
½ *teaspoon vanilla*
½ *teaspoon mace*
¼ *cup bourbon*
  assorted liqueurs

Prepare cake mix according to package directions, adding vanilla and mace, but use ¼ cup bourbon in place of ¼ cup of milk. Pour batter into 2 greased and floured 8-inch-square pans. Bake in preheated oven at 375 degrees for 25-30 minutes. Cool.

Cut into 2-inch squares. Cut a small ½-inch hole in center of each square (not all the way through). Brush inside of hole with Snow Frosting (see below) and let dry. Then, pour 1 teaspoon liqueur into each hole, using an assortment of liqueurs.

Now, cover top and sides with Snow Frosting, placing cakes on wire rack over wax paper and slowly pouring icing over all. Makes 32 small cakes.

Snow Frosting

2 *cups confectioner's sugar*
2 *tablespoons hot water*
1 *tablespoon bourbon*

Mix sugar with hot water and bourbon. Beat until smooth.

Raisin Cake

- 1½ cups white raisins
- 2 cups water
- ½ cup shortening
- 1 teaspoon mace
- 1 teaspoon grated lemon rind
- ¾ cup sugar
- 1 egg
- 1½ cups sifted flour
- 1 teaspoon soda
- ½ teaspoon cloves
- ½ teaspoon nutmeg
- ¼ teaspoon allspice
- ½ teaspoon salt
- 1 cup chopped pecans
- 2 tablespoons bourbon
- pecans for decoration

Cover raisins with water and simmer uncovered for 20 minutes. Drain, saving ¾ cup cooking liquid. Cool. Cream shortening, mace, lemon rind, and sugar together thoroughly. Beat in egg. Sift together flour, spices, soda, and salt. Blend into creamed mixture alternately with cooking liquid. Stir in raisins, nuts, and bourbon.

Pour into 2 greased 9-inch layer cake pans. Bake at 350 degrees about 25 minutes. Remove from pans; cool thoroughly. Frost tops and sides with Bourbon Hard Sauce (see below). Decorate with pecans.

Bourbon Hard Sauce

- ¼ cup butter
- 3 cups sifted confectioner's sugar
- 1 egg
- ¼ cup bourbon

Cream butter. Gradually beat in 3 cups sifted confectioner's sugar, egg, and bourbon.

Bourbon Nut Cake No. 1

1 cup butter
2 cups sugar
6 eggs
4 cups sifted flour
1 teaspoon salt
2 teaspoons baking powder
1 teaspoon mace
½ cup bourbon
1 lb. walnuts, chopped
1 lb. candied cherries, chopped
1 lb. candied pineapple, chopped
2 tablespoons bourbon

Cream butter; gradually add sugar and continue creaming till light and fluffy. Add eggs, one at a time, beating well after each addition. Sift 3 cups flour with salt, baking powder, mace; add alternately with bourbon. Mix nuts and fruits with remaining 1 cup flour. Add to mixture and put in 2 greased and paper-lined 9 x 5 x 3-inch loaf pans. Put them in the center of the oven with a pan of hot water below. Bake at 300 degrees for 2 hours; then reduce heat to 200 degrees and bake ½ hour longer or until done.

Cool and sprinkle with bourbon; decorate with nuts and cherries. Wrap and store in cool place.

Bourbon Nut Cake No. 2

2 cups granulated sugar
2¼ cups brown sugar
1½ cups butter
6 eggs
¼ teaspoon salt
1 teaspoon nutmeg
5½ cups sifted flour
2 cups bourbon
1 cup chopped walnuts

Combine white and brown sugar. Cream butter in large mixing bowl and add one-half sugar mixture. In separate bowl, beat eggs till light. Slowly beat in remaining sugar till smooth. Stir egg mixture into butter mix. Sift salt and the nutmeg with the flour. Add dry ingredients alternately with the bourbon. Stir in the chopped nuts. Pour into greased 10-inch tubular pan. Bake in preheated 300-degree oven for about 90 minutes. Cake is done when it shrinks slightly from pan. Cool in pan for 15 minutes before removing to cake rack.

Bourbon Orange Cake

1 cup butter
2 cups granulated sugar
2 tablespoons grated orange rind
½ teaspoon vanilla
½ teaspoon nutmeg
5 eggs
3 cups sifted flour
1 tablespoon baking powder
¾ cup fresh orange juice

Glaze
¼ cup butter
⅔ cup granulated sugar
½ cup bourbon

Preheat oven to 350 degrees. Butter and flour 10-inch tube pan. Cream butter and sugar until fluffy. Add grated orange rind, vanilla, and nutmeg. Add eggs, one at a time, beating well after each addition. Sift together twice flour and baking powder. Add dry ingredients alternately with orange juice, ending with juice, beating well after each addition. Spoon or pour into prepared pan. Bake 1 hour, or until cake springs back when touched.
  As soon as cake is taken from oven, combine glaze ingredients and heat until sugar is melted. Pour evenly over cake while it is hot, and leave in pan until cooled.

Flaming Peach Dessert Pancakes

    ½ cup sifted all-purpose flour
    1 egg
    1 tablespoon salad oil
    ½ cup milk
    ¼ teaspoon cinnamon
    1 tablespoon butter for frying
    2 cups sliced peaches
    ¼ teaspoon mace
    ¾ cup bourbon
    ½ cup sugar

Combine flour, egg, salad oil, milk, and cinnamon. Melt small amount of butter in 5½-inch skillet. Add about 2 tablespoons batter; tilt skillet so that batter covers bottom of skillet. Cook over low heat until lightly browned on both sides. Repeat, using remaining butter and batter.

Meanwhile, combine peaches, mace, ¼ cup bourbon, and sugar; mix well and let stand 15 minutes. Place some of peach mixture on center of each pancake. Fold pancake over peaches. Place seam side down in greased shallow baking dish. Bake in moderate oven (350 degrees) 15 minutes. Spoon remaining ½ cup bourbon over pancakes. Ignite and serve. Serves 4.

Bourbon Bars

    1 package yellow cake mix
    ¼ cup sugar
    2 teaspoons mace
    ½ cup corn oil
    ½ cup bourbon
    3 eggs, separated
    1½ cups chopped walnuts
    1½ cups cut-up seedless raisins

Grease a jelly roll pan (15 x 10 inches). Reserve 1⅓ cup cake mix. In mixing bowl, combine remaining cake mix, sugar, mace,

Flaming Peach Dessert Pancakes

oil, bourbon, and egg yolks. Mix at low speed until ingredients are moist. Beat at medium speed about 1 minute. Beat egg whites until stiff and fold into cake mixture.

Toss walnuts and raisins with reserved cake mix; fold into mixture. Turn into pan and bake at 325 degrees 35-40 minutes. Cool and cut into bars.

Date-Nut Squares No. 1

1 *cup chopped dates*
2 *tablespoons bourbon*
2 *eggs*
½ *cup sugar*
1 *teaspoon cinnamon*
¼ *cup sifted flour*
½ *teaspoon baking powder*
1 *cup chopped almonds*

Mix dates and bourbon and let stand half an hour. Beat eggs and gradually add sugar and cinnamon. Continue beating till mixture is light and fluffy. Stir in flour sifted with baking powder, almonds, and date mixture. Combine mixture and spread on bottom of buttered and floured 9-inch-square pan. Bake cake in 350-degree oven for 30 minutes. Let cake cool on wire rack for about 10 minutes; then cut into squares. Let squares cool and remove from pan.

Date-Nut Squares No. 2

½ *cup sugar*
2 *eggs, beaten*
2 *oz. orange rind*
¼ *cup sifted flour*
½ *teaspoon baking powder*
1 *cup walnuts, chopped*
3 *tablespoons bourbon*
1 *cup chopped dates*

¾ cup confectioner's sugar
3 teaspoons heavy cream

Add sugar and orange rind to eggs, beating till light. Sift together flour and baking powder and add to egg mixture. Add walnuts, dates, and 1 tablespoon bourbon. Spread in buttered 8-inch-square pan dusted with flour. Bake at 350 degrees for 30 minutes. Cut in squares. Remove squares and ice with mixture of confectioner's sugar, remaining 2 tablespoons bourbon, and heavy cream.

Butterscotch Cake

1½ cups all-purpose flour
1½ teaspoons baking powder
¼ teaspoon salt
1 cup chopped pecans
½ cup butter
1 cup brown sugar
2 eggs
1 teaspoon almond extract
2 oz. bourbon
2½ cups sifted confectioner's sugar
¼ cup bourbon
½ cup flaked coconut

Sift together flour, baking powder, and salt. Add chopped nuts and mix. Melt butter and remove from heat, adding to it the brown sugar and beating well. Beat eggs, one at a time, into sugar mixture. Stir flour mix into sugar mixture, adding almond extract, and mixing well. Turn into greased, 9-inch-square baking pan. Bake in 350-degree oven 20-25 minutes, or till cake tests done. Remove cake from oven and sprinkle 2 ounces bourbon over it.

Combine confectioner's sugar and ¼ cup bourbon and beat till smooth. Add coconut and spread mixture over cake. Cut into squares.

Cookies

Yuletide Cookies

- 3 cups flour
- 3 teaspoons soda
- ¼ teaspoon salt
- 1 teaspoon nutmeg
- ½ teaspoon allspice
- ½ cup shortening
- 1 cup brown sugar
- 4 eggs
- ¼ teaspoon lemon extract
- ½ cup bourbon
- 1 lb. candied cherries
- 1 lb. candied pineapple
- ½ lb. chopped dates
- ½ lb. white raisins
- 1½ lb. chopped walnuts

Cream shortening; add sugar, eggs, lemon extract, and bourbon. Let set for 10 minutes. Sift 2 cups of flour, soda, salt, and spices together. Add to creamed mixture. Add remaining cup of flour to fruit and mix; add nuts. Pour creamed mixture over nuts and fruit. Mix together well. Drop on greased cooky sheet. Bake at 300 degrees for 20 minutes.

Bourbon-Brown Sugar Cookies

¼ cup butter
¼ cup light brown sugar
2 eggs
¼ cup bourbon
¼ teaspoon vanilla
1 lb. chopped walnuts
1 lb. candied pineapple
1 lb. candied cherries
1 lb. white raisins
1½ cups flour
1½ teaspoons soda
1½ teaspoons cinnamon
½ teaspoon mace
½ teaspoon cloves

Cream butter. Add sugar gradually. Add eggs, one at a time. Beat well after each addition.
Sift flour, soda, and spices. Add to butter mixture.
Soak raisins in bourbon and vanilla at least 2 hours. Add to mixture with nuts and fruit. Drop from teaspoon on buttered cooky sheet. Bake at 375 degrees for 20 minutes.
Store in air-tight container or freeze.

Lizzies

1 15-oz. box raisins
½ cup bourbon
¼ cup butter
¾ cup brown sugar

2 eggs
2 cups flour
½ teaspoon powdered cloves
½ teaspoon cinnamon
½ teaspoon allspice
½ teaspoon salt
½ teaspoon soda
1 teaspoon grated lemon rind
½ lb. candied pineapple, chopped
¼ lb. candied orange, chopped
¼ lb. candied citron, chopped
¼ lb. glacé cherries, quartered
¼ lb. candied lemon, chopped
3 cups chopped pecans

Preheat the oven to 325 degrees.

Soak the raisins in the bourbon. Cream butter and sugar together. Beat in eggs.

Sift together the flour, cloves, cinnamon, allspice, salt, and soda. Add lemon rind. Fold into the batter.

Mix the soaked raisins and liquor with the remaining ingredients and stir into the flour mixture.

Drop by tablespoons on a greased cooky sheet and bake about 15 minutes, or until lightly browned. Cool on a rack and then store in an air-tight tin. Makes about 4 dozen.

London Strips

2½ cups flour
5 eggs, separated
6 tablespoons sugar
1 cup sweet butter
1 tablespoon vanilla
  strawberry jam
1 cup sugar
1 tablespoon bourbon
1 teaspoon vanilla
3 cups finely chopped pecans
  confectioner's sugar

Mix flour, egg yolks, 6 tablespoons sugar, butter, and 1 tablespoon vanilla, blending thoroughly. Spread dough in a 16 x 11-inch pan and flatten. Cover liberally with strawberry jam. Beat egg whites until stiff, gradually beating in 1 cup sugar, bourbon, and 1 teaspoon vanilla. Fold in nuts and spread over dough. Bake at 350 degrees for 40 minutes. Sprinkle with confectioner's sugar and cut into strips when cool. Makes 3-4 dozen strips.

Canestrelli

  1 *lb. unsalted soft butter*
1¼ *lb. flour*
    pinch salt
  1 *tablespoon bourbon*
  1 *cup white sugar*
  3 *egg yolks (save whites)*
  1 *oz. grated orange rind*
    powdered sugar

Place flour, sugar, and salt in large bowl. Add butter, orange rind, egg yolks, and bourbon. Mix together well, roll into a sheet ½ inch thick, and cut. Mix egg whites slightly and brush on each cooky with a pastry brush.

Bake at 375 degrees about 15 minutes, or until a light brown. Remove from oven and let cool on waxed paper. Sprinkle lightly with sifted powdered sugar.

Bourbon Brownies No. 1

Batter
¾ *cup sifted all-purpose flour*
¼ *teaspoon baking powder*
¼ *teaspoon salt*
2 *tablespoons water*
½ *cup sugar*
⅓ *cup sweet butter*
6 *oz. semisweet chocolate pieces*

1 teaspoon vanilla
2 eggs
½ teaspoon mace
1½ cups coarsely chopped pecans
4 tablespoons bourbon

Mint Frosting
½ cup sweet butter
green coloring and mint extract (optional)
2 cups sifted powdered sugar

Chocolate Glaze
3 tablespoons vegetable shortening
6 oz. semisweet chocolate pieces

Sift together flour, baking powder, and salt and set aside. Combine water, sugar, and butter. Bring to a boil, stirring constantly. Remove from heat and stir in chocolate pieces, mace, and vanilla. Beat until smooth.

Beat in eggs, one at a time. Add flour mixture and nuts. Spread in a greased 7 x 11-inch pan. Bake in moderately slow oven (325 degrees) for 25 to 30 minutes. Remove from oven and sprinkle with bourbon while hot. Cool.

To make frosting, cream butter and add coloring and extract if desired. Add sugar gradually. Spread over cooled brownies.

To make glaze, melt shortening and chocolate pieces over hot water. Spread over mint frosting. Cool before cutting into small squares.

Bourbon Brownies No. 2

⅓ cup margarine
2 oz. unsweetened chocolate
½ teaspoon almond extract
1 cup sugar
2 eggs

¾ cup all-purpose flour
¼ teaspoon salt
3 tablespoons bourbon

Melt margarine and chocolate in saucepan over low heat, stirring. Cool. Beat in almond extract and sugar. Add eggs, one at a time, beating well after each addition. Mix flour and salt and stir into chocolate mixture. Spread in greased 8-inch-square pan. Bake in slow oven, 325 degrees, about 25 minutes. Cool. When thoroughly cooled, crumble brownies into bowl. Sprinkle with bourbon; mix in with fingers. Shape into 1-inch balls or logs about 1 inch long. Store in air-tight container for a day before serving. Makes 3-3½ dozen.

German Christmas Cookies

1 cup butter
1 cup sugar
1 egg white
2 egg yolks
rind of ½ orange, grated
½ teaspoon mace
1 teaspoon vanilla
2 oz. bourbon
3¾ cups flour

Cream butter; add sugar gradually, continuing to cream. Add egg yolks, orange rind, mace, vanilla, and bourbon. Mix well. Slowly add the flour until mixture becomes a workable dough. Roll out and cut with Christmas cooky cutter; brush with egg white and sprinkle colored confetti sugar for decoration. Bake at 350 degrees until slightly browned.

Greek-Style Cookies

1 lb. butter
1 tablespoon shortening

2 cups sugar
6 egg yolks
2 whole eggs
juice 1 lemon
juice 1 orange
1 teaspoon lemon rind, ground
1 teaspoon orange rind, ground
2 tablespoons bourbon
10-11 cups sifted flour
3 teaspoons baking powder
1 teaspoon baking soda
sesame seeds

Cream butter and shortening; add sugar gradually, continuing to cream. Add whole eggs, juice, bourbon, and rinds. Sift baking powder and soda with flour. Mix well with butter-sugar-egg mixture. Pinch off pieces of dough and shape into rings, crescents, or stars. Brush tops of cookies with egg yolk to which a little milk has been added. Sprinkle with sesame seeds. Bake at 350 degrees for 20-25 minutes or until lightly browned on top. Makes about 80 cookies.

Fruit Snaps

1½ cups sugar
½ cup butter
3 eggs, beaten
3 cups flour
2 teaspoons cinnamon
1 teaspoon nutmeg
1 teaspoon allspice
½ teaspoon salt
½ teaspoon baking soda
¼ cup water
4 oz. bourbon
1 teaspoon vanilla
2 oz. orange juice
1½ lb. dates, chopped

1 lb. candied cherries, chopped
1 lb. candied pineapple, chopped
1 lb. walnuts, chopped

Cream together sugar and butter, adding eggs. Sift together flour and spices plus salt and add sugar-butter mixture. Add baking soda dissolved in water, bourbon, orange juice, and vanilla. Add chopped fruits and nuts to mixture. Mix well and drop with tablespoon on a greased cooky sheet dabs of about half an ounce each. Bake in 325-degree oven about 20 minutes.

Bourbon Tricorns

½ cup margarine
½ cup sugar
1 egg
1½ cups flour
½ teaspoon salt
3 tablespoons milk
½ cup shelled walnuts
¼ teaspoon cinnamon
1 tablespoon each brown and granulated sugar
2 tablespoons bourbon
1 teaspoon butter
confectioner's sugar
1 egg white

Cream margarine with sugar till light and beat in egg. Mix flour and salt; add to creamed mixture alternately with milk. Blend well and chill 2 hours.

Roll chilled dough a little at a time between lightly floured sheets of waxed paper. Dough should be about ⅛ inch thick. Remove top sheet. Cut in 2½-inch rounds and, with floured pancake turner, transfer to ungreased cooky sheet. Fold rounds in half, then in thirds to form tricorns, pinching corners together. Arrange 1 inch apart and set aside.

Grind walnuts which have soaked in bourbon and cinnamon mix for 24 hours and strain off bourbon, setting aside. Add brown and white sugar to ground nuts with teaspoon butter, melted. If mixture does not form a stiff paste, add a few drops of the bourbon. Roll mixture into small nut balls, dip in confectioner's sugar, and drop a ball in the center of each crown.

To glaze, brush sides and tops of tricorns with 1 egg white beaten slightly in 1 tablespoon water. Bake in 350-degree oven about 15 minutes. Makes about 2 dozen tricorns.

Bourbon Cookies No. 1

 1 *12-oz. box vanilla wafers*
 10 *ginger snaps*
 2 *heaping tablespoons cocoa*
 2 *tablespoons white syrup*
 ½ *cup chopped pecans*
 ¼ *cup bourbon*
 ½ *teaspoon vanilla*
 1 *teaspoon finely grated orange rind*
 powdered sugar

Grind cookies to crumbs and add all other ingredients except the powdered sugar. Mix thoroughly and roll into balls the size of walnuts. Roll in powdered sugar. Store in closed container a few days before using.

Bourbon Cookies No. 2

 1 *cup brown sugar*
 ½ *cup butter*
 4 *eggs*
 3 *cups flour*
 1 *teaspoon nutmeg*
 1 *teaspoon allspice*
 1 *teaspoon cloves*
 ½ *teaspoon salt*
 ½ *cup bourbon*
 3 *teaspoons soda*
 3 *tablespoons milk*

1 lb. candied pineapple
1 lb. candied cherries
1 lb. white raisins
1 lb. walnuts, chopped

Cream brown sugar and butter. Beat the eggs and add. Then mix the flour, spices, salt, bourbon, soda, and milk. Add flour mix to sugar-butter mix. Mix in the candied fruits, raisins, and nuts. Drop on greased cooky sheet and bake at 350 degrees till light brown.

Filled Bourbon Cookies

½ cup butter
½ cup sugar
½ teaspoon vanilla
½ teaspoon mace
1 egg
1½ cups flour
¼ teaspoon salt
3 tablespoons bourbon

Filling
¼ cup butter
1 cup confectioner's sugar
¼ teaspoon salt
1 tablespoon bourbon

Cream butter with sugar, vanilla, and mace until light; beat in egg. Mix flour and salt; add to creamed mixture alternately with bourbon. Blend well. Chill.

Roll dough out ¼ inch thick. Cut into rounds with glass or cooky cutter. With smaller cutter, cut center from half the rounds. (Reroll centers for more cookies, or bake separately.)

Bake on greased baking sheets in a preheated 400-degree oven 7-10 minutes, until golden. Remove to rack to cool.

To make filling: Blend butter and sugar; stir in salt and enough whiskey to make firm paste. Sandwich whole cookies with rings on top. Makes 2 dozen.

Bourbon Snaps

¼ lb. butter
½ cup sugar
¼ cup bourbon
1 cup sifted flour
½ teaspoon vanilla
¼ teaspoon ground mace

Cream butter with sugar well until fluffy. Add bourbon and vanilla alternately with flour. Sprinkle mace over. Mix thoroughly. Chill for at least 1 hour. Drop very small amounts of mixture off the tip of a teaspoon, about 2 inches apart, on an ungreased cooky sheet. Bake for 5 minutes or until edges are golden in an oven that has been preheated to 375 degrees. Cool slightly on cooky sheet. Lift cookies off carefully with a spatula, and place on cake rack to cool.

Crisp Cookies

6 egg yolks
1 teaspoon sugar
1 teaspoon lemon rind
½ teaspoon salt
⅓ stick butter
¼ cup sweet cream
1 teaspoon vanilla
1 tablespoon bourbon
3 cups flour

Mix flour, sugar, and salt. Add the yolks, butter, cream, and flavoring (bourbon, vanilla, and lemon rind) to make a stiff dough. Toss on floured board and roll very thin. Cut in strips 3 x 5 inches and make 4 1-inch gashes crosswise.

Lower strips into deep hot fat, and fry until light brown (about 2 minutes). Sprinkle with powdered sugar.

Bourbon Puffs

½ cup sweet butter
1 teaspoon bourbon

1　teaspoon vanilla
　　　2　tablespoons granulated sugar
　　　1　cup sifted flour
　　　1　cup walnuts, chopped
　　½-1　cup confectioner's sugar

Cream butter with bourbon and vanilla until light and smooth. Mix granulated sugar with flour and walnuts; blend well into butter mixture. Roll into small balls between palms; place on ungreased baking sheet. Bake in preheated 350-degree oven for 15 minutes. While still hot, roll balls in confectioner's sugar until well coated. Cool on rack. Makes 24 puffs.

Grecian Butter Cookies

　　1　lb. (2 cups) sweet butter
　　¼　cup confectioner's sugar
　　½　teaspoon almond extract
　　1　egg yolk
　　6　cups sifted all-purpose flour
　　1　oz. caraway seeds
　　1　oz. bourbon
　　¼　cup finely chopped blanched almonds, toasted

Cream butter until very light. Add confectioner's sugar, almond extract, and egg yolk. Beat 2 minutes. Add flour and caraway seeds gradually, mixing constantly. Add bourbon; blend well. Knead dough on lightly floured board until smooth but crumbly.

Add nuts; continue kneading until nuts are thoroughly blended into dough. Pinch off small amounts of dough, or use a teaspoon; shape in crescents.

Place on ungreased cooky sheet ¾ inch apart. Bake in 350-degree oven about 20 minutes. Sift additional confectioner's sugar over cookies while hot. Makes about 6 dozen.

Sweet Cookies

　　1　lb. unsalted butter
　　2　egg yolks

½ teaspoon vanilla
4 tablespoons confectioner's sugar
2 oz. bourbon
4-6 oz. pecans, chopped
5-6 cups flour

Beat butter with electric mixer for 20-25 minutes, until light and fluffy. Add egg yolks, vanilla, sugar, and bourbon. Mix well; then add pecans. Start adding flour, mixing by hand. Mix well as you blend and add enough flour so dough will be soft but not sticky.

Shape into rounds and bake on greased pan at 350 degrees about 15-20 minutes, until very lightly browned. Allow to cool; then sprinkle with sifted confectioner's sugar. These keep well in airtight containers. Makes 40-50 cookies.

Christmas Cookies

1 cup brown sugar, firmly packed
½ cup butter
4 eggs
3 tablespoons milk
3 teaspoons soda
¾ cup bourbon
3 cups flour
1 teaspoon cinnamon
1 teaspoon mace
1 teaspoon allspice
1½ lbs. chopped walnuts
1 lb. raisins
1 lb. candied pineapple
1 lb. candied cherries
1 can coconut

Mix nuts, fruits, and coconut and pour bourbon over them. Cream butter and brown sugar. Add nuts, fruits, and coconut, and mix. Add eggs, one at a time, flour, milk, soda, and spices. Mix well. Drop by teaspoonful on greased cooky sheet and bake at 300 degrees for 22 minutes.

Listy

    4 *egg yolks*
    1 *tablespoon sugar*
    3 *tablespoons sour cream*
    1 *tablespoon bourbon*
    1 *teaspoon nutmeg*
  ¼ *teaspoon vanilla*
  ½ *cup ground pecans*
1¼ *cups all-purpose flour*
     deep fat for frying

Beat egg yolks till lemon-colored. Add sugar, sour cream, bourbon, nutmeg, and vanilla; mix well. Stir in flour and nuts; work dough with hands till it does not stick to the fingers.

Divide dough into 8 equal parts. Roll each portion very thin on lightly floured board. Cut into strips 1 inch wide by 3 inches long. (There will be about 18 to 25 strips to each portion.) Make a lengthwise slit in each strip.

Drop strips, no more than 4 at a time, into deep fat preheated to 375 degrees. Fry a few seconds; turn quickly. Fry a few seconds longer. Quickly remove from fat; drain on paper towel. Makes about 12 dozen.

Breads

Sweet Potato Biscuits

   ¾ *cup mashed sweet potatoes*
   1 *tablespoon brown sugar*
   1 *tablespoon lime rind*
      salt to taste
   ¼ *cup melted butter*
   ⅓ *cup milk*
   ⅓ *cup bourbon*
 1¼ *cups flour*
 2½ *teaspoons baking powder*
   1 *teaspoon salt*
   1 *teaspoon cinnamon*

Season potatoes with sugar, lime rind, and salt. Stir in butter, milk, and bourbon. Toss dry ingredients and gradually work into potato mixture. Pat dough ½ inch thick on waxed paper and cut into small rounds. Bake in a 450-degree oven about 15 minutes, until golden brown and crusty. Serves about 12.

Corn Muffins

  ¾ cup flour
  ¼ cup light brown sugar
  2 teaspoons baking powder
  1 tablespoon lemon rind, grated
  1 teaspoon salt
  ¼ cup butter, melted
 1½ cups yellow cornmeal
  2 eggs, beaten
  ½ cup milk
  ¼ cup bourbon

Sift flour, baking powder, and salt together. Mix in cornmeal, lemon rind, and brown sugar. Combine eggs and milk; drip bourbon in slowly as you stir, and blend into flour mixture. Stir in butter. Pour into buttered and floured, preheated, heavy (preferably iron) muffin pans or 9-inch-square ovenproof dish. Bake in 425-degree oven for 30 minutes. Makes about 8 muffins or squares.

Bourbon Rolls No. 1

  2 cups milk
  1 package yeast
  1 teaspoon sugar
  2 tablespoons water
  ½ lb. butter or margarine
  ¾ cup sugar
  5 eggs, beaten
 4½ cups flour
  7 tablespoons bourbon
  2 tablespoons powdered sugar

Scald milk and cool. Soften yeast with water and 1 teaspoon sugar. Add 4 cups flour to cooled milk and mix. Add yeast and cover. Let rise two hours. Cream butter; add ¾ cup sugar and eggs. Gradually add remaining ½ cup flour alternately with 5 tablespoons of bourbon. Blend well and add to yeast mixture. (At this stage, mix may be stored in refrigerator as long as 3 days.)

Let entire mixture rise again, about 2 hours. Spoon into greased muffin pans and let rise 15-30 minutes. Bake at 425 degrees about 12 minutes or until lightly browned. Remove from pan, add a thin glaze of 2 tablespoons of bourbon and 2 tablespoons of powdered sugar, and serve hot. Makes 36 small rolls.

Bourbon Rolls No. 2

- 1 *package dry yeast*
- ¼ *cup warm water*
- ¾ *cup scalded milk, cooled to lukewarm*
- ½ *teaspoon salt*
- ⅛ *pound (½ stick) butter*
- 3 *tablespoons sugar*
- 1 *teaspoon grated lemon rind*
- 1 *cup raisins*
- 1 *egg, lightly beaten*
- 4 *cups flour*
- *Bourbon Sauce (see below)*

Stir yeast in warm water to dissolve and add milk in large bowl. Add salt, butter, lemon rind, sugar, raisins, and egg. Stir well and add ½ cup flour. Beat until smooth. Stir in remainder of flour and beat to form stiff dough. Place in large greased bowl and cover with tea towel.

Let rise in warm place until double in bulk.

Turn onto lightly floured board and knead until smooth and elastic. Cut off equal portions and form balls to put in greased muffin pans. Fill muffin cups. Cover and let rise in warm place until doubled. Bake in 425-degree oven for 15-18 minutes. While rolls are hot, brush with Bourbon Sauce. Makes 18.

Bourbon Sauce

2 *tablespoons bourbon*
2 *tablespoons butter*
2 *tablespoons sugar*

Combine bourbon with butter. Simmer with sugar.

Bourbon Bread Loaf

½ *cup milk*
1 *cup and 1 tablespoon bourbon*
2 *tablespoons sugar*
2 *teaspoons salt*
3½ *tablespoons butter*
1 *cup warm water*
1 *package dry yeast*
4-5 *cups flour*
shortening, melted

Heat milk and ½ cup bourbon. Stir in sugar, salt, and 2½ tablespoons butter. Cool to lukewarm. Measure warm water into mixing bowl. Sprinkle dry yeast over water and stir until dissolved. Add lukewarm milk mixture. Stir in 3 cups flour. Beat until smooth. Continue stirring in flour until dough is easily handled.

Turn out on lightly floured board. Knead until smooth and elastic. Place in greased bowl; brush lightly with melted shortening. Cover and let rise in warm place until double in bulk (approximately 1 hour and 20 minutes). Punch down and form into a loaf shape. Place in a greased loaf pan 9 x 5 x 3 inches, or shape into 3 small loaves.

Cover and let rise in warm place about 55 minutes. Bake in 400-degree oven about 50 minutes for a large loaf or 30-35 minutes for small loaves. Turn out immediately. Brush loaf all over with mixture of remaining butter and bourbon.

Fried Bread

8 *slices bread*
4 *eggs*

½ cup sugar
1 lemon rind, grated
4 tablespoons bourbon
  butter for frying
4 tablespoons confectioner's sugar
8 teaspoons lemon marmalade

Mix the eggs, sugar, and bourbon. Toss in the lemon rind. Let bread soak in this mixture. Fry the bread in butter until both sides are brown. Spread marmalade on fried bread and sprinkle with confectioner's sugar. Serve warm.

Bourbon French Toast

12 eggs
4 teaspoons sugar
1 teaspoon cardamom
1½ teaspoons salt
1¼ cups bourbon
1½ loaves French bread
   cooking oil
1 cup confectioner's sugar
1 tablespoon cinnamon
48 strips bacon
   maple syrup

Beat together eggs, sugar, cardamom, and salt. Add 1 cup of the bourbon and mix well. Fill large frying pan (preferably cast iron) with ⅜ inch cooking oil and heat to boiling point. Cut French bread into ½-inch slices. Using a long-handled fork, dip bread in batter, then slip into hot oil. Fry until crisp and brown.

Drain quickly on paper towels. Place 3 pieces on each plate, dust with confectioner's sugar mixed with cinnamon, and surround with bacon. Serve with hot maple syrup to which ¼ cup of bourbon has been added. Serves 16.

Bourbon Pancakes

    3 *eggs*
    ⅔ *cup sugar*
    ¼ *lb. butter*
    ¾ *cup flour*
    ⅓ *cup bourbon*
    2 *tablespoons water*
    2 *teaspoons cinnamon*

Beat eggs and sugar for ½ hour. Melt butter; when cool add bourbon and water. To sugar and eggs, alternately add flour, mixed with cinnamon, and liquid, ending with flour. If mixture is too thick (it should be the consistency of crepe batter), thin with bourbon or water.

To make each pancake, pour 2 tablespoons of batter into pan and cook until brown. Remove and roll immediately around handle of wooden spoon. Will keep well.

Orange-Bourbon Nut Bread

    2½ *cups sifted flour*
    3 *teaspoons baking powder*
    1 *teaspoon salt*
    ¼ *teaspoon nutmeg*
    1 *cup sugar*
    ¼ *cup butter*
    ½ *cup bourbon*
    ½ *cup orange juice*
    1 *egg*
    1 *tablespoon grated orange rind*
    1 *cup coarsely chopped walnuts*

Sift flour, baking powder, salt, nutmeg, and sugar into a bowl. Cut in shortening as for piecrust. Add bourbon, orange juice, and egg. Mix lightly, just until dry ingredients are dampened. Stir in orange rind and nuts.

Turn batter into greased 9 x 5 x 3-inch loaf pan, spreading into corners. Let stand for 20 minutes.

Bake in preheated 350-degree oven about 1 hour, or until tester inserted in center comes out clean and bread has pulled away from sides of pan. Let stand in pan 5 minutes and then turn out on rack. Cool completely before slicing.

Bourbon Date-Nut Bread

½ cup chopped dates
½ cup coarsely chopped walnuts or pecans
¼ cup bourbon
1 13¾-oz. box hot roll mix
2 eggs, slightly beaten
¼ cup sugar
¼ cup melted butter
flour

Soak dates and nuts in bourbon for ½ hour or longer. Prepare hot roll mix dough as directed on package, using 2 eggs and stirring in sugar and butter. Work date-nut mixture into dough, which will be soft and sticky. Cover bowl with towel and let dough rise in a warm place until doubled, about 1 hour and 15 minutes. (*Note:* This bread takes longer to rise than plain hot roll mix.)

Turn dough out of bowl onto a well-floured surface. Sprinkle top with flour. Knead dough lightly for about 1 minute. Turn into a greased 9 x 5 x 3-inch loaf pan or 2-pound coffee can. Cover and let stand until dough doubles, about 1½ hours.

Bake in preheated 350-degree oven 45-50 minutes, until top is nicely browned and sounds hollow when lightly tapped. Cool in pan about 10 minutes; then turn out on rack to cool completely.

Bourbon
The Whiskey for Sippin'

The origins of whiskeymaking in America are sketchy, with fiction often rivaling fact. It is known that an enterprising distiller tried his hand at making whiskey on Staten Island in New York Harbor back in 1660. But there apparently were not enough takers to make the venture a success. For the next hundred years or so, the colonists made do with rum made in New England or the rare kegs of scotch or irish that found their way to the colonies in the hold of some ship. Whiskey did become available in Pennsylvania in the late 1700s, when Scotch-Irish farmers who were old hands with the pot still began making rye.

The question as to who made the first bourbon has never been answered successfully. Some reports say it was innovated by Evan Williams, a Pennsylvania distiller who set up shop in Louisville in 1783 and sold his potent spirits without waiting for them to age or mellow. Others give credit to a frontiersman named Wattie Boone who was said to have operated a rig on Cox's Creek in Nelson County, Kentucky, around 1785.

There seems to be solid agreement, however, that one of the first to make true bourbon was the Reverend Elijah Craig, a Baptist preacher with an educated palate. Craig was said to have set up a still in Georgetown, Kentucky, where he had been operating a corn-grinding mill on the side, in 1789, the year George Washington became the first president of the United States. Craig, who also kept active preaching fiery sermons, is credited by many historians with creating the authentic bourbon formula. Lest one get the impression that the Reverend was something of a hypocrite, it might be noted that in 1795 one Kentucky church carried on a spirited debate over the question of who should make whiskey. The parish came to the conclusion that it was in fact "consistent with true religion. . . . to carry on a distillery of spirits." It could be further noted that during those early days, frontier parishes often paid their parsons in whiskey.

Whiskey served many purposes in those days. Besides being a frontier beverage, it was used by many pioneering families as a principal ingredient in their folk medicines. A charming sidelight on this has turned up in the archives of the venerable Henry McKenna Distillery, which has been turning out bourbon in the same plant and in much the same way in Fairfield, Kentucky, for 119 years.

A sales letter written by Henry McKenna in 1878 cited the medicinal properties of his spirited product. "Dear Sir," wrote Mr. McKenna, "as the Fishing Season is near at hand, now is the time for all who expect to enjoy that delightful sport to prepare for the journey and camp. You know—and all 'old fishermen' know—that it is very dangerous to be out in the cold and damp without something to prevent one from taking cold and having chills, so you should not delay in getting a supply of H. McKenna's old-fashioned Hand Made Sour Mash Whiskey to take with you; also have it always in your house, for it is recommended by the leading physicians for Medicinal and Family use." A distiller could hardly lose with that approach!

Kegs and barrels of whiskey also served in frontier regions as a medium of exchange. Specie was scarce and bank notes were suspect, but a barrel of whiskey was a popular commodity with a known and stable value. When Abraham Lincoln's family went from Kentucky to Indiana in 1816, his father is supposed to have sold his 30-acre Knob Creek farm for $20 cash and 400 gallons of whiskey valued at $640.

Bourbon: The Whiskey for Sippin'

Over the years, a controversy has blown up as to the state in which bourbon was first conceived: Kentucky or Virginia. In the early days, Bourbon County, where Rev. Elijah Craig kept busy turning out his whiskey, was part of Virginia under the English crown grants. But the county was later officially named part of Kentucky. This question of geography has stirred up more than one dispute among bourbon buffs.

Processing can be a fighting word in the world of bourbon. It can also be somewhat confusing. For instance, one of the best-known American whiskeys, made generally according to the bourbon formula, is Jack Daniels. But because at the distillation it is filtered through a bed of charcoal, the federal government does not accept the resulting whiskey as bourbon. One bourbon, however, Bourbon Supreme, is mellowed by charcoal during the distillation in a process approved by the federal government.

To take another example of confusion, Old Fitzgerald, Jim Beam whiskeys, and Mr. McKenna's cold remedy are referred to as sour mash bourbons. For that matter, so is Jack Daniels. But a number of estimable bourbons are not so classified, and the term does not mean the whiskey is actually sour. It merely means that some of the residue left in the bottom of the still from the previous day's run is added to the yeast in the fermenting tub. Thus, say advocates of the sour mash process, an unbroken chain of distinctive flavor is maintained. Fooey, say the opposing school members. Sour mash is no different from any other bourbon. Among the disciples of sour mash bourbon, the author might add, were Lucius Beebe, the famed gourmet and boulevardier, and novelist William Faulkner.

One thing that indisputably does give bourbon its unique taste and color is the charred barrel in which it is aged. Again the true origins of the process are obscured by myth. The most logical theory is that since most available barrels in the early days had already served as containers for dried fish, salt pork, vinegar, or flour, charring their interiors was an essential process. Later on, charring new barrels was suggested to prevent development of blisters in the wood that might spoil the aging whiskey. Whatever the reason, one fact remains. Whiskey makers soon found out that spirits aged in a charred barrel were far more mellow than those in regular kegs. It seems that when the whiskey expands and contracts it seeps through the charred surface, beneath which a reddish sap has formed. The spirits draw flavor and their distinctive amber-red color from this charcoaled oak.

Bourbon seems to have arrived at its distinctive quality through a series of such experiments, or accidents. For instance, during the California Gold Rush, it was found that whiskey hauled in covered wagons during the blistering heat of the day and piercing chill of the prairie night showed a considerable improvement in flavor as it neared the West Coast. This discovery inspired distillers to load kegs of bourbon in the holds of clipper ships bound on long voyages around Cape Horn during which they were subjected to both equatorial heat and Antarctic cold.

Measuring the alcoholic content of bourbon is another process that had some odd beginnings. Under the original "whiskey tax" of 1791, the federal government levied duties ranging from nine to twenty-five cents per gallon on six classifications of proof or alcoholic content. But aside from the practice of judging whiskey good, indifferent, or poor, little attention had been given as to how strong it was. Distiller and buyers might taste a whiskey and assess the strength by how much it burned as it went down. But the favorite method was to mix a little of the liquor with gunpowder, then touch a flame to it. If the mixture blew up, it was too strong. If it failed to burn, it was too weak. But if it burned with a steady blue flame, it was "proved perfect" and could be marked as "bearing proof of gunpowder."

The government quickly decided that both the taste and gunpowder methods were inadequate and they dispatched an army of revenue collectors each armed with a gauge and hydrometer to measure strength. This was not only far more accurate but resulted in a greater standardization of bourbons. Today they are usually either 86 or 100 proof.

The word bourbon crops up all through early American history, a fact which inspired author Bernard De Voto to comment that "in the heroic age, our forefathers invented self-government, the Constitution and Bourbon."

As the pioneers trail-blazed their way westward during the last century, they usually took along a few kegs of the amber-colored liquid to keep out the night chill and to fortify themselves against snakebite, insect sting, or whatever. So fond were these stalwarts of the American spirit that U.S. historian George Bancroft's famed line "Westward the star of empire takes its way" was paraphrased by Mark Twain to read "Westward the *jug* of empire takes its way."

Bourbon seemed to bring out the wry wit in Twain. When the famed writer was making a journey abroad, a customs inspector opened his luggage and in one suitcase spotted a bottle of the whiskey. Looking reproachfully at Twain, he said, "I thought you said there was nothing in here except clothing."

"I did say that," replied Twain. "You're looking at my nightcap!"

During the Civil War (as in all wars) there was a good deal of drinking on both sides, and warriors often took a supply of spirits into battle with them. Historian Gerald Carson in his *Social History of Bourbon* notes that Farwell Gould, a Confederate hero from the Ozark Hills, rode into the fray at Pea Ridge with a jug in his arms because, as he said, "there wasn't no safe place to set it down."

The most famous anecdote about whiskey during the Civil War recalls Abraham Lincoln's reaction when a Missouri congressman complained to him about General Ulysses S. Grant's fondness for bourbon. Lincoln was said to have retorted sharply, "I wish I knew what brand of whiskey he drinks. I would send a barrel to all my other generals."

Bourbon has been the favorite drink of a distinguished roster of Americans. They include Daniel Webster, Presidents Grant, Franklin D. Roosevelt, and Harry S. Truman and Vice-Presidents John Nance "Cactus Jack" Garner and Alben Barkley.

One less illustrious but no less faithful devotee was a great-aunt of mine who belonged to the Kentucky branch of the family. At age twelve, I first saw this withered little woman, whose Irish ancestry asserted itself in a passion for tea so strong you could stand a spoon in it. It was midwinter when I paid that first visit and I well remember the small figure, swathed in shawls, huddled beside the big iron kitchen stove with a bubbling teapot in handy reach. From time to time she would pour herself a cup, adding a spoon of coarse brown sugar, a couple of cloves, and a spoon of bourbon "to keep the chill out." When nobody was watching she gave me a furtive sip. I don't suppose the old lady drank more than an ounce and a half a day, but it seemed to give her comfort and strength. To this day, when it is raw outside, I like to brew a cup of tea and add a bit of bourbon to warm the marrows.

It is doubtful that any other liquor has been the subject of as many eulogies as bourbon. "Cactus Jack" Garner, who lived to the ripe old age of ninety-eight, referred to drinking the whiskey as "striking a blow for liberty." Alben Barkley likened fine bourbon to a good story. "If you don't use too much it will never hurt you." Sir William Osler, the famed Canadian physician and teacher, called it "the milk of old age." But the eulogy to end all eulogies was coined by Henry Morton Robinson in his novel *Water of Life*, in which he described bourbon as "Elixir and Opiate, Tonic and Pain Killer, Running Riddle and Fluid Answer, Destroyer and Preserver, Universal Solvent and Mortal Strain, Setter-on of the Dream and Taker-Away of the Performance . . ."

How do you tell a good bourbon? Some old-timers tell you to hold the bottle to the light. If the color is clear and deep amber-red, it is bourbon of good breeding. Shake the bottle and if small beads form around the neck and remain a long time, you've got good stuff, they claim.

Such tests are not taken seriously by anyone in the industry, however. For one thing, the deep red color is no longer characteristic of bourbon. The public demand for lightness in whiskeys has resulted in lighter-colored bourbons. As for the beads, say the experts, brandy or scotch will also produce bubbles if you shake them long enough. The best definition of quality a distiller will give is: "All bourbons are good. But some are better."

What's the best way to enjoy bourbon? Some take it straight, others toss it off with a beer chaser, and some take their bourbon in Manhattan cocktails, which call to mind a story. Winston Churchill's mother, American-born Jennie Jerome, first introduced the cocktail to New York society at a reception in the Manhattan Club in the 1870s. Hence the name.

Perhaps the most famous bourbon drink is the mint julep, which inspired Judge Soule Smith of Lexington, Kentucky to comment that "who has not tasted one has lived in vain."

The proper way to make a julep has touched off many a heated debate. One school of thought says to get the right flavor, you must crush the mint. Others insist that the drink should consist of just bourbon, sugar syrup, and shaved ice. Then, at the last minute, stick a sprig of mint in the top to tickle your nostrils. Personally, I like my mint crushed and the bourbon muddled in it before the ice is added.

One way to set a julep lover quivering with rage is to make the

Bourbon: The Whiskey for Sippin'

drink with some other kind of whiskey. Kentucky's famous humorist, Irvin S. Cobb, once snarled that a man who made a julep with rye would not be above putting a scorpion in a baby's cradle.

Whatever the drink, julep, neat, or mixed with a little "branch water," bourbon must have something going for it. It has soared in sales to almost 90 million gallons a year and, counting the bourbon used anonymously in blends, it easily passes the 100 million gallon mark, which is ahead of any other spirit, domestic or imported.

Bloody Marys, daiquiris, and the like are all right for some. But for true drinking pleasure, one should have bourbon.

Drinks

Mint Julep

There are almost as many ways of making a mint julep as there are southerners. Here is one popular version.

    4 *mint leaves*
    1 *lump sugar*
    1 *tablespoon water*
    2 *oz. bourbon*
       crushed ice

Muddle mint leaves, sugar, and water in a tall glass or tankard. Fill with crushed ice and add bourbon. Do *not* stir. Garnish with fresh mint sprig.

Fish House Punch

This is a variation of a drink that was popular back in colonial days.

>   juice of 12 lemons
> 1 quart water
> 1 cup powdered sugar
> 1½ quarts cognac
> 1 pint peach brandy
> 1 pint bourbon

Pour all ingredients over ice in punch bowl. Stir well and garnish with slices of orange.

Morning Lift

A soothing pick-me-up created by Henri Jabeneau of Chicago's Ambassador Hotel.

> 2 oz. bourbon
> 1 oz. crème de cacao
> 1 egg
> 3 oz. milk

Shake well, ice, and serve to the patient.

Eggnog

Here is a tasty version of an old Yuletide favorite.

> 12 egg yolks
> 12 oz. bourbon
> 12 tablespoons sugar, divided
> 12 egg whites
> 1 pint whipping cream
> 1 tablespoon powdered sugar

Beat egg yolks till thick and lemon-colored. Continue to beat. Slowly add bourbon, beating constantly. Slowly add 8 tablespoons sugar and continue beating till mixture is smooth.

Whip egg whites till stiff but not dry, adding 4 tablespoons sugar a little at a time. Set aside. Put beaten egg whites in chilled punch bowl. Whip cream, adding one tablespoon powdered sugar. Put whipped cream on top of beaten egg whites. Pour egg yolk mixture over this and carefully fold all ingredients together. Serves 15-20.

Milk Punch

- 2 *cups vanilla ice cream*
- 1 *cup milk*
- 2 *oz. cognac*
- 4 *oz. bourbon*
- 2 *oz. light rum*
- *nutmeg*

Mix the ingredients in a blender for about 10 seconds and pour into a cold pitcher. Serve with a dash of nutmeg atop each glass. Serves 6.

Bourbon Sour

This is a great favorite down around Louisville, Kentucky.

- *juice of ½ lemon*
- 1 *teaspoon sugar syrup*
- 2 *oz. bourbon*
- *stick fresh pineapple* or *orange wedge*

Shake lemon, syrup, and bourbon well with ice and strain into glass. Decorate with pineapple stick or orange wedge.

Bourbaree

This drink was invented by Capt. Henry E. Bernstein (U.S.N., ret.).

    1 *oz. lime juice*
    1 *oz. honey*
    3 *oz. bourbon*
      dash bitters
    6 *ice cubes*

Mix in blender with ice. Makes two generous-sized cocktails.

Hot Buttered Bourbon

This is a comforting brew after a chilly afternoon on the ski slopes.

    1 *lump sugar*
      boiling water
    1 *pat butter*
    2 *oz. bourbon*

Put sugar into heated whiskey glass and slowly fill with boiling water till it is about ⅔ full. Add pat of butter and 2 ounces bourbon to hot water and sugar. Stir and grate nutmeg on top.

Hot Mulled Cider

Grandpa used to warm this up with a hot poker.

    ½ *gallon sweet cider*
    2 *cinnamon sticks about 3 inches each, broken up*
  10 *allspice berries*
  10 *whole cloves*
    1 *pint bourbon*
    1 *oz. lemon juice*

2 oz. orange juice
5 orange slices, halved
10 whole cinnamon sticks

Bring cider to boil with spices and simmer 30 minutes. Strain into mugs and add bourbon and fruit juices. Garnish with orange slices and cinnamon stick stirrers. Serves 10.

Bourbon Spiced Coffee

This one picks up where Irish coffee leaves off.

3 pints freshly brewed coffee
1/8 teaspoon powdered ginger
1/4 teaspoon mace
dash lemon extract
1/8 teaspoon allspice
1 piece stick cinnamon
8 oz. bourbon
4 teaspoons sugar

Combine coffee, ginger, mace, lemon extract, allspice, and cinnamon in a saucepan. Pour coffee into 8 serving mugs. Add 1 oz. bourbon and 1/2 teaspoon sugar to each cup. Stir and serve.

Bourbon Spiced Coffee, Served with Whipped Cream and Dessert

Index

All-Purpose Barbecue Sauce, 155
All-Purpose Sauce, 152
Apricot-Raisin Sauce, 161
Avocado Salad, 41

Baked Carrot Pudding, 204
Baked Ham with Apricots, 122
Baked Kidney Beans, 145
Bananas Flambé, 170
Bananas Flamed with Bourbon, 169
Barbecue Sauce for Country-Style Spareribs, 117
Barbecue Sauce for Venison, 154
Bean Soup Flambé, 34
Beans for Barbecues, 146
Beef and Bourbon Aspic, 102
Beef Bourbon Supreme, 96
Beef Bourbonnaise, 96
Beef-Eggplant Casserole, 100
Beef Slivers on Toast, 101

Beef Tenderloin with Rice and Chicken Livers, 90
Berry Bourbon Jelly, 211
Black Bean Soup, 33
Black Gold Bourbon, 197
Bootlegger's Dream, 230
Booze Pudding, 205
Bourbaree, 279
Bourbon Angel, 177
Bourbon Apple Jelly, 212
Bourbon Aspic No. 1, 21
Bourbon Aspic No. 2, 22
Bourbon Baked Chicken, 85
Bourbon-Banana-Bacon Tidbits, 29
Bourbon Barbecue Sauce, 151
Bourbon Bars, 244
Bourbon Beef Balls No. 1, 22
Bourbon Beef Balls No. 2, 23
Bourbon Beef Roast Flambé, 97
Bourbon Black Bean Dip, 30
Bourbon Bread Loaf, 265

283

Index

Bourbon-Brown Sugar Cookies, 249
Bourbon Brownies No. 1, 251
Bourbon Brownies No. 2, 252
Bourbon Burgers, 100
Bourbon Burgers with Confetti Rice, 103
Bourbon Butter Cream, 237
Bourbon Cake, 237
Bourbon Cheese Fondue, 48
Bourbon Cheese Soup No. 1, 36
Bourbon Cheese Soup No. 2, 36
Bourbon Cheese Spread, 25
Bourbon Chicken, 84
Bourbon Chili No. 1, 106
Bourbon Chili No. 2, 106
Bourbon Chocolate Sauce, 44
Bourbon Clam Dip, 30
Bourbon Cloud, 178
Bourbon Cookies No. 1, 256
Bourbon Cookies No. 2, 256
Bourbon Cream Cake, 239
Bourbon Cream Pie, 186
Bourbon-Cured Peaches, 169
Bourbon Custard, 207
Bourbon Custard Sauce, 163
Bourbon Date-Nut Bread, 268
Bourbon Delight Pie No. 1, 182
Bourbon Delight Pie No. 2, 182
Bourbon Dessert Sauce, 160
Bourbon Drops, 218
Bourbon Flamed Quail, 136
Bourbon French Toast, 266
Bourbon Fudge Balls, 216
Bourbon Glaze for Ham, 158
Bourbon Goose, 73
Bourbon Graham Cracker Pie, 185
Bourbon Hard Sauce, 163
Bourbon Hard Sauce for Raisin Cake, 241
Bourbon Hors d'Oeuvres, 31
Bourbon Hot Dogs, 28
Bourbon Ice Cream Cake, 238
Bourbon Lemon Cake, 236
Bourbon Marinade, 99
Bourbon Marinade for Roast, 154
Bourbon Marshmallow Pie, 183
Bourbon Mincemeat Pie, 191
Bourbon Mist Pâté, 19
Bourbon Mold, 214
Bourbon Molds, 171
Bourbon Mushrooms on Toast, 144

Bourbon Mushrooms with Peas, 143
Bourbon Nut Cake No. 1, 242
Bourbon Nut Cake No. 2, 242
Bourbon Nut Pie, 189
Bourbon Omelette ala Moana, 43
Bourbon, Orange, and Beans, 149
Bourbon Orange Cake, 243
Bourbon-Orange Pork Loin, 119
Bourbon Pancakes, 267
Bourbon Pâté Balls, 20
Bourbon Pâté No. 1, 17
Bourbon Pâté No. 2, 18
Bourbon Pâté No. 3, 18
Bourbon Pecan Pound Cake, 231
Bourbon Petits Fours, 240
Bourbon Pie, 185
Bourbon Pralines, 220
Bourbon Pudding, 201
Bourbon Puffs, 258
Bourbon Rolls No. 1, 263
Bourbon Rolls No. 2, 264
Bourbon Sauce, 159
Bourbon Sauce for Mocha Soufflé, 45
Bourbon Sauce for Turkey, 156
Bourbon Seafood Sauce, 158
Bourbon Seafood Shells, 60
Bourbon Skewered Steak, 93
Bourbon Snaps, 258
Bourbon Soufflé, 43
Bourbon Sour, 278
Bourbon Spiced Coffee, 280
Bourbon Squash, 145
Bourbon Squirrel, 135
Bourbon Stew, 105
Bourbon Stroganoff, 95
Bourbon Sugar Balls, 216
Bourbon Sweet Potatoes, 144
Bourbon Swiss Fondue, 50
Bourbon Tricorns, 255
Bourbon Walnut Cake, 232
Bourbon-Walnut Mushrooms, 29
Bourbon Watermelons, 167
Bourbon Wieners, 28
Bourbonnaise Sauce, 157
Brace of Wild Ducks, 138
Braised Turkey, 80
Bread Pudding with Fruit, 200
Breaded Country Ham, 123
Breast of Capon with White Grapes, 71

Index

Breast of Chicken with Bourbon, 64
Broccoli Egg Divan, 142
Broiled Shrimp, 53
Broiled Top Round, 92
Brown Rice, 90
Browned Butter Frosting, 229
Brownie-Bottomed Bourbon Pie, 183
Burning Apples, 172
Butterflied Leg of Lamb, 108
Butterscotch-Bourbon Fondue, 49
Butterscotch Cake, 247

Canestrelli, 251
Canned Ham with Home Glaze, 123
Carrots Bourbonade, 143
Carrots Newburg, 140
Cepes à la Bordelaise, 141
Charcoal Venison, 134
Charlotte Russe, 204
Cheddar and Bourbon Mix, 25
Cheddar Cream Spread, 26
Cheese Coquettes, 25
Cherries Jubilee, 171
Cherry Bourbon Cake, 235
Cherry Bourbon Sauce, 162
Cherry Jelly, 210
Chestnut-Almond Torte, 234
Chicken Cacciatore, 67
Chicken-Cream Pâté, 19
Chicken Ginger, 71
Chicken in Orange-Lemon Sauce, 69
Chicken Salad with Bourbon, 40
Chicken Sauté Bourbon, 68
Chiffon Pie, 188
Chili Bourbon Beans, 148
Chinese Walnut Chicken, 70
Chocolate Bavaroise, 208
Chocolate Icebox Pie, 193
Chocolate Parfait American, 178
Chocolate Walnut Pie, 181
Christmas Cookies, 260
Cioppino, 59
Clam Corn Soup, 34
Cocktail Sandwich Filling, 28
Cocoa Bourbon Balls, 217
Coffee Baked Beans, 147
Coffee Bourbon Balls, 218

Coffee Pie, 190
Concord Grape Bourbon Balls, 217
Confetti Rice, 103
Corn Muffins, 263
Corn-Oyster Chowder, 32
Cornish Hens, 72
Country-Style Spareribs, 117
Crab Bisque, 39
Crabmeat au Crème, 62
Crabmeat Bourbonnaise, 60
Crabmeat Kentucky Chowder, 33
Cranberry Apple Pie, 194
Cream of Shrimp Soup, 37
Crème Anglaise, 158
Creole Chicken, 69
Crepe Sauce, 163
Crisp Cookies, 258
Crown Roast of Lamb, 109
Crown Roast of Lamb au Bourbon, 110
Cups of Gold, Flambé, 206

Daily Double, 177
Date-Nut Squares No. 1, 246
Date-Nut Squares No. 2, 246
Derby Delight, 208
Dessert Sauce, 160
Deviled Lobster Tails, 55
Drunken Figs, 168
Drunken Hot Dogs, 27

Economy Roast Marinade, 152
Eggnog, 277
Eggnog Mousse, 179
Eggnog Pie No. 1, 186
Eggnog Pie No. 2, 187
Eggnog, Russian Style, 203
Eggnog Squares, 239
Eggnog Walnut Pie, 187

Festival Freeze, 175
Fiery Bean Pot, 148
Fig Fancy, 179
Filled Bourbon Cookies, 257
Fish House Punch, 277
Flag Cake, 226
Flamed Veal Scallopini, 127
Flaming Cherry Sauce, 160

Index

Flaming Peach Dessert Pancakes, 244
Flaming Peaches, 168
Flaming Pecan Pumpkin Pie, 192
Flank Steak, Bourbon County Style, 94
French Onion Soup Flambé, 38
Fried Bread, 265
Frozen Lee, 174
Frozen Mincemeat Pie, 191
Fruit Bourbon Kuchen, 196
Fruit Cake, 222
Fruit Garnish for Bourbon-Orange Pork Loin, 119
Fruit Nuggets, 225
Fruit Sauce for Pears 'n' Chicken, 67
Fruit Snaps, 254
Fruit Tart, 165
Fruited Duo, 211

German Christmas Cookies, 253
Glazed Ham Steak, 122
Golden Cheese Fondue, 50
Golden Fried Chicken, 83
Gourmet Baked Apples, 172
Gourmet Roast Beef Bourbon, 99
Grapefruit-Orange Marmalade, 213
Grecian Butter Cookies, 259
Greek-Style Cookies, 253

Ham au Poivre Vert, 121
Ham Bourbon Balls, 22
Ham Pie, 120
Ham Soufflé, 46
Hard Sauce for Plum Pudding, 199
Hoisin-Bourbon Marinade, 153
Holiday Meat Balls, Flambé, 24
Hot Buttered Bourbon, 279
Hot Dog Cocktail Sauce, 154
Hot Fruit Compote, 170
Hot Mulled Cider, 279
Hot Sweet Sauce, 164

Jellied Old-Fashioneds, 213
Julep Lamb Chops, 111

Kentucky Bourbon Pudding, 202
Kentucky Burgoo No. 1, 128
Kentucky Burgoo No. 2, 129
Kentucky Burgoo No. 3, 130
Kentucky Burgoo No. 4, 131
Kentucky Burgoo No. 5, 131
Kentucky Cassoulet, 149
Kentucky Corn Dip, 31
Kentucky Duck, 74
Kentucky Duckling, 75
Kentucky Pecan Bourbon Cake, 233
Kentucky Sweets, 144

Lamb and Vegetable Jumble, 113
Lamb Chops with Sauce, 112
Lamb Kebabs Hoisin, 111
Lamb Racks with Bourbon, 109
Lamb Scallopini, 114
Lamb Sesame, 114
Lamb Steaks with Bourbon Sauce, 113
Lamb Stroganoff, 112
Lamb Teriyaki, 111
Limestone Lettuce Flambé, 41
Liquor Butter, 155
Listy, 261
Lizzies, 249
Lobster au Whiskey, 58
Lobster Grand Marnier, 56
Lobster Queen Anne, 58
London Broil, 95
London Strips, 250

Macaroon Delight, 179
Marinade for Beef Roast, 152
Marinade for Steak, 153
Marinated Duck, 74
Meat Loaf en Croûte, 132
Mignons of Tenderloins Flared in Bourbon, 89
Milk Punch, 278
Mince-Apple Deep Dish Pie, 195
Mincemeat Pork Savories, 116
Mint Julep, 276
Mint Parfait, 175
Mocha Soufflé with Bourbon Sauce, 45
Morning Lift, 277

Index 287

Mount Vernon Pot Roast, 99
Mrs. Dean Rusk's Fruit Cake, 221
Mushroom Omelette, 46
Mushrooms Flamed with Bourbon, 142

Old Bourbon Soufflé, 47
Old-Fashioned Steamed Pudding, 200
Onion Casserole, 141
Onion Soup, Italian Style, 38
Onion Soup, Kentucky Style, 37
Orange-Bourbon Nut Bread, 267

Partridge Casserole, 137
Peach Butter, 212
Pears 'n' Chicken, 66
Peppermint Bourbon Mousse, 176
Pepperpot Soup, 35
Pheasant au Crème Bourbon, 138
Picnic Roast, 98
Piquant Steak Marinade, 153
Plum Pudding, 198
Poached Apricots in Bourbon, 168
Polish Pound Cake, 235
Polynesian Beef, 97
Pumpkin Bourbon Pie, 191
Pumpkin Mousse, 180

Quick Bourbon-Chicken Liver Spread, 20

Raisin Bourbon Fruit Cake, 230
Raisin Bourbon Soufflé, 44
Raisin Cake, 241
Raspberry-Bourbon Sauce, 162
Ribs 'n' Bourbon, 119
Roast Beef Oriental, 94
Roast Beef with Bourbon Sauce, 102
Roast Pork with Wild Rice, 117
Roast Turkey, Julep Style, 77
Roast Turkey with Bourbon Stuffing, 78
Rock Lobster Tails Inferno, 56
Roquefort Spread, 26

Saint Patrick's Day Cake, 227
Sauce Anglaise, 72
Sausage and Bacon Tidbits, 27
Sautéed Chicken Livers, 91
Seafood Louisiana, 62
Seafood Special, 51
Shrimp and Mushrooms with Whiskey, 53
Shrimp Bisque, 33
Shrimp Calypso, 55
Shrimp Flambé, 52
Shrimp in Bourbon, 52
Shrimp Orleans, 54
Sirloin Steak Flambé No. 1, 87
Sirloin Steak Flambé No. 2, 88
Sirloin Steak Flambé No. 3, 88
Sirloin Steak Flambé No. 4, 89
Snow Frosting, 240
Snowball Ice Cream Mold, 175
Sour Cream Dip, 30
Southern Fried Chicken, 82
Southern Yule Cake, 228
Spaghetti Sauce, 156
Spanish Baked Beans, 147
Spicy Bourbon Sauce, 155
Spiked Cheese Pastries, 26
Satin Fudge, 219
Steak au Poivre Flambé, 91
Steak au Poivre Vert, 92
Steak Bourbon, 93
Strawberry Bourbon Sauce, 162
Strawberry Omelette Flambé, 42
Sugared Ham, 121
Sweet Cookies, 259
Sweet Potato Biscuits, 262
Sweet Potato Pie, 192
Sweet Potato Pudding, 206
Syllabub, 211

Teriyaki Appetizers, 27
Thanksgiving Turkey and Dressing, 76
Tipsy Apple Pie, 194
Tipsy Balls, 216
Tipsy Bits, 215
Tipsy Bourbon Sauce, 159
Tipsy Cake, 224
Tipsy Christmas Kisses, 224
Tipsy Pudding, 204
Tipsy Ribs, 118
Tomato Pea Soup, 36

Index

Turkey and Bourbon, 76
Turkey Hash St. Germain, 81
Turkey Tetrazzini, 80

Veal Amandine Flambé, 125
Veal Cutlets with Bourbon, 126
Veal Scallopini au Bourbon, 126
Venison Ragout, 135

Walnut Cream Pie, 189
Walnut Crumb Crust, 188
Walnut Pie Shell, 189

Walnut Pudding, 207
Watermelon Cheer, 167
Whiskey Cake, 228
Whiskey Chicken, 85
Whiskey Fried Chicken, 83
Whiskey Pie, 184
Whiskey Pork Chops, 120
Whiskey Sauce for Bread Pudding, 201
Whiskey Sauce for Pudding, 161
Wild Oriental Shrimp, 54

Yuletide Cookies, 248